THE POWERS OF LAW

Comparative studies can reveal much about how law is formed out of social reality and political power by exploring these interactions in different national contexts. In this work Mauricio García-Villegas compares ideas about law, power and society in France and the United States, demonstrating different approaches to sociopolitical legal studies. Using the interdisciplinary tools of the sociology of law, critical legal theory, and socio-legal studies, García-Villegas builds up an insightful overview of what constitutes law and society theory and practice in France and the United States. He brings together diverse perspectives and practices that generally do not communicate well with one another, as is often the case between the critical theory of law of jurists and the legal sociology of sociologists. This study will allow readers to understand the sociology of law in a comparative perspective and sets out a new research agenda for the field of sociopolitical legal studies.

MAURICIO GARCÍA-VILLEGAS is Professor at Universidad Nacional de Colombia, Instituto de Estudios Políticos y Relaciones Internacionales (IEPRI), and an Honorary Fellow of the University of Wisconsin, Madison Institute for Legal Studies.

CAMBRIDGE STUDIES IN LAW AND SOCIETY

Founded in 1997, Cambridge Studies in Law and Society is a hub for leading scholarship in socio-legal studies. Located at the intersection of law, the humanities, and the social sciences, it publishes empirically innovative and theoretically sophisticated work on law's manifestations in everyday life: from discourses to practices, and from institutions to cultures. The series editors have longstanding expertise in the interdisciplinary study of law, and welcome contributions that place legal phenomena in national, comparative, or international perspective. Series authors come from a range of disciplines, including anthropology, history, law, literature, political science, and sociology.

Series Editors

Mark Fathi Massoud, *University of California, Santa Cruz*

Jens Meierhenrich, *London School of Economics and Political Science*

Rachel E. Stern, *University of California, Berkeley*

A list of books in the series can be found at the back of this book.

THE POWERS OF LAW
A Comparative Analysis of Sociopolitical Legal Studies

Mauricio García-Villegas
National University of Colombia

CAMBRIDGE
UNIVERSITY PRESS

CAMBRIDGE
UNIVERSITY PRESS

University Printing House, Cambridge CB2 8BS, United Kingdom

One Liberty Plaza, 20th Floor, New York, NY 10006, USA

477 Williamstown Road, Port Melbourne, VIC 3207, Australia

314–321, 3rd Floor, Plot 3, Splendor Forum, Jasola District Centre, New Delhi – 110025, India

79 Anson Road, #06–04/06, Singapore 079906

Cambridge University Press is part of the University of Cambridge.

It furthers the University's mission by disseminating knowledge in the pursuit of education, learning, and research at the highest international levels of excellence.

www.cambridge.org
Information on this title: www.cambridge.org/9781108482714
DOI: 10.1017/9781108584975

First published in English by Cambridge University Press 2018 as *The Powers of Law*

This adaptation and translation was originally published in French as *Les pouvoirs du droit* by Mauricio García-Villegas, Paris, LGDJ, 2015

Printed in the United Kingdom by Clays, St Ives plc

A catalogue record for this publication is available from the British Library.

ISBN 978-1-108-48271-4 Hardback

To Eric Rambo

CONTENTS

TABLES

PREFACE

Our ideas are largely dependent on the events of our lives and on the history of our existence. Every thought, Nietzsche said, is the confession of a body, the autobiography of a living being. This book is no exception to this assertion. The ideas of law and politics that I present here are, mainly, the product of the life I have lived, first as a student in Latin America and Belgium, then as a professor at various universities and research centers in France, the United States, and Latin America.

The contrasting populations, histories, cultures, and political struggles of the countries where I have lived have shaped my own conceptions of law and its relation to political power. My academic experience in such different countries has allowed me to see how dependent legal thought is on the national setting and, from this evidence, how doubtful the idea of the political neutrality of law is.

Nonetheless, this experience also showed me that we should not dissolve legal thinking into the social and political reality of each country. The law is not only a system of ideas built by the tools of a technical rationality (the science of law) but also the result of the political and cultural relations underlying such rationality.

This book would not have been possible without the help and support of many colleagues and friends. I would first like to extend my thanks to Jacques Commaille, who asked me to write this book in 2010, when I was doing research in France, and who has honored me with his friendship and advice throughout most of my academic career. I also wish to thank Liora Israël, who patiently read the first draft of the French version of this book and gave me important critical feedback. I thank Aude Lejeune, who commented on the first version of this book and coauthored an early version of Chapter 5.

I wrote a good portion of this volume during my stays at the University of Grenoble in France. These visits were made possible thanks to several invitations from the Centre d´Etudes et de Recherches sur le Droit, l´Histoire et l´Administration Publique (CERDHAP), and the Institut d´Etudes Politiques (IEP) over the last decade. Jean-Charles

Froment, who directed these institutions at various times in recent years, invited me to teach comparative sociology of law and provided me with valuable advice and friendship.

This book is a shortened and revised version of a book published in France in 2015 under the title *Les pouvoirs du droit*. I want to thank Morgan Stoffregen who reviewed the English version and María Adelaida Ceballos who reviewed the final version of the manuscript.

Many colleagues and friends in France, the United States, and Latin America have read and commented on one or more chapters. I apologize in advance to those who are the victims of my bad memory. In Europe, I thank André-Jean Arnaud (who passed away in December 2015), Wanda Capeller, Laurence Dumoulin, Cécile Vigour, Antoine Vauchez, Martin Kaluszynski, Claire Galembert, Nicolas Kada, Pierre Mura, Marcel Tercinet, Michel Carraud, Carlos Miguel Herrera, Jean-François Davignon, Jérôme Pelisse, Céline Torrisi, and Diana Villegas. I also thank my friends Monique Perriaux, Florence Perriaux, and François Marie Delhaye, all of whom took me in at different times during my stays in Europe. In addition, Marie Delhaye read and edited the final manuscript of the French version of this book.

In the United States, where I did an essential part of the research, I wish to thank several colleagues. Howard Erlanger, director of the Institute for Legal Studies at the University of Wisconsin Law School, welcomed me several times as a visiting professor. I am also deeply grateful to Professors Gay Seidman and Joe Thome, who were always willing to advise me and lend a hand whenever I needed. Particular thanks are due to the Tinker Foundation for extending me two invitations, in 2004 and 2008, to serve as a visiting professor. This latest invitation allowed me to complete much of the manuscript. During my stay at the Sociology Department at the University of Wisconsin–Madison, I received valuable comments from my colleagues Ivan Ermakoff, Heinz Klug, Joe Conti, Sida Liu, Erik Olin Wright, Francisco Serrano, Elizabeth Mertz, Alexandra Huneeus, and Joe Thome, as well as my friends Lisa Mackinnon and Eric Rambo, to whom I dedicate this book. I had the opportunity to discuss some of the ideas in this book, particularly those related to the Law and Society, with Susan Silbey, during various meetings in Paris, thanks to invitations by Liora Israël and Jacques Commaille. Her advice and comments were very helpful to me.

I would like to express my deepest gratitude to members of LACIS (the Latin American, Caribbean, and Iberian Studies Program), particularly its director, Francisco Scarano, and its associate director, Alberto Vargas, for their encouragement. LACIS also funded the English translation of most of the chapters of this book, which were used in my seminar.

In Latin America, I would like to thank Carlos Mario Perea and Fabio López de la Roche, both directors of IEPRI (the Instituto de Estudios Políticos y Relaciones Internacionales) at the National University of Colombia, and Rodrigo Uprimny, director of the Center for the Study of Law, Justice, and Society–Dejusticia, for facilitating my frequent international trips to Madison and Grenoble. I also thank my friends and colleagues César Rodríguez, Fernando Escalante, José Reinaldo de Lima Lopes, Néstor Raúl Correa, José Rafael Espinosa, Helena Alviar, María Adelaida Ceballos, Julieta Lemaitre, Javier Revelo, Catalina Pérez, René de la Vega, Rodolfo Vázquez, Martin Böhmer, Roberto Gargarella, Juan Carlos Henao, Oscar Vilhena, Catalina Botero, María Paula Saffón, Camilo Sánchez, Carolina Villadiego, Nicolás Torres, Alejandro Cortés, Antanas Mockus, Gabriela Vargas, and Vivian Newman.

Finally, without the support of my family – Ángela, Julia, and Emilio – none of the personal biography that allowed me to write this book would have been possible.

CHAPTER ONE

A SOCIOPOLITICAL UNDERSTANDING OF LAW*

INTRODUCTION

Classical sociologists (including Karl Marx, Emile Durkheim, and Max Weber) understood law as closely related to social reality and political power.[1] This can be seen in classical social theory and jurisprudence. Law was, for them, an essential element of social cohesion, collective identity, and economic development. Durkheim, for instance, argued that to understand the character of a society, one had to understand the type of law that prevailed in it:

> [W]hen one wants to know the way in which a society is divided politically, the way in which these divisions are composed, the more or less complete fusion which exists between them, it is not with the aid of a material inspection and by geographical observations that one arrives at an understanding; for these divisions are moral as well as having some basis in physical nature. It is only through public law that it is possible to study this organization, for it is this

---

* An earlier version of this chapter was published in the *Annual Review of Law and Social Science, 12,* 25–44, as "A Comparison of Sociopolitical Legal Studies."
[1] On Marx, see Cain & Hunt (1979); Hall (1996); Hunt (1982); Stone (1985). On Weber, see Hunt (1978); Lascoumes (1995); Pollak (1988); Treviño (1996); Trubek (1972); Weber (1922, 1978). On Durkheim, see Chazel (1991); Cotterrell (1991); Hunt (1982); Treviño (1996). For a general explanation, see Commaille (2003a, 2003b); Commaille & Duran (2009). For a general analysis, see Treviño (2010).

law, which determines it, just as it determines our domestic and civil relations (1963, p. 12).[2]

Law, power, and society were intimately linked – so much so that the study of each one was crucial for their mutual comprehension. Thus, classical sociology was also a political sociology of law.[3]

On the other hand, jurisprudence and classical legal thinking also viewed law, society, and politics as interconnected. Indeed, the great majority of legal thinkers, from Plato to Immanuel Kant, envisaged law as intimately linked to social order, justice, and the defense of the political community (Berman, 1983, 2003; Del Vecchio, 1964; Hespanha, 2005; Sabine, 1961; Tamanaha, 2001; Villey, 1975). They understood law and politics not only as two interlocked elements but also as essential instruments for justice and the common good.[4]

The idea that law, society, and politics were closely intertwined (what I refer to as a sociopolitical vision of law) gained strength in both sociology and jurisprudence at the beginning of the twentieth century, as a reaction to the formalist conceptions of law that had previously dominated in Europe and the United States.[5] In the United States, this vision became known as "the sociological movement in law."[6] In Europe, a similar reaction spurred by the emergence of social and socialist legal ideologies arose against the French codification

---

[2] Weber, on the other hand, saw a close relationship between types of legal thought (substantive, formal, rational, irrational) and types of legitimacy of political regimes (Lascoumes, 1995; Rheinstein, 1954; Trubek, 1972).

[3] The same idea can be applied to other classical authors, such as Ehrlich (1922); Geiger (1969); Gurvitch (1942); Maine (1861); Petrazycki (1955); Romano (1946); Savigny (1815); Spencer (1898); Sumner (1940); Timasheff (2007).

[4] See Aristotle (1974); De Aquino (1988); Kant (1797). More generally, see Bobbio (2005); Del Vecchio (1964); Tamanaha (2006). On the classic idea of the interconnection between law, society, and politics, see Tamanaha's (2006) concept of noninstrumental theories of law.

[5] Here, I am adopting the English terminology that differentiates formalist and antiformalist theories of the law; the former include those that regard law as a collection of norms organized in a coherent, rational, and politically neutral manner. On this subject, see Duxbury (1995); Minda (1995). According to Duncan Kennedy, formalism supposes that all questions in law can be resolved through deduction – that is to say, without recourse to politics (1997, p. 105). On the debate regarding legal formalism, see Cotterrell (1998); Nelken (1996).

[6] Its main representatives were Oliver Wendell Holmes, Roscoe Pound, and Karl Llewellyn. For a discussion of these authors, see Hunt (1978); Treviño (1996).

movement and the school of exegesis.[7] I will develop this point in further detail in Chapter 2.

Sociopolitical visions of law began to lose ground in both Europe and the United States after the Second World War, as conservative ideas and legal formalism once again took hold. At the same time, the social sciences began to distance themselves from legal thinking. Until that point, economics, political science, and sociology – relatively young disciplines – were quite often promoted and even taught by lawyers, which could have led legal science and lawyers to claim paternity of these disciplines. Thus, in their quest for disciplinary autonomy, these new social sciences excluded the law from their methods and objects, fearing that its presence would threaten their recently conquered independence (Deflem, 2010; Pécaut, 1996).

Nevertheless, despite formalism in legal theory, and sociologists' withdrawal from law, the sociopolitical perspective was never obliterated. Its advocates, however, did not face the same fate everywhere: they were more or less successful in the United States, aided by a more dynamic and political conception of legal practice, but they failed in Europe and Latin America, in particular between the Second World War and the end of the twentieth century, when the integrity of the law was preserved by a caste of jurists and professors who benefited from great social power (Boigeol & Dezalay, 1997; Bourdieu, 1989, 1991; Dezalay, 1992; López, 2004).

Today, once again, we are witnessing a renaissance of social and political visions of law in Europe and Latin America, and even in France, the country that was the greatest defender of legal formalism.[8] This renaissance, nonetheless, is founded on "disciplinary niches" that differ from country to country: while in France it has flourished largely in departments and institutes of sociology and political science,[9] in

---

[7] On the codification movement and the school of exegesis, see Bonnecase (1924); Jestaz & Jamin (2004); Matteucci (1988). On the influence of social ideas in law, see Herrera (2003a, 2003c).

[8] In 1986, Pierre Bourdieu published *La force du droit*, and in 1990, the French Sociological Association dedicated its annual colloquium to the question of the law. See Chazel & Commaille (1991); Garapon & Papadopoulos (2003); Israël (2008a); Israël et al. (2005a, 2005b); Jamin (2012).

[9] On the side of political science, see Chevallier (2003); Jamin (2012); Lochak (1989a, 1989b). On the side of the theory of law, see Caillosse (2011); Troper (2000). And on the side of sociology and anthropology, see Assier-Andrieu (1996);

Latin America, in countries such as Brazil, Colombia, and Argentina,[10] it has prospered primarily in law schools. It must be added, however, that formalist visions continue to dominate in most law schools, even in the United States, where the law is, prima facie, more open to social sciences. Similarly, in the overall context of international legal knowledge, the new sociopolitical visions are relatively marginal.

My objective in this chapter is twofold: first, to propose an interdisciplinary concept for the comparison of sociopolitical perspectives in law, and second, to set up the basis for comparing these perspectives in the United States and France.

THE SOCIOPOLITICAL VISION OF LAW

The Core Idea

In spite of their differences, these two approaches (European and American) share the idea that law cannot be understood outside of its sociopolitical dimension (Griffiths, 2006). They also share three fundamental theoretical premises.

First, they reject the two central tenets of legal formalism: (i) legal autonomy in relation to society and (ii) legal neutrality in relation to political power. The critique of legal autonomy assumes that law is embedded in society and therefore is not a self-sufficient knowledge that determines its own truth. The critique of legal neutrality means that law is not an expression of the people's will, interpreted and applied in a technical and impartial way by politically disinterested legislators, judges, or bureaucrats. Sometimes these rejections are radical and reduce the law to either society or politics, whereas othertimes they are moderate and lead to the recognition of relative legal autonomy or relative legal neutrality. Not all of these critiques reject both legal autonomy and legal neutrality. Some focus on only one of these formalist legal features. I develop these ideas in the next section.

Second, these sociopolitical approaches draw on the idea that the law is a language composed primarily of words and symbols that reflect

---

Bancaud & Dezalay (1984); Champy & Israël (2009); Commaille & Duran (2009); García-Villegas & Lejeune (2011); Lascoumes (1991); Vauchez (2006).

[10] See, for example, García-Villegas & Ceballos (2016); Gargarella (2005); Olivera (2015); Rodríguez-Garavito (2015); Sieder & Ansolabehere (2017)

society's core values, such as justice, equality, order, cooperation, and freedom. They claim that legal language and values do not have a fixed meaning and that the reality of the law depends to a large extent on the political ability of social actors and institutions to determine the meaning of legal texts in an adversarial legal field (García-Villegas, 2014). The symbolic dimension of legal norms is grounded in the fluidity of legal meaning – that is, in the malleable understanding of legal words, and particularly of legal rights. A good portion of the current legal mobilization is founded in what Scheingold (1974) calls "the myth of rights," which is the fight for rights as banners of political mobilization used by social movements. Rather than simply law, rights are political and moral symbols whose interpretation depends on a political struggle for the final meaning of legal texts. Such a meaning is reached at the intersection of several discourses and approaches: "Most of what is articulated as 'law' and 'rights'," Dudas, Goldberg-Hiller, & McCann (2015, p. 369) argue, "is a complex mix of generically legal, moral, religious, technical and other logics."[11]

Third, these two approaches are cross-disciplinary.[12] Most of the time, they exhibit not only methodological flexibility and creativity but also a combination of critical reflection and empirical research.

A New Concept: Sociopolitical Legal Studies

Thus, despite their heterogeneity, these new socio-legal perspectives share many practical and theoretical similarities. For this reason, I propose grouping them under the more general label of "sociopolitical legal studies" (SLS). I use the term "studies" in a broad sense, including not just legal theories but also empirical analyses of law. This general label comprises a collection of transdisciplinary research, theories, and

---

[11] The symbolic idea of law is a concept that goes beyond the practice of interpreting rules and standards in the process of legal adjudication. This is why the difference between the law's symbolic efficacy and its instrumental efficacy does not necessarily coincide with the difference between an internal (technical) point of view and an external point of view (Hart, 1961). As has been shown by critical legal theories, the political dimension of law is embedded in the internal and technical point of view, due to the fluidity of legal meaning (Kennedy, 1997; Tushnet, 1984). Therefore, the symbolic efficacy of law encompasses the entire legal phenomenon, which makes it the key concept for understanding the political dimension of law. For a development of these ideas, see García-Villegas (2014).

[12] Generally speaking, they are based on sociology, anthropology, political science, and legal theory.

studies that see law as a sociopolitical phenomenon that is central to the understanding of power and society.[13]

It is worth noting that there have been other efforts to bring together critical, sociological, and socio-legal scholars. Good examples in the United States include the book series *Crossing Boundaries*, edited by Austin Sarat and others (1998); of particular interest in this collection is Munger´s "Mapping Law and Society." A book edited by David Clark (2012a), *Comparative Law and Society*, is also worth mentioning.[14] In Europe, Volkmar Gessner and David Nelken (2007a) and particularly Nelken (2016) have published an interesting collection of articles in which scholars from different disciplines compare European law with other legal systems.[15] The works of Reza Banakar and Max Travers, which seek to bring the classical sociological approach to law, are also part of this endeavor (Banakar & Travers, 2002; Travers, 1993). Likewise, scholars working in specific subfields have attempted to do the same. This is evident in Michael McCann's work on the dialogue between social movement scholars and legal mobilization scholars (Dudas et al., 2015; Lovell, McCann, & Taylor, 2016; McCann, 2006). Some integrative efforts have also been made at the regional level. In France, the recent multiauthor book *Le "moment 1900"* embarks on an important comparative effort, as do the works of Frédéric Audren and Jean-Louis Halpérin (2013), Jacques Commaille (2016), and Rafael Encinas de Muñagorri et al. (2016). In Latin America, particularly in Colombia, Mexico, Argentina, and Brazil, there is a growing interest in law and society scholarship (see, e.g., García-Villegas, 2010, 2014; Junqueira, 2001; Lemaitre, 2015; Lopés & Freitas, 2014; Rodríguez-Garavito, 2003, 2011, 2014; Santos & Rodríguez-Garavito, 2005).

I am aware of the fact that the concept of SLS might not fully capture the cultural aspects of contemporary scholarship on law and society and critical legal studies, particularly in the United States,

---

[13] Transdisciplinarity is the intellectual posture that is, at the same time, between, across, and beyond all disciplines (Morin, 1994; Nicolescu, 2002). For a discussion of transdisciplinarity in law, see Arnaud (2013a); Chassagnard-Pinet et al. (2013); Van de Kerchove (2013).

[14] See also Calavita (2010); Darian-Smith (2013); García-Villegas (2003a, 2003b, 2009a); Israël (2013); Nelken (1984, 1986).

[15] Of particular interest in this collection are the introduction by Gessner & Nelken (2007b), and chapters by Cotterrell (2007), Garapon (2007), and Kagan (2007).

where there is significant academic production on the cultural dimen-sion of law (Coombe, 1998; Geertz, 1983; Harris, 1993; Kahn, 1999; Sarat & Kearns, 1998; Silbey, 2012; White, 1990). I made a good effort to seize this cultural dimension through the concept of law's symbolic value; however, this is a very large and complex subject worthy of a book in its own right.[16]

This book seeks to contribute to this literature not only by deepening the disciplinary connections within SLS but also by expanding the geographical scope of comparison of SLS. As for disciplinary connec-tions, this book takes up the old idea of classical sociology according to which the law cannot be understood independently of society and power. As for the latter, my analysis benefits from the advances made by SLS in Europe and Latin America.

More specifically, the idea of SLS reveals the existence of a trans-verse field of studies between three academic areas: the sociology of law, legal theory, and socio-legal studies, which, in spite of multiple con-nections, rarely communicate with one another. From a comparative perspective, the adoption of this general and inclusive terminology has several advantages.

First, it helps overcome the lack of communication between the three aforementioned academic disciplines and, in doing so, highlights the multiple relationships between their legal scholarship. Replacing the conventional expressions sociology of law, socio-legal studies, and critical theory of law (susceptible to being appropriated by jurists as well as sociologists) with the more neutral SLS helps avoid disciplinary quarrels, particularly common in countries with civil law traditions, between a sociology of law crafted by jurists and one crafted by sociologists.[17] Assuming a more general point of view than that of the disciplines at stake (law, political science, and sociology) can help not only make peace in disciplinary battles (Wallerstein, 1999) but also

---

[16] I tried to do just that in my book *La eficacia simbólica del derecho* (García-Villegas, 2014).

[17] On this subject, see Arnaud (1998b); Banakar & Travers (2002); Caillosse (2011); Commaille (2003b); Israël (2008a, 2008b); Loiselle (2000); Travers (1993); Treves (1995). More recently, see the two volumes of *Droit et société* dedicated to this debate: the first of them (vol. 69/70) from the sociological perspective, organized by Israël, and the second (vol. 75) from the juridical perspective, organized by Brunet and Van de Kerchove. It must be said that these divisions can sometimes also be found in the United States and England; see, for instance, Banakar & Travers (2002); Deflem (2010, p. 275); Sarat & Ewick (2015); Travers (1993).

help one better understand, from a comparative perspective, the multiple connections between schools of legal scholarship that barely communicate with one another (Nelken, 2016).

Second, this more inclusive perspective highlights the fact that the great contribution of these new visions of the law resides less in the methodological or epistemological enrichment of each of these disciplines than in the analysis of certain fundamental social and political problems of the contemporary world. This can be seen in the tendency of SLS authors toward the study of subjects such as the politicization of justice, the globalization of law, human rights activism, the politicization of the juridical profession, the increasing contestation of the law, and the pervasiveness of juridical pluralism, among others. All these issues are traversed by the double phenomenon (disciplinarily unclassifiable) of the increased judicialization of politics and of the politicization of justice, which characterizes a great deal of current social relations. In short, instead of beginning with the disciplines and moving to the problems, SLS begins with the problems, moves toward the disciplines, and then returns to the problems.

On this point, I share not only the surprise of scholars (especially American ones) upon observing the persistence and even virulence of disciplinary debates between jurists and sociologists that take place in France around the existence of sociology of law, but also their concern for the unfavorable consequences that such debates have for the construction of cooperative academic communities.[18]

Third, the inclusive nature of this perspective can help overcome a kind of legal and socio-legal knowledge that is too parochial, too focused on the nation-state, and too limited to local and domestic law (Assier-Andrieu, 1996; Darian-Smith, 2013; Santos & Rodríguez-Garavito, 2005; Twining, 2009). SLS not only relativizes the dependency of law in relation to the nation-state but also expands the notions of time and space that we need to address modern issues of globalization and the weakening of nation-states (Pogge, 2008; Rodotà, 2013; Singer, 2004).

Finally, with this label, I believe we will more easily reach the objective pursued by some sociologists of law, particularly Commaille in France, of recovering the perspective of classical sociologists (and, I add, of classical legal thinkers) in order to better understand

---

[18] On this subject, see Arnaud (1998b); Caillosse (2004); Treves (1995).

the close connections that exist between power, legal norms, and social relations.[19]

This book seeks to compare ideas on the relationship between law, political power, and society in the United States and France. These two countries exhibit very different conceptions and practices of law vis-à-vis their historical, economic, social, and political situations.[20] It is not my intention to compare legal norms or legal doctrines as comparative legal scholars do (Legrand, 1999; Legrand & Munday, 2003). On the contrary, this book proposes a critique of the conventional idea that a country's national legal norms and doctrines – as reflected through domestic debates, authors, schools, and internal movements – account for the explanation of the law that prevails in that country. This idea undermines the strong connections that exist between the intellectual life of law and the material and social conditions in which the law operates. In the words of Karl Mannheim, stated more than a century ago:

> The sociologist in the long run must be able to do better than to attribute the emergence and solutions of problems of a given time and place to the mere existence of certain talented individuals. The existence of and the complex interrelationship between the problems of a given time and place must be viewed and understood against the background of the structure of the society in which they occur (1936, p. 109).

Drawing on this point, my task will be to compare the various sociopolitical legal cultures underlying legal norms and legal doctrines, bearing in mind that in each of these cultures a certain type of relationship between law, power, and society is established and that such relationships are the reference points around which those norms and doctrines are constructed, interpreted, and lived.[21]

---

[19] See Commaille (2015); Commaille, Demoulin, & Robert (2010); a similar vision can be found in the writings of Hunt (1978, 1982, 1993).

[20] For a theoretical essay on this point, see Costa (2012). More generally, see Herrera & Le Pillouer (2012).

[21] There is a vast literature on the concept of legal culture. See Mezey (2015); Sarat & Kearns (1998). Scholars often distinguish between two types of legal culture: one internal and the other external. The first is related to ideas and the professional practice of law within the legal field, whereas the second concerns the place given to law within a national (or local) culture. For an overview, see Audren & Halpérin (2013); Cotterrell (2006); Friedman (2005); Kagan (2007); Legrand (1999); Merryman (1994); Nelken (1995, 2016); Van Caenegem (1987). This notion of culture,

To set the stage for these ideas, the remainder of this chapter is divided into two sections. The first section formulates two theoretical presuppositions that inspire the comparison, and the second section addresses some disciplinary questions.

BASIC IDEAS FOR THE COMPARISON OF SOCIOPOLITICAL LEGAL STUDIES

Oliver Wendell Holmes, Jr. once said that "the law embodies the story of a nation's development through many centuries, and it cannot be dealt with as if it contained only the axioms and corollaries of a book of mathematics" (1881, p. 1). More than an ensemble of valid legal norms, the law is the political history and legal culture that lie behind such norms. In order to compare these sociopolitical cultures, I propose relying on the differences between the two Western legal traditions – civil law (or Roman law) and common law – bearing in mind that such differences reside more in the implicit political culture of each tradition than in the greater or lesser primacy that they give to judges or legislators.[22] The main idea here is that these cultures are the political and epistemological reservoirs that nourish SLS.

It must nevertheless be said that the variances between these traditions have been softened over the course of the last two decades, as will be shown in the following chapters. This is due to multiple factors. First, there has been a growing influence, on the one hand, of legislated law in common law countries and, on the other, of judges in civil law countries. Additionally, globalization has created more flexible and porous national borders, which has affected the rigidity of national legal systems. Furthermore, and most importantly, rights as political tools have acquired enormous significance in civil law countries, France among them (Commaille, 2003b; Hirschl, 2004; Israël, 2009a, 2009b; Pelisse, 2005; Santos & García-Villegas, 2001; Spanou, 1989).

rooted in social reality, takes a certain distance from what is called "the cultural turn" in socio-legal studies, or at least the most micro and subjective version of it. For a similar analysis as it relates to the economy, see Fourcade (2009, p. 15). For an analysis of the cultural turn in law, see Sarat & Simon (2003).

[22] According to Legrand (1999), law offers a perspective of the world through which society represents itself. See also Garapon (1996); Merryman (1994). This is why judges in England and the United States, as well as professors in continental Europe, are, each in their own manner, political instruments for the conservation and reproduction of the political and social systems (Van Caenegem, 1987, p. 157).

But despite this, law remains, in essence, linked to nation-states and national legal traditions. The identities of the common law and the civil law have been shaped by the social, political, and institutional contexts that have accompanied their historical development in each country. For example, it is impossible to grasp the specificity of the difference between the French and American legal systems without considering the changing relationships between the state and the legal system in each of these countries from the mid-eighteenth century onward (Fourcarde, 2009; Kagan, 2007). But since this historical enterprise is too ambitious, I will focus on two aspects that I consider particularly important: first, the competition between actors in the legal field for capital and symbolic power and, second, the conception of the state and its relation to law that prevails in each country.

Sociology of Actors in the Legal Field

A sociopolitical vision of law grasps law in terms of legal fields, nationally and historically constituted. It supposes that legal and socio-legal ideas are shaped, to some extent, by the distribution of symbolic and social capital among legal actors (lawyers, law professors, legislators, judges, and so on) and by the relationships that these actors maintain with actors in the political field (Bourdieu, 1986, 1997; Foucault, 1975).[23] Since the internal struggle among legal actors for the appropriation of symbolic power is not independent of the political context in which that power is produced, the connections between the political and legal fields are multiple and mutually constitutive (Commaille, 2003a, 2013).

These power relations among actors in the legal field differ according to legal traditions, as explained by Weber (1922) in a classical text. While in France and other civil law countries law professors enjoy the most prestige, in common law countries judges and lawyers do.[24]

The success of professors of (civil) law and of law schools in France and Germany comes from their capacity to present themselves as the

---

[23] According to Bourdieu, "The juridical field is the site of a competition for monopoly of the right to determine the law. Within this field there occurs a confrontation among actors possessing a technical competence which is inevitably social and which consists essentially in the socially recognized capacity to interpret a corpus of texts sanctifying a correct or legitimized vision of the social world" (1987, p. 4).

[24] For a detailed explanation of the differences, see Bourdieu (1986); Legrand (1999); Rheinstein (1954); Van Caenegem (1987).

keepers of state knowledge. They have thus acquired not only great visibility and political significance but also great autonomy vis-à-vis political power (Dahrendorf, 1969). Furthermore, they draw their symbolic capital from a situation of ambivalence: being at once close to and distant from political power. They are close to this power in that they are tasked with educating the state elite, and distant in that they belong to universities and are supposed to produce a science of law. This ambivalence allows them to simultaneously approach the state as an external political entity and to justify the state by identifying it with the law, understood as a politically neutral object.[25]

By contrast, the success of lawyers and judges in the United States is due to their role as social engineers in the resolution of conflicts and in a wide range of sociopolitical questions. I will come back to these differences in Chapter 2.

In short, a comparative socio-legal assessment of the authors, debates, and movements in the legal field must keep in mind the legal tradition in which they operate, the political struggles among legal actors, and the social and political context in which they succeed or fail in their search for symbolic power (Bourdieu, 2012; Dezalay, 1990; Garth & Sterling, 1998). Only thus can we appreciate the reasons for which certain ideas, authors, or movements are accepted while others are rejected (López, 2004; Nelken, 2001). By bearing in mind this complex web of connections, we can avoid both what Lawrence Friedman calls the "internalist school"[26] – that is, the temptation to explain the evolution of a discipline (in this case, law) by tracing the vicissitudes of its arguments, movements, and ideas – and the materialist approach that reduces legal thought to the economic context in which it arises.[27]

The Relationship between the State and the Law

The particular identities of common law and civil law were shaped by the debate around the concept of sovereignty in the seventeenth and

---

[25] For German legal positivism – from Jellinek (1981) to Kelsen (1997) – the state is nothing more than a legal norm.

[26] According to Friedman, this perspective "observes law as the lawyer or the jurist observes law" (1989, p. 10).

[27] This reductionist vision is adopted by both orthodox Marxism and contemporary perspectives from the law and economics movement.

eighteenth centuries in England and France (Bourdieu, 1997; Elias, 1986; Tilly, 1990). The two countries had different ideas on this subject. In the French tradition, which came out of absolutism, law was the expression of the sovereignty of the state, represented by the monarch (Van Houtte, 1986). Under this conception, law does not precede the state but is its expression. The French Revolution did not change this tradition. On the contrary, it emphasized the idea of popular sovereignty, initially proposed by Emmanuel Joseph Sieyès (2002) and subsequently taken up again by the party of Maximilien Robespierre (1970). Between the old and new regimes, only the person of the sovereign changed: before the French Revolution, it was the king; after, it was the people. The old expression *un roi, une foi, une loi* ("one king, one faith, one law") varied merely in form, maintaining its content as a symbol of national unity. In the civil law tradition, popular sovereignty is expressed in the Civil Code,[28] which seeks to create a consciousness of all belonging to a single nation, governed by one sole law and one sole will. According to John Henry Merryman, "the French Code of 1804 was conceived as a sort of book of the people which could be placed on the shelf next to the Bible" (1994, p. 28).

The common law tradition rests, conversely, on the medieval conception of mixed constitution,[29] according to which the law belongs to the people, almost as an attribute of the group or a common possession that helps the group maintain its unity (Sabine, 1961).[30] The legal culture is thus founded on practices and common sense, not on general principles (Nelken, 2016). This is why it is supposed that common law

---

[28] According to article 4 of the Declaration of the Rights of Man and Citizen of 1793, the law is an expression of the general will.

[29] In England, the adoption of the tradition of the mixed constitution, inherited from the Middle Ages, was an antidote to the idea of sovereignty. See Blanco Valdés (1998); Fioravanti (1999, 2001); Matteucci (1988); Zagrebelzki (1992). In the seventeenth century, the Stuarts failed in their attempt to import the French model of sovereignty. The Glorious Revolution of 1688, which ran counter to this French tradition, adopted the idea of the separation of power between Parliament and the king.

[30] For example, in the United States, although the popular will might play an important role in times of constitutional crisis (marked by radical changes of political regimes), once this crisis is over, the sovereign people withdraws and acts through the powers established by the Constitution (Ackerman & Rosenkrantz, 1991).

has always existed and must be discovered and ceaselessly adapted.[31] Law is like the script of a play where every character has her role and acts accordingly. Indeed, Pierre Legrand observes that "Common Law is a form of social solidarity, inherent to a historical process by virtue of which a community is constituted" (1999, p. 41). In the common law tradition, law, and particularly rights, are close to individuals. John Locke (1946), for instance, argued that the foundation of political power came from the inalienable rights of individuals, who, at any moment, could revoke the mandate of those in power. Conversely, for Jean-Jacques Rousseau (1762), both law and rights were defined and granted by the state.

In short, there is a neat differentiation between the law as resulting from essential rights embedded in human nature (England) and the law resulting from the representatives of the people, who are the only ones capable of establishing the content of fundamental rights (France). In the first case, rights are natural rights; therefore, they are autonomous from political power, and legal norms can be the object of an institutionalized legal critique, developed within the juridical system, without putting the social contract into question. In the second case (France), law has no autonomy in relation to politics, and legal critique, to be effective, must question the entire social contract.

All of this has a direct impact on the political conception of law and on the social and political uses of rights. Legal critiques in Europe have a tendency to neglect legal analysis by subordinating law to political power. Conversely, in the United States, the critique of legal norms is natural and therefore does not involve a critique of the political order. In France, the conceptual separation between the state and the exercise of power is more tortuous than in England, where the state is more related to natural law and therefore is not affected by historical facts.[32]

Moreover, whereas in continental Europe the political struggle around law is concentrated on the lawmaking process, in the United

---

[31] In the common law tradition, George Sabine explains, law is "found" rather than "created," and it is inappropriate to say that there exists a body of people whose task is to create law (1961).

[32] The autonomy of the state in France was built from the supremacy of the public administration, as an expression of the Civil Code (Carré de Malberg, 1922; Jellinek, 1981).

States this struggle extends beyond lawmaking to adjudication, in which citizens and social movements are involved.[33]

The social and political visions expressed in these traditions have led to the formation of two different types of SLS, each one with a particular conception of the relationship between law and sociopolitical realities. As a result, two different ideas of legal critique have emerged, as well as two particular conceptions of the relationship between law and social sciences.

One caveat is in order. First, these differences are valid from a *longue durée* perspective. Today, the globalization of the economy, the constitutionalization of rights, the legalization of politics, and the rise of a European legal field, among other factors, have produced a significant homogenization across legal fields.

TRANSDISCIPLINARITY

SLS should echo the lack of differentiation of the social sciences and the need for social imagination in the contemporary world (Wright Mills, 1959). Disciplinary divisions have frequently become straitjackets that prevent us from understanding problems and social realities that are increasingly complex, multidimensional, and interconnected (Abbott, 1995, 2001). In fact, most intellectual traditions do not correspond to objective borders in social reality. All social understanding is porous and interconnected with other social knowledge and disciplines. Encasing them in borders, or cataloguing them, is problematic (Hunt & Colander, 2013). Disciplines reveal as much as they conceal, as Santos (1995a, 1995b) says, or, in Andrew Abbott's (2001, p. 18) terms, disciplines correct one another's mistakes.

The case for methodological flexibility is particularly important today in light of the fact that socio-legal phenomena have become diffuse, complex, and difficult to grasp from a disciplinary perspective, due mostly to the state's loss of its monopoly on legal creation and legal interpretation. In these circumstances the legal phenomenon is often a diffuse and complex feature that cannot be grasped from one discipline alone. Indeed, monodisciplinary analyses of contemporary socio-legal

---

[33] This dichotomy can be a little reductive in relation to certain works that, especially in France, tend to show that public engagement with law exists during legal implementation. See Baudot & Revillard (2014); Lejeune (2011a, 2011b).

problems tend to be, most of the time, incomplete or even misleading.[34] As Roger Cotterrell (2004, p. 15) states, "[S]ocial theory can no longer be considered the preserve of any particular academic discipline. It has to be defined in terms of its objectives rather than particular traditions that have shaped it."

Recognition of the sociopolitical dimension of law involves a delicate interdisciplinary balance that does not fall into either of two extremes: one that converts the social sciences into a legal servant without any possibility for questioning legal rationality, and another that dissolves the specificity of law in the contents of sociology, political science, or any other social science (and thus overriding any degree of autonomy of the legal system).

A monodisciplinary perspective is particularly problematic when it comes to the study of legal phenomena. Paul Amselek is right when he affirms that

> [p]roperly speaking, there cannot be a "study of law," or "study of legal norms," but only a study of man, an anthropological science that studies a categorical sector of human deeds, those which constitute the legal experience of people: the deeds of elaboration, promulgation, diffusion, reception, utilization, study, theorization, etc., of legal norms. It is the deeds of humanity, and not directly legal instruments, which are susceptible to being the object of a scientific treatment (1997, p. 341).

The epistemological flexibility of SLS not only entails more diffuse and porous borders between law and social sciences but also implies a certain disregard for the state's centrality in legal analysis (Cotterrell, 2004, p. 25; Twining, 2009, p. 13). As stated earlier, legal doctrines are historically tied to the nation-state and the idea of sovereignty. That is why the validity of international law and of the "minimum content of Natural Law" (Hart, 1961, p. 193), in spite of these laws' cosmopolitan substance, has been conditioned by the adoption of constitutions at the domestic level.

Over the last fifty years, however, this connection between law and the nation-state has lost its strength. This is due, first, to a deficit of regulation in the global sphere – not only in economic matters but also in political and social ones. By the very nature of their functions, states

---

[34] Israël (2008a, 2008b, p. 381) is close to the interdisciplinary vision when she proposes a "methodological indifferentiation" for the sociology of law. See also Arnaud (2013a, 2013b); Levine (1990); and the Belgian debate on the relationship between law and context in *Revue interdisciplinaire de droit* (vol. 70, 2013). See also Mottini, Brunet, & Zevounou (2014).

today are unable to provide the regulation that is needed. In other words, the surplus of global problems faces a deficit of legal tools. Second, this regulatory deficit comes from a model of economic globalization that is imposed by a powerful minority, scattered around the world, against which there is no majority able to oppose it. This model supposes an international order based on sovereign and free states that coordinate their actions in order to solve global problems. Inequality, war, uncertainty, and the lack of democratic regimes are seen as dysfunctions or externalities that can be solved. However, it is becoming increasingly clear that these problems concern the nature of the regulatory model itself (i.e., economic globalization) and that they cannot be solved in the absence of a new regulatory system (Held & Roger, 2013; Lemaitre, 2015; Pogge, 2008).

We have markets without law and law without democracy. To that extent, industrialized countries are copying the world's periphery. Not only did the modernist illusion of the mid-twentieth century – according to which economic development, democracy, and the rule of law would be extended from Europe and the United States to the rest of the world – turn out to be false, but all signs point to the opposite happening: legal pluralism, the inefficiency of the state, social violence, and the capture of state institutions by private interests – typically Third World phenomena – are colonizing developed countries. I will come back to these ideas in Chapter 6.

Under these circumstances, SLS can help us understand how today's global regulation deficit is a type of political order that is leading the planet down a possibly disastrous path. In the face of such a dramatic situation, we need to think not only in global terms but also in terms of humankind – and, I would add, in cosmopolitan terms (see Chapter 6). We need to imagine new connections between law and political power that can be efficient in terms of problem solving, as well as moral and just in humanitarian terms.

***

This book is divided into six chapters, with this introduction serving as the first chapter. Chapter 2 explores the concept of "symbolic uses of law," which refers to the mobility of the meaning of legal language and the possibilities that emerge from a political interpretation and use of legal rules. In this symbolic use lies the engine behind the politicization of the law and the interest – both academic and practical – in SLS. Chapter 3 embraces a more historical emphasis. It explains how the development and strengthening of the sociopolitical dimension of law in France and the United States have been, to a large extent, determined by the two theoretical assumptions defined earlier in this introduction – that is, by the conception of the state and its relation-ship with the law and by the tensions among protagonists of the legal field. This history has resulted in a conception of the law that is more or less autonomous with regard to the social sciences and social life, and more or less neutral in relation to political decisions. The more autonomous and neutral we envision the law to be, as is the case in France, the more problematic the relationship between the law and the social sciences/social struggles becomes, and the more radical and removed from the legal field antiformalism and SLS become. These early chapters provide background information and set the stage for a more substantial discussion of the field of sociopolitical legal studies, which is put forward in the chapters on France and the United States.

Chapter 4 describes recent developments in SLS in the United States. It shows how the law's proximity to social phenomena and the social sciences has made way for a wide spectrum of SLS – that is, of movements, groups, tendencies, and schools that address the sociopolitical dimensions of law. These developments have been espe-cially present in law schools, where, thanks to legal realism's triumph over legal formalism, critical thought and socio-legal studies have flourished. The chapter aims, among other things, to demonstrate the richness and diversity of SLS in the United States and to demonstrate the need for the different visions of SLS to better communicate among themselves and to construct broader, more comprehensive, and more radical sociopolitical theories. Chapter 5 describes SLS in France in recent decades. It explains how SLS has suffered a more difficult fate, particularly in law schools, where legal formalism and the myth of law as an expression of popular will have nurtured a conception of the law that is politically neutral and autonomous in relation to social reality. Nonetheless, in recent years, and particularly in social science settings, SLS has undergone important developments. The chapter illustrates those developments, as well as SLS's achievements and limits.

Finally, Chapter 6 takes stock of the discussions from previous chapters. It proposes a typology of SLS based on the types of socio-political visions of the law that dominate in each country. In addition, it addresses the future of SLS in a world that is increasingly globalized, more uncertain, and less prone to organization on the basis of the traditional nation-state structure.

CHAPTER TWO

THE SYMBOLIC USES OF LAW
At the Heart of a Political Sociology of Law*

> *Words are more mysterious than facts.*
> – Pierre Mac Orlan, *La Petite Cloche Sorbonne*

The political dimension of the law arises from legal language. This language has an open, as opposed to fixed, texture (Hart, 1961) – that is, it can be interpreted in a range of ways. But what is the legitimate or correct way? For centuries, legal philosophers have debated whether valid interpretations actually exist (Dworkin, 1977). However, this is a normative problem. From the descriptive point of view, it is clear that many of these interpretive conflicts – which, far from being exceptional, are part of the daily life of law – are decided on in a political manner based on the subjective conceptions of those tasked with making such decisions. Interpretation is not a mechanical or rational exercise (as believed by the exegetes of the Napoleonic Code) but instead a hermeneutic one, necessarily connected to politics.

Thus, interpretation implies a political struggle over the fixing of meaning of legal texts.[1] Some of these words in these texts – such as justice, liberty, dignity, security, and rights – are where the very

---

* This chapter is a summary of my book *La eficacia simbólica del derecho* (2014).

[1] The mobility of legal sense is part of the general phenomenon of the mobility of the meaning of language; consequently, the political dimension of legal language is part of the political dimension of language in general. The symbolic efficacy of law comes from the fact that the law is made of words and, as such, is inseparable from the mobility of meaning (Austin, 1962; Barthes, 1980; De Saussure, 1945; Perelman & Olbrechts-Tyteca, 1976; Wittgenstein, 1988); in law, see a recent book of Lauren Edelman (2016). A full explanation of the function fulfilled by the law cannot omit the fact that legal language, like any language, has both an instrumental function and a symbolic function.

structure of social life is defined. That is why the task of interpreting and fixing the meaning of legal language (not only by judges and public officials but also by social actors) is a controversial and fundamentally political one, which represents the very essence of law.

The struggle to fix the meaning of legal language means that the distinction between the language of the law and the language of politics is a fuzzy one. According to this distinction, while legal language ensures that things happen in a certain way by defining specific mech-anisms (such as judicial processes), political language promises that things will go a certain way but without establishing any specific guarantees to this end. Thus, the argument goes, the law entails an instrumental linkage to the future, through legal proceedings, while politics merely implies a symbolic linkage, through images.

The problem with this distinction, however, is that the law does not always manage to secure the future, due to the impossibility of fixing the true meaning of legal language. The issue is not that the law fails to establish any meanings (as claimed by some postmodern lines of legal thought) but rather that it defines much less than it aims to. It is in this deficit where we find the political dimension of the law.

The law is thus a cultural system of meaning as well as a system of instrumental controls. Its force lies not only in the threat or reward it promises but also in its ability to produce speech that people perceive as legitimate, true, and authoritative. While the instrumental efficacy of legal language determines conduct as a result of its obligatory character or its technical capacity to regulate and organize society, the symbolic efficacy of legal language achieves its objectives through the communi-cation of images of justice, equity, security, and other values perceived as essential for social life.

The symbolic efficacy of law determines the symbolic uses of law — that is, the utilization of legal language for political purposes. The symbolic uses of law are therefore an essential part of the sociopolitical vision of law. A good portion of both socio-legal scholarship and legal mobilization consists of fights for rights as banners of political mobiliza-tion used by social movements. Rather than simply law, rights are political and moral symbols whose interpretation depends on a political struggle for the final meaning of legal texts. Such a meaning is reached at the intersection of several discourses and approaches: "Most of what is articulated as 'law' and 'rights,'" Jeffrey Dudas et al. explain, is "a complex mix of generically legal, moral, religious, technical, and other logics" (Dudas, Goldberg-Hiller, & McCann, 2015, p. 369).

The symbolic idea of law is a concept that goes beyond the practice of interpreting rules and standards in the process of legal adjudication.[2] This is why the difference between law's symbolic efficacy and its instrumental efficacy does not necessarily coincide with the difference between an internal (technical) point of view and an external one (Hart, 1961). As has been shown by critical legal theories, due to the mobility of legal meaning, the political dimension of law is embedded in the internal and technical point of view (Kennedy, 1997; Tushnet, 1984). Therefore, the symbolic efficacy of law encompasses the entire legal phenomenon and is the key to understanding the political dimension of law.[3]

The symbolic efficacy of law is at the heart of the sociopolitical legal study (SLS) described in Chapter 1. It enables us to better understand the meaning of political struggles among social and legal actors within the legal field (Bourdieu, 1986). In addition, the study of the symbolic dimension of law can elucidate the moral and political relationships that each actor establishes with the legal system. As Michael McCann explains, "the symbolic manifestation of law, as both a source of moral right and a potential threat of outside intervention, invests rights discourse with its most fundamental social power" (2004, p. 514).[4]

In this chapter, I will focus on the symbolic uses of law, understood as a strategy adopted by protagonists of the legal field (such as lawmakers, lawyers, and judges) or by citizens who use rights or other legal norms to achieve their political goals. These actors perform a kind of political battle for the meaning of legal texts, either by reducing or enlarging that meaning.

The discussion that follows is divided into three sections. The first section provides an overview of existing perspectives on the symbolic

---

[2] Law, of course, has other functions that are not political, including social techniques, regulation, and coordination (Delpeuch, Dumoulin, & De Galembert, 2014).

[3] In theory, two political dimensions of law – internal and external – can be distinguished. The first one, as explained by critical legal theory, is related to the margin of legitimate interpretation in legal adjudication and, generally, in the technical uses of law. The second one extends beyond legal interpretation to the political uses of law, connecting the legal field with the political field. In the first case (internal dimension), the political dimension of law is framed by legal doctrine, while in the second (external dimension), legal doctrine is determined by political power. It is worth pointing out, however, that this is an analytical distinction and that the line between these two dimensions is not always easy to establish in practice.

[4] See also Somers & Roberts (2008); Spanou (1989).

efficacy of the law; the second presents a typology of political uses of the law; and the last section discusses the political potential of legal language.

PERSPECTIVES ON THE SYMBOLIC EFFICACY OF LAW

The symbolic dimension of law is usually acknowledged in legal studies. This is the case with constitutional law,[5] criminal law,[6] labor law,[7] and environmental law.[8] Studies on the symbolic dimensions of law are also common in theoretical reflections on law.[9] Nevertheless, there is no unified vision, whether in legal doctrine or in the social sciences, on the meaning of the symbolic efficacy of law. Conceptualizations vary according to authors, countries, and disciplines. To clarify this vast and scattered panorama, I begin by distinguishing three approaches to this symbolic dimension.

Liberal Perspective

In the modern state, legitimacy derives from legality.[10] Hence the English statement, "It is not the king who makes the law, but rather the law that makes the king."[11]

---

[5] In the United States, one can find a dense bibliography on the symbolic effects of constitutions. See, for example, Brigham (1987); Edelman, M. (1971); Edelman, L. (2016); Lemaitre, (2008, 2009); Lerner (1973); Scheingold (1974); Sutton (2013); Tyler & Boeckmann (2014). For Europe, see Priban (2007). According to Lauren Edelman, for instance, "an important reason for continuing racial and gender inequality in the working place is that employers create policies and programs that promise equal opportunity yet often maintain practices that perpetuate the advantages of whites and males" Edelman (2016: 3).

[6] See, for example, Berger, Searles, & Neuman (1988); Grattet & Jenness (2008); Jenness & Smyth (2011).

[7] See, for example, Moore & Newman (1985).

[8] See Bart, Van Beers & Poort (2016); Lane (1998); Lascoumes (1991).

[9] On the philosophy of law, see, for example, Coskun (2007); Lenoble & Ost (1980); Noreau (2009). On the sociology of law, see Calavita (1996); Chevallier (2003); Dos Santos (1987); Faria (1988); Macaulay, Friedman, & Mertz (2007); Santos (1977, 1995a, 1995b). On legal semiotics, see Kelsall (2009); Witteveen (1999).

[10] According to Rousseau, the strongest is never strong enough to be the master unless he transforms obedience into duty, and strength into law (1964). See also Weber's famous definition of the state: an entity that is able to successfully claim a monopoly of legitimate violence within a given territory (1992, p. 1057). For a deeper discussion of state legitimacy, see Corten (2003).

[11] Similarly, the historical preference for a "government of laws" over a "government of men" (according to the famous Greek distinction) is a reflection of the

The most extraordinary power of the law is its ability to transform the use of force into a legitimate exercise of authority. This power allows us to differentiate between, for example, an organized gang of thieves that imposes respect for its orders and a state that does likewise (Bobbio, 2005, p. 254; Hart, 1961). This legitimizing power is, above all, a symbolic power.

There is an inherent symbolic force in the legal system that is essential for power to be respected. Without it – without the blessing it gives to the state's raw exercise of power – political domination would be impossible. The law is the language through which legitimacy is produced and reproduced. Thus, under this view, power and legal rhetoric exist in a kind of symbiosis: state actions are justified through juridical norms, and juridical norms are upheld when they enjoy the support of the state. The legitimizing power of the law relies on the actual power of the state (i.e., its physical strength), and vice versa.

This liberal version of the symbolic efficacy of law has been developed by authors as diverse as Jean-Jacques Rousseau, John Locke, Max Weber, Herbert Lionel Hart, Hans Kelsen, and Jürgen Habermas.[12] For Weber (1922), for instance, the law is able to rationalize and justify the use of force. The symbolic is also closely linked to what Hart (1961) calls the acceptance of the law from the internal point of view – that is, respecting legal norms based on the fact that they are a set of socially accepted rules.

The Marxist View

The Marxist vision of law, like the liberal vision, assumes that legal norms incarnate a symbolic power that reproduces the majesty of power (i.e., its legal and just character). However, unlike the liberal conception, the Marxist vision maintains that this power is one of indoctrination – one that masks the existing reality behind legal concepts.[13] The law is an institutional power that creates an alienated consciousness, or false consciousness, from social reality. As a result, political domination

---

legitimizing importance of law (Bobbio, 2005, p. 2005). See also Ayres & Braithwaite (1992); Tyler (1990).

[12] See Guibentif (2010). For a critical perspective, see Gupta (1995); Migdal (2001, 2011); Rajagopal (2005).

[13] See the classic text by Marx (1842) on thieves of wood. See also Beirne & Quinney (1982); Pasukanis (1979).

appears as something natural (not constructed) – something that has always existed and thus ought to be respected (Gabel, 1980). The law, according to Marx and Engels, has a double function: repressive (punitive) and symbolic (ideological). The symbolic function overshadows the repressive function of legal norms (Pavlich, 2011, p. 98).

Social institutions such as law and religion are thus elements constructed by the bourgeoisie to protect its economic interests. This occurs through the "commodification" or "objectification" of norms: norms are perceived (by workers and the bourgeoisie alike) as part of the existing natural order and therefore as things that are durable and solid. According to Engels, the legal system "appears as an independent element, that is justified by its mere existence ... by its intrinsic fundamentals ... such that people forget that the law comes from the economic conditions of life" (1955, p. 623).[14] It is in this forgetfulness that Anatole France (1894) was inspired to pen his famous phrase, "In its majestic equality, the law forbids rich and poor alike to sleep under bridges, beg in the streets, and steal loaves of bread."

These ideas regarding the symbolic efficacy of law were developed by critical legal movements, such as the critical legal studies movement in the United States, the *critique du droit* movement in France, and the *crítica jurídica* movement in Latin America. For many authors of these movements, the law was an instrument for legitimizing domination through symbols of unity, justice, and equality in a society ruled by the most privileged group. Peter Gabel and Paul Harris describe this power of law as an attractive spectacle of macabre and perverse symbols (1983, p. 372).

This version of the symbolic efficacy of law proposes that the liberal view, centered on rights, ought to be replaced by a critical view centered on domination (Hutchinson, 1992; Kairys, 1998; Sutter, 2017; Tushnet, 1984). It is important to note that the disqualification of law as a political instrument of domination does not always find its roots in Marxist thinking. Michel Foucault (1980b) is also an important source of inspiration for this type of criticism.[15]

---

[14] In *The Manifesto of the Communist Party*, Marx and Engels wrote, "[Y]our own ideas are the product of relations of production and bourgeois property, just as your law is nothing but the will of your class made into law; will whose content is determined by the material conditions of existence of your class" (2000, p. 57).

[15] See Golder & Fitzpatrick (2009); Pavlich (2000); Valverde (2010).

In the 1970s, an intense debate occurred within Marxism regarding the autonomy of the state (and its ideological apparatuses, the law among them) vis-à-vis economic power. In this debate, marked largely by the intervention of American feminists and African Americans,[16] there was an inevitable tension between those who emphasized the cultural dimension of political legitimation and those who emphasized the structural dimension of the economy (Barrow, 1993). Some adhered to the position of Nicos Poulantzas (1972, 1973), according to whom the autonomy of the state was relative, and the legal order was determined "in the last instance" by the structure of the capitalist mode of production. According to this vision, the possibility of social emancipation through progressive legal reform was virtually nonexistent.[17] Others, however, supported a Marxist analysis with a cultural focus, arguing that the law provides social movements with a margin for maneuver, which compels the state to make concessions in order to maintain or increase its legitimacy.[18] While the first position emphasizes the determinant character of the economic structure, the second underscores the need to legitimize the state through culture and symbols.

At the beginning of this debate, economic structuralism was the dominant trend. The majority of authors in the 1970s (in the United States and France) posited that the symbolic effects of law worked to the benefit of state institutions and their goals of political manipulation (Kairys, 1998; Kennedy, 1995; Novoa Monreal, 1980; Roelofs, 1982; Tushnet, 1984). However, this excessive emphasis on the radical unitary character of state domination was ultimately seen by some as promoting a rather simplistic view of the law, in which the law was a mere institutional mechanism of social control. Thus, in the 1980s, other authors, less radical and more willing to accept some cultural autonomy in the symbolic use of law, accepted that under specific circumstances, individuals and social movements could equally rely on the symbolic dimension of law to strengthen their struggles (Calavita, 2010; Santos, 2002).

---

[16] On legal feminism, see MacKinnon (1982); Smart (1989). On legal criticisms of race, see Crenshaw et al. (1995).
[17] See, for example, Balbus (1996).
[18] See, for example, Hunt (1985). For a detailed discussion of the debate in Marxism on the relative autonomy of the law, see Tomlins (2007).

Constructivist Visions

The previous two visions regard law as an instrument that affects an external reality.[19] Despite their ideological differences, they share the same instrumentalist conceptualization of law, which remains in the formal and positive dimension of legal norms (Trubek & Esser, 1989).

In the 1980s in the United States and Europe, some scholars promoted new visions of law nourished by social constructivist theories according to which both subjectivity and objectivity (as well as institutions and social realities) enjoy a reciprocal relationship marked by communication and culture (Berger & Luckmann, 1966; Bourdieu, 1977; Giddens, 1984). Under this perspective, the law is a space for symbolic construction between different positions and interests struggling to settle the meaning of legal texts (Bourdieu, 1986; Kahn, 1999). The emphasis is no longer on the capacity of legal norms to determine human behavior but on the law's ability to produce meaning in social relationships (Mertz, 1994).

Constructivist theories of law are, to a certain degree, a reflection of changes that have occurred in the legal system over the last few decades, such as the loss of the legal code's centrality, the presence of judges in political life, the growing importance of international human rights, and the transnationalization of law and social movements. These phenomena have reinforced political uses of law and, above all, of rights.

A good illustration of a constructivist vision can be found in Scheingold's 1974 book *The Politics of Rights*. Scheingold was one of the first to examine the relationship between rights and social change, which he did in the case of the civil rights movement in the United States. Can rights interpreted and applied by judges produce social change? An adequate answer to this question, according to Scheingold, requires taking into account two ideas of rights: rights as myths and rights as politics. These two concepts are part of the reality of rights.

The myth of rights emerges from the ideology that places trust in the political efficacy and ethics of law (Scheingold, 1974, p. 17). This confidence is based on the idea, shared by a large number of American citizens, that rights and the US Constitution are not just symbolic manifestations of justice but living realities. People believe that what is written in the Constitution is something that exists in reality.

---

[19] Only their purposes change: while the liberalist vision seeks order and development, the Marxist vision seeks to consolidate a model of political domination.

As Scheingold argues, such confidence in the effectiveness of rights is often an illusory hope. Not only people believe that: "As courts increasingly equate symbolic structures with the achievement of civil rights ‑ Lauren Edelman explains ‑ they render law endogenous and condone forms of compliance that are unlikely to produce racial and gender equality" (Scheingold 2016, p. 238).

Scheingold notes, however, that not all rights are empty and harmless. The presence of rights also provides a political space for contestation and collective mobilization that allows one to fight for their effectiveness. Rights cease to be myths, instead becoming realities. This is what Scheingold calls "the politics of rights," or "rights as politics." He proposes looking to the Constitution and rights as tools for political mobilization.[20]

Hence, the symbolic efficacy of the law serves not only to maintain physical structures of political domination but also to strengthen the struggle against political power. The law, as the god Janus, has two faces: one of domination and another of emancipation (García‑Villegas, 2014, 2017). This duality makes symbolic efficacy a key concept, both from a political point of view – encompassing the defense and critique of power – and from a theoretical point of view – as a practice that is determined by the material conditions of power and the capacity of social and legal actors to affect and even transform these structures.

SYMBOLIC USES OF LAW

The symbolic use of law helps explain the way law functions as a political resource. This is the reason why the symbolic efficacy of law is at the heart of SLS – it is an essential component of the struggles of social actors in the legal field when they try to settle the meanings of legal norms. Lawmakers are not the only ones who benefit from this type of use. Those responsible for the application of legal norms (judges, for instance) can also introduce a symbolic dimension that goes beyond the freedom of interpretation accorded to them by legal doctrine. The symbolic use of law might equally be associated with

[20] This is the position adopted by some theoretical movements critical of the specific political agendas that use the law as a strategic tool to achieve their goals. In this regard, see, for example, the case of critical race theory (Crenshaw et al., 1995) or queer theory (Halley, 1993).

citizens, who are the recipients of legal norms. For example, social movements can turn a norm originally intended not to be applied into the banner of a great political cause.

Thus, the symbolic efficacy of law is a strategy that can be differentiated according to two perspectives: the type of actor (either officials responsible for interpreting and applying legal norms, or social actors who make political use of these norms) and the political position (either conservative or progressive) of these actors.

The difference between conservatism and progressivism in law is complex[21] and requires differentiating two dimensions: the socioeconomic dimension and the personal autonomy dimension. The first dimension refers to the classical distinction between left and right, while the second concerns the distinction between paternalism and liberalism. There may be people, such as judges, who adopt progressive (i.e., leftist) positions in the first dimension and conservative positions in the second, and vice versa. One can find, for example, Catholic judges who support agrarian reform (on the basis of the social doctrine of the Church) but who oppose abortion rights and gay rights. One can also find judges who are neoliberal on economic issues and opposed to the legalization of social rights; but because they are liberal in political philosophy, they defend the decriminalization of drugs or abortion.[22]

When both of these dimensions (actor and political vision) are taken into account, four symbolic uses of the law emerge: (i) state-conservative; (ii) state-progressive; (iii) social-conservative; and (iv) social-progressive.

A state-conservative use of law occurs when public officials use legal norms for political purposes. In the United States, for instance, it is relatively common for local officials to use their powers to reverse the decisions of judges (Brisbin, 2010; Miller & Sarat, 1980; Tyler, 2006). Another example is the legislative practice known in the United States as "filibusterism," which consists of preventing a decision through the abusive extension of congressional debate.

There are other examples, such as criminal laws on drugs designed to satisfy the punitive spirit of a society. In a classic text, Joseph Gusfield

---

[21] For an explanation of these complexities, see Fraser (1998, 2000); García-Villegas (1997).

[22] The contrasts are seen more clearly in countries with strong and activist constitutional courts, such as Germany, South Africa, and Colombia. See García-Villegas (2012a, p. 201); Gargarella (2011a, 2011b); Lemaitre (2009); Uprimny (2011).

TABLE 1   Symbolic uses of law

	Vision	
Actor	Conservative	Progressive
State	State-conservative	State-progressive
Society	Social-conservative	Social-progressive

(1963) demonstrates how the true sense of norms that outlawed the use of alcohol in the United States during Prohibition was found less in the idea that these norms would be respected than in the idea of their being promulgated. On the other hand, progressive constitutional norms on social rights (for which protection is very costly) are sometimes interpreted and applied by the government (which has limited resources) in a way that disregards the original objectives set in the constitution.[23]

The state-progressive use of law occurs when officials employ the law as a tool for social justice. This happens, for example, when a judge uses the law to achieve social change (which is not directly embodied in these norms) for the marginalized classes. In 1898, Paul Magnaud, a French judge famous for his mercy and defense of feminism, acquitted a young single mother who had stolen bread from a baker because she was hungry.[24]

The rest of this section will focus on the two remaining uses of law: social-progressive and social-conservative.

The Social-Progressive Use of Law

The social-progressive use appears when individuals or leftist social movements use rights as a part of their political strategy. In the words of E. P. Thompson (1975), those who are in power can become "prisoners of their own rhetoric" when their subordinates learn how to use the same rhetoric as a political weapon. A classic historical example of this turnabout is the use of the text of the British Magna Carta of 1215 during the Glorious Revolution of 1688. Recent

---

[23] This occurs most frequently in criminal law. See, for example, Abramovich & Courtis (2002); Patiño Santa (1992); Rubio (1999); Uprimny, Guzmán, & Parra (2012).

[24] Magnaud based his decision on article 64 of France's Criminal Code, which provided that a person was not guilty of a crime if he "was in a state of dementia at the time of his actions."

examples of this legal strategy can be found in the civil rights move-ment in the United States and in the anti-apartheid movement in South Africa; and more recently, in movements fighting for the rights of women, the LGBT community, people with disabilities, victims of discrimination, animals, and so forth.[25] One part of these movements' strategies could also include making demands for the instrumental efficacy of laws.

The progressive use of the law is founded on the possibility of social emancipation through the law. Here it is important to clarify two aspects: the concept of "emancipation" and the political convenience of legal strategies for emancipative struggles.

Regarding the first aspect, I embrace a broad and rather weak con-ception of emancipation,[26] which allows my analysis to include a series of progressive social battles with a simple reformative scope. This preference deviates from strong visions according to which the only possible emancipation is that which implies a full rupture with the established order.[27] According to these visions, partial changes and reforms not only are not conducive to true transformations but also can have the contradictory effect of legitimizing the status quo and delaying change. They are also founded on the dubious idea that when things improve for the poor, the conformity of this class increases – in other words, hope produces nothing but submission, less class consciousness, and less energy for battle. I will expand on this issue at the end of this chapter.

These visions echo *The Manifesto of the Communist Party*, which says that revolution will take place when the proletarians have "nothing to lose but their chains" (Marx & Engels, 2000).[28] According to this view,

---

[25] For a vast review of the literature on this theme, see Abel (1995a); Beckett & Hoffman (2014); Ewick & Silbey (1992); Handler (1992); Israël (2009a); Lemaitre, (2008, 2009); McCann (1994, 2004); McCann & March (1995); Merry (1990); Sarat & Scheingold (2005); Somers & Roberts (2008); Spanou (1989); Teitel (1997). On counterhegemonic battles through law, see Santos & Rodríguez (2005). On international activism, see Keck & Sikkink (1998).

[26] On the concept of emancipation and its rapport with the law, see Santos (1998, 2002).

[27] The classical radical vision was developed by Marx in "On the Jewish Question" (1978), among others.

[28] Substantial evidence has been mounted to refute this understanding of the mani-festo. See, for instance, Gurr (1970); McAdam (1982); McAdam, McCarthy, & Zald (1996); Taylor (1988); Tilly (1978, 2005).

numerous countries could experience revolutions if the increase in injustice and oppression foments popular insurrection. Yet it seems even more probable, as Alexis de Tocqueville (1856) said in his text on the French Revolution, that the opposite could happen: there is a greater chance that a revolution will take place when people are better off, because such amelioration allows them to perceive possibilities of improvement that they otherwise would not foresee. The Marxist hypothesis is not only empirically questionable but also morally doubt-ful insofar as it involves a certain justification of human tragedy – as if it were necessary to support purgatory in order to obtain the final release. I am conscious of the fact that in very unjust societies, such as those of certain Latin American countries, it is important that radical voices speak on behalf of human dignity. But it seems to me that we should not give up the radical idea when the emancipatory potential of legal reforms seeking the improvement of the social condition of the marginalized is accepted.

This brings me to the second point, which is the political con-venience of legal strategies for emancipative struggles. This question has been intensely debated within progressive social movements. Why fight for rights in courtrooms when the struggle can be brought to the streets? One of the arguments put forth by skeptics of legal strategies relies on the paradoxical character of this battle.[29] According to these critics, using legal mechanisms established by the state amounts to the legitimation of the same state that activists wish to attack. Stephen Ellmann notes that "[t]hose who seek to challenge unjust states by using the law of those states against them are very likely to feel tarnished by the need to speak in terms of laws they despise" (1995, p. 339). Richard Brisbin refers to the same problem when he states that "[t]he inside strategy for resist-ance requires an investment in tactics that pit legality against itself" (2010, p. 31).

On the other hand, one must not forget the possibilities of reaction among the most powerful sectors of society and the state in the face of decisions reached under the pressure of social movements. According to McCann, "Legal mobilization efforts have generated backlashes in virtually every part of the world where social movements have attempted to challenge hierarchical social power and authoritarian

---

[29] For an analysis of these paradoxes in the French context, see Spanou (1989).

state rule" (2004, p. 516). We must always take into account the possibility that a counterrevolution erupts when social movements question traditional values, such as order, religion, and social hierarchies.

These doubts about the convenience of legal strategies are founded on the ambivalent and elusive character of the law (Sarat & Ewick, 2015). As Richard Abel notes, the law is simultaneously government and politics, ideology and reality, neutral and partisan, above the fray and in the midst of it (1998, p. 69). More concretely, the law has two faces: on one side is a power that regulates, imposes, and requires obedience, and on the other is a group of rights that citizens can invoke to limit and control state power.[30]

This ambiguity reveals the delicate equilibrium (both empirical and political) that exists between the costs of legitimating a system through litigation and the benefits that can be obtained by using the legal process against the state (Bisharat, 1990; Keck, 2014). This equilibrium is difficult to evaluate, notably because it may be the case that one of the principal benefits obtained by a movement that fights for its rights is a symbolic benefit consisting of greater cohesion in these rights. There can thus be a social movement that fails in its legal dispute but that obtains, from this litigious experience, the political unity and determination needed to win other future battles. This is one of the advantages – and risks – of symbolic (political) battles: in their production of meaning, they go beyond the specific issue they address; they re-signify both the battles and the actors. "Rights," says Martha Minow, "can give rise to a 'rights consciousness' so that individuals and groups can imagine and act on rights that have not been formally recognized or enforced" (1987, p. 1867).[31]

The Social-Conservative Use of Law
Lastly, the social-conservative use of law can be found among conservative groups and movements that employ the law to protect their interests. For example, some movements, inspired by the defense of

---

[30] This ambiguity is particularly evident, as demonstrated in Chapter 1, in the continental European tradition of law due to the fact that there is only one word to express these two aspects (e.g., *droit*, *derecho*, *recht*, *diritto*).

[31] See also Brigham (1996); McCann (2004); Piven & Cloward (1979); Zackin (2014).

religious beliefs, fight against the legalization of abortion,[32] while others engage in legal battles against the liberalization of drugs.[33] Another example is that of users and sellers of firearms in the United States, who, backed by the National Rifle Association, invoke the Second Amendment to argue that citizens have a right to bear arms. Further, Kitty Calavita refers to California's Proposition 187 (also known as the "Save Our State" initiative), a 1994 ballot measure that sought to restrict the rights of undocumented immigrants by denying them health services and preventing their children from attending school (2010, pp. 105–106). Despite the fact that it was clear that the norm would be declared unconstitutional by judges, proponents urged people to vote for the proposition in order to "send a message" that they were fed up with illegal immigration. The initiative won 59 percent of the votes, but the norm was never applied because of its unconstitutionality. Such a contradiction (proposing a law that would ultimately be declared unconstitutional) reflects the main intention of the campaign: to send a message (a symbol) against immigration. Moreover, the massive vote was a political message against the judiciary that would declare the norm unconstitutional.

***

Finally, it is worth mentioning that certain contexts can be more or less favorable to certain types of symbolic use. Authoritarian regimes in Latin America – especially those that still have some semblance of democratic formality, as is the case of "delegative democracies" (Acemoglu & Robinson, 2012; Centeno & Ferraro, 2013; O'Donnell, 1994) – create favorable contexts for the state-conservative use of law.

The state-progressive use, by contrast, is particularly prosperous in countries where judicial independence is strong (especially within the high courts) and where there is a progressive aspirational constitution with a generous bill of rights (García-Villegas, 2002, 2012a). This institutional environment is also conducive to the social-progressive use of law.

---

[32] In the United States, the struggles of millionaire Tom Monaghan, particularly against the legalization of abortion, invoke the Catholic cause. For the Colombian context, see Garzón & Botero (2012); Hoyos (2005).

[33] With regard to the consumption of alcohol, see Gusfield (1963). For a look at Catholics who defend the idea of protecting their rights through the courts, see Smart (1989).

It is worth nothing that these two types of progressive uses are closely connected in practice. Progressive constitutional courts (in constant tension with the executive and legislative powers) and progressive social movements can establish symbolic and political alliances for mutual support.[34]

Another context that favors the symbolic use of these progressive legal strategies is the existence of legal support networks, which are able to translate the demands of social movements into legal actions. In countries with progressive judicial activism, such as the United States and Canada, the existence of a legal structure to support social movements is crucial for the success of this activism. Charles R. Epp (1998) explains how the so-called rights revolution in the United States, which occurred at the time of the civil rights movement, was made possible not only by the existence of a bill of rights, progressive Supreme Court judges, and a civic culture conducive to the protection of such rights, but also thanks to lawyers and legal support for mobilized citizens' networks.[35] Without all these factors – norms, judges, culture, and social mobilization – the rights would not have led to real changes. Similarly, McCann and Helena Silverstein argue that in the United States, the success of "public interest lawyers" (lawyers who defend the causes of social movements, also known as cause lawyers) depends on factors such as the organizational structures within which these lawyers work, the role that lawyers play in these organizations, the types of opportunities available in legal firms, and the lawyers' experience (1998, p. 278).

THE TWO FACES OF SYMBOLIC EFFICACY

Every legal system must achieve two fundamental objectives: the adaptation of its general legal norms to social reality, and legal certainty – that is, the predictability of legal texts for future judicial cases. Any system, according to Nikas Luhmann (1983), must strike a balance between the need for justice and the need for legal certainty. To achieve these objectives, the legal system uses words and concepts that do not have a fixed meaning but instead are contestable symbols, giving

---

[34] In a piece on the effectiveness of the policy decisions of the Colombian Constitutional Court, Uprimny and I propose a model for understanding the emancipatory dimension of progressive jurisprudence (Uprimny & García-Villegas, 2004).

[35] For an opposite vision, see Rosenberg (1991); Waldron (2006).

rise to very different political and social uses. As Dudas et al. argue, rights discourses are complex, contradictory, contested, and, above all, constitutive (Dudas et al., 2015, p. 367).

The symbol of hope has a double face: it can calm our minds, but it can also stimulate them. This ambivalence is reflected in the fantasy tale of Ramón Gómez de la Serna, which tells the story of a man condemned by God for all eternity except for one day. After having spent a hundred years in purgatory, waiting for heaven, the condemned man prays to God to send him to hell. "Kill my hope, kill this hope that thinks always of the final and distant date," pleads the prisoner (Gómez de la Serna, 2014, p. 190). God takes pity on him and sends him to hell, where the man finally releases his despair. Priests are familiar with this double face of hope: they know that belief can feed both resignation in the face of life's adversities and the courage to fight against these misfortunes. But priests are not the only experts on this matter. Politicians also know that their promises can promote not just resignation but also mobilization. Unhappiness is more readily accepted when people believe that the future will be better. As Francis Bacon (2001, p. 41) once said, "The political and artificial nourishing and entertaining of hopes, and carrying men from hope to hope, is one of the best antidotes against the poison of discontentment." On the other hand, when people know that their situation is capable of improving, they often make every effort to achieve change. In the words of Samuel Johnson (1751, p. 165), "Where there is not hope, there can be no endeavor." Hope can also make people willing and courageous.

Hope, then, is a symbol that sometimes favors the passive acceptance of reality and sometimes favors action.[36] The implications of one or the other are essential for the political life of law: the first is a remedy against rebellion, the second a remedy against conformism.

Thus, for example, the promulgation of a progressive constitution can be a remedy against popular uprisings as well as a remedy against conformism. Too often, governments try to temporarily separate these two effects: constitutions are enacted to immediately obtain a calming effect, with the idea that, in the future, popular mobilization can be constrained through a restrictive interpretation of the constitution. The same thing happens when parents lure their child to bed with the promise of a gift for the next day, in the hope that the child will

---

[36] In a book documenting the experiences of people seeking justice through the courts, Merry (1990) shows the contrast between frustration and hope.

forget the promise. This strategy, however, fails when the child is perceptive enough to demand that the promise be fulfilled. In the same manner, generous legal rules to legitimize political power can be used by social movements against the same power.

The second fundamental legal symbol is dependency – in other words, the idea that individuals depend on the social group. This is also a polysemic symbol that evokes opposing images: on the one hand, dependency can be perceived as a factor of submission to society and, consequently, as a reason for seeking liberation and detachment from the social group; on the other, dependence can be seen as a factor of compromise to the social group and therefore as a reason for commitment and obligations. These two images, detachment and compromise, have important political consequences: the detachment makes us passive and indolent toward the group, while compromise makes us active and supportive.

In short, the law, viewed in terms of its symbolic efficacy, is a double-edged sword[37]: it can be a tool to appease the population so that things remain as they have always been, or it can be a signal to demand social change. It can be a symbol for us to submit to the social order or a symbol for us to fight for collective values. More than a valid norm or an obligation, the law is a box of symbolic resources for taking action, particularly political action, which is limited and vast at the same time.

CONCLUSION

Democratic politics have changed significantly in recent decades. Not only has the traditional way of doing politics through political parties and social movements evolved, but the political balance between the political branches of government and the judiciary has been modified as well, particularly in civil law countries. A good portion of political power has migrated from traditional institutions (the parliament and executive branch) to the courts (Dudas et al., 2015, p. 369). These changes – like others that have occurred on the world stage, such as the internationalization of human rights and social struggles – have given greater visibility and political significance to the law. This does not mean that the new balance between law and politics is better, or that legal authorities provide better solutions to current problems – just that

---

[37] For an illustration of this idea, see Mertz (2007, pp. 130–137).

the power has changed, and in this change the politics of law plays an increasingly important role. It also does not mean that rights mobilization is always profitable for social movements. As Dudas et al. posit, "[R]ights speak both to equality and inequality, to empowerment and disempowerment, often concurrently" (2015, p. 372).

Given these changes, the promises of the law are no longer limited to securing law's instrumental effectiveness. More than a regulator of social reality, the law is a resource, a political arena within which social realities are constructed (Commaille & Duran, 2009; Israël, 2009a). It is in this political arena that state bodies and social groups compete, each trying to use the law to serve their own interests.

Most of the time, this struggle is uneven, favoring the government and powerful economic groups. But, the result of this clash is not always set in advance. This is why, in order to avoid not only the optimism of liberal views that perceive society as a reflection of values set by legislators and great jurists, but also the Marxist pessimistic view that sees law merely as a reflection of economic conditions in society, we need to do empirical research, to see how and under which circumstances counterhegemonic forces can win the battle for the interpretation of legal meaning.

In contemporary democracies, struggles for rights have acquired great importance (Delpeuch et al., 2014; Larson & Schmidt, 2014; Rodríguez Garavito, 2014; Sarat & Ewick, 2015). Today, almost all social and political problems pass through the filter of law – hence Jacques Commaille's (2010) description of the "legalization of politics." This is why the idea of the symbolic efficacy of law is not only central in the political arena of contemporary societies but also a key concept for SLS that aims to explain the political uses of law in those societies.

CHAPTER THREE

LEGAL FIELDS AND THE SOCIAL SCIENCES IN FRANCE AND THE UNITED STATES*

Ever since Alexis de Tocqueville's famous text *Democracy in America*, the differences between French and American legal fields have been widely studied in political science. Here, too, I attempt to compare the two legal fields by bearing in mind the concept of symbolic uses of law explained in Chapter 2 and drawing on the two theoretical assumptions developed in Chapter 1. The first assumption relates to the understanding of law as a social field, closely connected with the political system, in which different actors (judges, legislators, lawyers, teachers, social movements, and so on) with varying levels of material and symbolic power compete for the legitimate interpretation of legal texts. Given that the resulting legal debates in this competition implicate the distribution of power and social goods, as opposed to being primarily intellectual or technical, they are largely political in nature. In that sense, this analysis of the legal field is also a sociopolitical legal study (SLS). The second assumption refers to the idea that the fate of legal fields – and, more specifically, the fate of the symbolic uses of law – depends, in part, on the legal tradition to which they belong (common law or civil law) and on the type of relation between the legal tradition and the conceptions of state and sovereignty embedded within it.

* This chapter is a modified version of my article "Comparative Sociology of Law: Legal Fields, Legal Scholarships, and Social Sciences in Europe and the United States," published in *Law and Social Inquiry* (García-Villegas, 2006). A French version of this piece was published in *L'Année sociologique* (García-Villegas, 2009a).

In this chapter, I will argue that the structure of legal fields in contemporary continental Europe and the United States, as well as their connection to the political field, took shape as the result of a process of accommodation and internal restructuring that began in the early nineteenth century. The structuring of the French legal field was marked by a legal doctrine considered autonomous and neutral, which gave way to a minimal or nonexistent application of the symbolic uses of law. On the other hand, the structuring of the American legal field was marked by a legal practice connected to social reality and the political field, which resulted in a less autonomous and neutral doctrine that was more amenable to political uses of law. It is true that during the last decades this contrast has been substantially attenuated. However, these differences continue to play an important role in the two countries, not only in relation to the conception of law but also in terms of its practice.

The chapter is divided into three sections. The first explores the sociopolitical visions of law that were in place in the early twentieth century; the second offers an analysis of the evolution of the French and American legal fields; and the third concludes with a brief commentary on the main sociopolitical differences between these two legal fields.

My approach hinges on a combination of deductive logic and thick description aimed at capturing the specificities of the historical events under examination while seeking to draw general theoretical conclusions from them. I undertake a detailed study of historical evidence in order to single out elements within these historical events that call for theoretical reconstruction.[1]

My analysis in this chapter is a long-term one, aimed at grasping the dominant features of the legal cultures of these two countries so that the contrasts and similarities between them come to light. It must be said at the outset that these legal cultures are neither monolithic nor hegemonic – and less so with the strong globalization of law that has been occurring since the 1990s.[2] Although both France and the United

---

[1] Therefore, this chapter does not agree with a type of comparative sociology that is based on inductive logic and that seeks to draw generalizations from a systematic comparison of observed cases based on a limited number of variables. See Skocpol & Somers (1980).

[2] Economic globalization has certainly reduced the contrast between traditions and legal fields (Dezalay & Garth, 2002; Garapon, 1995). In this sense, I agree with

States have had a dominant legal culture, each one of them has continuously been challenged – sometimes significantly so – by other legal visions.[3]

On the other hand, it should be noted that these cultures change according to different socio-legal domains. What happens in law schools and in the sites of production of legal doctrine is one thing; what takes place in the professional milieus of lawyers, judges, and public officials is another. In France, even within law schools, there is a marked difference between the legal culture of civil law professors and that of public law professors. Such contrasts are particularly important due to France's clear separation between the world of legal education (law schools) and that of legal practice. I will develop this point in Chapters 4 and 5.

THE ANTIFORMALIST CHALLENGE

At the beginning of the twentieth century, legal scholarship in France, Germany, and the United States was struggling to define its place between two diametrically opposed positions. On one side were formalist and conservative ideas, as exhibited by the school of exegesis (*école de l'exégèse*) in France, conceptualism in Germany, and classical legal thought in the United States. The other pole was occupied by critical visions of law spearheaded by the school of free law (*Freirechtsschule*) and legal pluralism in Europe and by legal realism in the United States (Belleau, 1999; Chassagnard-Pinet, 2013).[4]

These two contending positions proposed opposite solutions to the tension between the autonomy of law and law's adaptation to social reality. While the first group underlined the autonomy of law, the

Gessner and Nelken's criticism of my 2006 article, which they published in the introduction to *European Ways of Law* (2007b). However, in line with Kagan (2007), I argue here that there are still a number of important differences and that only a long-term vision allows us to highlight them.

[3] In this regard, see the recent book on French legal culture by Audren & Halpérin (2013), as well as Belleau (1999). Other authors, however, are less willing to characterize the French legal culture in this flexible and changeable manner; for these views, see Cohen-Tanugi (2007); Garapon (1995); Garapon & Papadopoulos (2003); Muir-Watt (2000).

[4] For a detailed explanation of the importance of law's social aspects at the beginning of the twentieth century in Europe and the United States, see Jouanjan & Zoller (2016).

second emphasized social adaptation and law's dependency on social practice. I will refer to the first as "formalist" and the second as "antiformalist." Legal formalism, as stated in Chapter 1, narrowed the concept of law to state law. At the foundation of this theoretical current lies the idea of law as a comprehensive and coherent system of positive norms that do not require interpretation; deductive reasoning is seen as the best, if not the only, method of adjudication, which leads to the belief that judicial decisions are neutral – in other words, not politicized. These differences also reflected the political tensions of the time between the followers of a vision of society based on individualism and laissez-faire and the proponents of a new society based on solidarity and collectivism (Hespanha, 2005; Kennedy, 1976).

The French Revolution wanted the new law, unlike that of the *ancien régime*, to be simple and clear so that people could understand it and use it to their benefit. A "law within the grasp of those who have to obey it," as Maximilien Robespierre used to say (1970). With this spirit in mind, during the first part of the nineteenth century, the law was identified with legislation – and, more specifically, with the 1804 Civil Code, which was seen as a perfect expression of the popular will (*volonté générale*). Any interpretation was forbidden. It is said that when Napoleon learned that Jacques de Maleville, one of the code's authors, had published a text titled *Analyse raisonnée du Code Civil*, Napoleon exclaimed, "My code is ruined" (Arnaud, 1975, p. 47). To preserve this ideal, the state did everything it could to block the development of a legal thought independent from political power.

By mid-century, however, in an era of great social and political change, it had become clear that the idea of the "self-sufficiency of positive law" was unsustainable and that commentaries on legislation were necessary. The school of exegesis arose in that context.[5] Its followers acknowledged the need for an analysis of law, but only with

---

[5] Despite being named "schools," these areas did not adhere to unified principles, nor did they share a clearly defined orientation. Exegesis was an attempt to understand and explain the Civil Code, beginning with an extremely detailed reading of its texts and the extraction of principles drawn strictly from the letter of the code. Among its main proponents were Étienne Delvincourt (*Institutions de droit civil français*), Alexandre Duranton (*Traité des obligations et contrat en général*), Antoine Demante (*Programme de cours de droit civil français*), Jean Baptiste Duvergier (*Collection des lois, décrets, ordonnances, règlements et avis du Conseil d'Etat*), and Victor Marcadé (*Explication théorique et pratique du Code de Napoléon*). On this point, see Arnaud (1975); Jestaz & Jamin (2004).

the aim of clarifying its meaning and scope through the meticulous examination of legal texts. Legislators and the Civil Code would continue to be not only the protagonists of the legal field but also a founding element of French national identity. The Civil Code was the legal source of truth and the object of veneration and republican pride in the political realm. For that reason, legal analysis was guided more by legislated law than by scientific description. The law was viewed not as a science but as a discipline, and it was this conception that prevailed in France until the last decade of the nineteenth century (Arnaud, 1975, p. 47; Audren, 2016).

In Germany, by contrast, codification came late, in part because of the reaction against the imperialist influence of Napoleonic France and its code. Instead, the "historical school of law," led by Friedrich Karl von Savigny and Georg Friedrich Puchta, flourished.[6] This school, which was opposed to the glorification of lawmakers, advocated the "people's law," as expressed in customary practices and systematized into a science by law professors. The interpretation and conceptualization of law were thus a product of universities.[7] Law faculties trained and educated professors (in addition to jurists and judges) with the idea that they were the holders of a "learned" and scientific knowledge destined to serve as an essential source of law.

But the historical school of law also defended a critical position against legal formalism. Savigny advocated for customary law over the legalist and statist idea of codification (Dufour, 1974). According to Savigny, all positive law was, in one sense or another, law that arose from the people (*Volksrecht*). He claimed that law transformed itself in the same way that language and morals did. Only at a later stage in social development was law manifested as legislated law.[8]

---

[6] The historical school of law opposed the 1814 codification project inspired by the French model and led by Anton Friedrich Thibaut. Another representative of the school was Rudolf von Ihering, considered to be the father of the "school of interests," which promoted a method of interpreting the law based on the interests at stake. He famously defined subjective law as "judicially protected interests." Notable among his works are *Geist des römischen Rechts* (1865a), *Der Kampf um's Rechts* (1865b), and *Der Zweck im Recht* (1877). See also Ihering (1901).

[7] See the work of Savigny (2001) on German universities.

[8] This transformation, according to Savigny, was necessary because the *Volksrecht* needed to address its lack of clarity by formalizing its premises in the form of legislated law. Nonetheless, even positive law was just a stage of the *Volksrecht*.

Savigny was a conservative man, but his idea of the "people's law" inspired a new generation of progressive legal thinkers (in both France and Germany) who published their works during the first decade of the twentieth century. In particular, Savigny influenced scholars such as Eugen Ehrlich, Hermann Kantorowicz and Philipp Hech in Germany,[9] Santi Romano in Italy, and Georges Gurvitch in France.[10] These scholars advocated "social law," opposed legal formalism, and proposed a new approach to law that enshrined social rights, social self-determination, and political progressivism.[11]

They critiqued legal formalism in three key ways. First, they were opposed to the traditional reduction of law to official law produced or recognized by the state. In contrast to this conception (the state as the only source of law), they claimed that official law was part of a phenomenon of legal pluralism (both official and nonofficial sources of law). According to Ehrlich, "Legal Provisions cannot possibly cover the entire law" (1922, p. 141).[12] Second, they rejected the notion of law as a rational, coherent, and autonomous system – that is, a system oblivious to the existence of gaps and contradictions. Legal doctrine understood as a unified and coherent system of knowledge driven by logic and deduction did not exist, they argued; lacunae and gaps were pervasive in the legal system.[13] Finally, they argued that "living law" was the primary source of official law. "The great mass of law," explained Ehrlich, "arises immediately in society itself in the form of a spontaneous ordering of social relations, of marriage, the family

---

[9] Ehrlich and Kantorowicz are considered to be the founders of modern sociological jurisprudence in Germany. Ehrlich's most important follower in Germany is Raiser (1999).

[10] See volume 94 of *Droit et société*, which is dedicated to the work of Gurvitch; see particularly Commaille (2016); Le Goff (2016).

[11] On the idea of social law, see Ewald (1986); Gaillet (2016); Gurvitch (1931); Herrera (2003b, 2016); Kennedy (2006).

[12] Ehrlich is acknowledged as the most renowned spokesperson of the school of free law. He demonstrated a certain sympathy for the system of common law, in which he saw ideas and instruments against legal formalism represented in codification. His work was introduced in the United States by the German refugee jurist Kantorowicz, another representative of the school, and later by Roscoe Pound (1912, 1927, 1943). See also Gurvitch (1931).

[13] Hart argues, with reference to Holmes, Pound, and Ihering, that despite their differences, they were united in the belief that "legal concepts are closed and precise, in the sense that it is possible to provide a complete and exhaustive definition in terms of a set of necessary and sufficient conditions" (1970, p. 113).

associations, possession, contracts, succession, and most of this Social Order has never been embraced in Legal Provisions" (1922, p. 100).

To summarize, legal pluralism, incoherence, and living law were three essential features of the European challenge to formalism, all of them in opposition to a law conceptualized as state legislation.

The historical school, especially Savigny's work, also had a significant influence in the United States. Legal thinkers such as Oliver Wendell Holmes, Jr., Roscoe Pound, and Karl Llewellyn found inspiration in the school of free law and European antiformalist scholars.[14] Under the banner of legal realism, they advanced a pragmatic and skeptical jurisprudence, countering the use of conceptualism and formalism in law schools. In the United States, the arrival of laissez-faire in the second half of the nineteenth century implied a new concept of adjudication based on logical deduction and syllogism. This kind of legal formalism was born with the program and the teaching method developed by Christopher Langdell at Harvard in the nineteenth century, called "the case method of instruction" (Tamanaha, 2006).

Admittedly, legal realism was not a unified movement. According to Neil Duxbury (1995), it was nothing more than an intellectual mood – but it was a very influential "mood" in American law schools. In hindsight, legal realism appears to be, by far, the most influential legal perspective in the United States (Fisher, Horwitz, & Reed, 1993).

Legal realism was marked by three distinguishing features.[15] First, realists advocated a social devaluation of law, particularly of legal

---

[14] Pound was a major advocate of European antiformalist ideas during the 1920s and 1930s, especially through his work *Interpretation of Legal History* (1967; originally published in 1923). He introduced sociological jurisprudence in a speech at the American Bar Foundation in 1906. He admired authors such as François Gény, Éduard Lambert, and Raymond Saleilles. See Duguit et al. (1916); Reimann (1993). See also Cohen (1937). Llewellyn was very familiar with the work of Ihering and Ehrlich; see, for example, his text "A Realistic Jurisprudence" (1930). Also, as Duxbury (1995) explains, Holmes's *The Common Law* is clearly indebted to the nineteenth-century historical jurisprudence of Savigny and Sir Henry Maine; see Ganne (2016); Jouanjan (2016a).

[15] Regarding the core of realist jurisprudence, see Hart (1983); Schlegel (1995); Tamanaha (2006). It is always difficult to define the core of realist thought. According to Twining (1985), if there is any agreement among those who have studied this movement, it would be regarding the movement's heterogeneity and dispersion. A less critical view can be found in Ackerman (1984); Hunt (1978). See also Hart (1983). Cotterrell (1989) distinguishes three types of legal realism: political scientific realism, radical skepticism, and radical constructive realism.

norms. As Llewellyn argued (1930), these norms were much less important than people thought. Second, and in line with the first idea, realists refuted the supposedly determining character of legislation, instead looking to judicial decisions as the real law – hence Holmes's famous statement that "predictions on what the courts will actually do is what I understand by law, and nothing more pretentious" (1897, p. 461).[16] Third, they called into question law's neutrality and thus postulated its political nature. Llewellyn insisted that legal forms were "vital ruling practices" that produced "official manipulation of the rules" (1994, p. 266).

In sum, marginality, indeterminacy, and political bias were the central points of antiformalist realism.

From this comparison of the two antiformalist movements we can identify three dichotomies that help explain their reciprocal emphasis: legal pluralism/marginality, incoherence/indetermination, and living law/political bias. These dichotomies would mark the theoretical and disciplinary tensions that came to characterize SLS in subsequent years. They question the two central tenets of legal formalism: the autonomy of law vis-à-vis social reality and the neutrality of law vis-à-vis the political field. In the following section, I will show the different fates of the antiformalist movement in France and in the United States and the resulting different development of SLS in the two countries.

LEGAL DOCTRINE IN FRANCE

An attempt to find a middle ground between formalist and antiformalist positions in law arose in France, as well as in Germany, during the first three decades of the twentieth century (Audren & Halpérin, 2013, p. 157; Encinas de Muñagorri et al., 2016; Jouanjan & Zoller, 2016). France's political environment at the time (between the two world wars) was characterized by, among other things, the desire of French lawyers and law schools to claim civility and defend the French legal tradition against German legal culture and legal authoritarianism (Audren & Halpérin, 2013, p. 160; Jouanjan, 2016a).[17] This attempt

---

[16] Llewellyn's article "A Realistic Jurisprudence" distinguishes between "paper rules" and "real rules" (1930, p. 12).

[17] Paradoxically, this desire led to support of the Vichy regime among many lawyers and law schools. See Lochak (1989a, 1989b). See also Audren & Halpérin (2013, p. 213).

gave birth to French classical legal doctrine. Among its main proponents were Léon Duguit, François Gény, Éduard Lambert, Marcel Planiol, Henri Capitant, and Louis Josserand.[18] These men wrote during the 1920s and 1930s, which was a period of rapid industrialization and increasing social complexity characterized by critiques of liberal individualism, the adoption of social and collective values, and the influence of the social sciences.[19]

These authors opposed the glorification of the law[20] and demanded the inclusion of customary practice as a formal legal source.[21] The analysis of texts was no longer the point; what aroused scholarly interest was the interpretation of law in light of knowledge drawn from economics, statistics, history, anthropology, and – especially – sociology.

The classical vision differed significantly not only from the traditional legal view (legal formalism) but also from the one developed by antiformalist critics, such as the school of free law (Belleau, 1999). The main interest of classical thinkers was constructive rather than critical. They wanted to integrate the social dimension into law without damaging law's autonomy vis-à-vis political power and social reality. In this era between the world wars, there was a particular interest in the social sciences and economics. However, according to Frédéric Audren and Jean-Louis Halpérin, these fields were "relegated to the borders of the civil law, and remained there, conceived as a simple complement of general culture" (2013, p. 185).

Classical legal thinkers sought to develop a third way between those who saw legislation as the only source of law and their critics who espoused legal pluralism and dissolved law into politics. Classical scholars' enthusiasm for the social and their sympathy for antiformalist

---

[18] See Capitant (1898); Duguit (1889, 1922); Gény (1899); Josserand (1927); Lambert (1928); Planiol (1899).

[19] During this era, the idea arose that social relations should be based less on principles of autonomy and individual responsibility than on the notion of solidarity (Durkheim, 1993). The influence of sociology was evident in Maurice Hauriou's theory of institution (1910). See, for example, Duguit (1889). For a general overview of the period, see Arnaud (1998); Chassagnard-Pinet (2013).

[20] At the end of the nineteenth century, many thought that the Civil Code had grown hoary; some, such as Demogue (1911) and Saleilles (1904), went further in opining that the code represented an obstacle to social progress.

[21] The classical text is that of Gény (1899), which lays out the bases of a pluralist theory of legal sources. See also Demogue (1911).

thought were clearly manifested but not unbounded. These were conservative men (*hommes d'ordre*) who wanted to preserve and exalt French law (particularly civil law) in a context of national struggle against Germany. While they were open to change, they desired a kind of change based on the preservation of the past and the glory of the national tradition of French law.[22]

At the end of the century, Gény asked if this emphasis on social aspects would lead to the dissolution of law and the predominance of arbitrary standards. If the codes were no longer the basis of law, he asked, "does this not expose us to all the dangers of empirical or case-by-case decisions and in this fashion sacrifice this primordial, absolute, indisputable need for the security of law, from which the security of life in society is derived?" (1899, p. 185).

Gény's (1899) response to both legal criticism and legal formalism was the consolidation of a scientific legal body of thought that was fully autonomous from the state, political parties, and social interests (Arnaud, 1975). Thus appeared a tradition that conceived of law as an "inexact, but hard science," in the words of Philippe Jestaz and Christophe Jamin (2004, p. 174). This middle way could only be developed by university law professors.[23] The new scholarship, called "legal doctrine," was defined as an authorized study of positive law in which the internal tensions of law were resolved with the aim of working out solutions applicable in practice (Chevallier, 1993; Jestaz & Jamin, 2004, p. 174).

But in reality, Gény's idea of the *libre recherche scientifique* was never accomplished. Instead, a conservative reaction emerged to defend the autonomy of law and the doctrinal model. Thus, as explained by Jamin, after the Second World War, the French model acquired its current

---

[22] This is why they distanced themselves from the leftist lawyers of the time. In Germany, the latter, inspired by Karl Marx, Friedrich Engels, and especially Ferdinand Lassalle, had a significant impact on the legislative reforms implemented during the Weimar Republic in 1929. See also Lassalle (1964); Ledford (1996); Menger (1899). In France, there were also leftist lawyers who used the law to fight for socialism – for example, Blum (1965), Duguit (1922), Hauriou (1910), Jaurès (1964), and Lévy (1909). They were interested in legal practice and doctrine, but their movement was too weak to challenge legal formalism (Israël & Mouralis, 2005). For a vision of this movement, see Herrera (2003a, 2003b, 2003c).

[23] A good example is the *Traité pratique de droit civil français*, by Marcel Planiol and Georges Ripert. For an explanation of the importance of these books and manuals, see Jestaz & Jamin (2004).

face, "based on a distribution of subjects within law schools, between the learning of legal technology and the knowledge of general culture, the first outweighing the second" (2012, p. 65).

Two consequences resulted from the birth of legal doctrine in France: (i) the creation of a priestly caste of legal scholars and (ii) the distancing of the autonomy of law from the social sciences.

Law Professors

With the creation of legal doctrine in the mid-twentieth century, law professors and legal formalism consolidated their hegemonic position in the French legal field.[24] Once again, European universities became intellectual centers destined to stabilize and, as Michel Foucault would say, normalize legal power.[25] Although the task of producing a unified body of law had been largely achieved with the adoption of the Civil Code during the nineteenth century, it was legal doctrine during the twentieth century that played the leading role.[26]

Law professors, especially civil law professors, acquired not only high visibility and great political influence, as mentioned in Chapter 1, but also a high degree of autonomy vis-à-vis political power. However, it must be mentioned that law schools have lost most of their influence in recent decades; they no longer have a monopoly on elite education, and law professors do not enjoy a privileged position in public and political life in today's France.[27] On the other hand, the left's arrival to

[24] It is true that the difference between the lawyer, the judge, and the professor is not always clear. In France, professors of civil law sometimes become lawyers, as judges can become lawyers. See Milet (2000); Serverin (1985). It also seems clear that during the Third Republic (1871–1940), the political influence of law professors was rather limited compared to the political influence of lawyers (Dulong, 1997). In administrative law, the role of judges and judicial decisions seems as important as the role of law professors. For an explanation of the special character of administrative law, see Jestaz & Jamin (2004, p. 202). With regard to civil law, the privileged position of jurisprudence still prevails in the French legal field.

[25] During the late Middle Ages, the university had already fulfilled this task of unification when it worked to restore Roman law and, through this route, consolidate the absolutist regime (Anderson, 1979).

[26] The Paris Law School played a fundamental role in this consolidation; for a socio-historical perspective of this institution, see Gazzaniga (1994); Halpérin (2011a, 2011b).

[27] In this regard, see Israël & Vanneuville (2014). See also Biland & Israël (2011). An example of law professors' zeal in retaining their status is reflected in the rules governing the entry into professorship (Mouly & Atias, 1993). After obtaining a doctoral degree, candidates must pass the *aggregation*, a test whose characteristics

power in 1981 not only implied a very difficult situation for critical movements (as government and domination were intrinsically embedded in their theories) but also a loss of power of formalists and law schools with regard to the *énarques* (Audren & Halpérin, 2013, p. 243).[28]

Law and the Social Sciences

The victory of a conception of law based on legal technique and legal positivism in France was also the result of the subordination, or even distancing, of social sciences with regard to law (Audren & Halpérin, 2013; Encinas de Muñagorri et al., 2016).

At the beginning of the Fifth Republic, in 1958, lawyers imposed a kind of sociology of law that viewed sociology as a servant of law.[29] At that time, a project seeking to give visibility to law and law schools was born in the Ministry of Justice and was given voice by various prestigious law professors. The project, conceived by Jean Foyer, the minister of justice, and Jean Carbonnier,[30] a law professor, aimed to reform legislation based on the results of the national Enquête d'Opinion Législative (survey of legislative opinion).[31] Sociology was perceived as a necessary tool for the study of law, although subordinate to lawyers' points of view.[32]

However, the reception of sociology in law schools at that moment is a rather exceptional event in the contemporary history of French law schools,[33] and one that is mostly explained by the role of Carbonnier.

---

and challenges are proof of the mastery of the field to which they aspire (Charle, 2003).

[28] In France, the term *énarques* is used to refer to those who hold a degree from the École Nationale d'Administration, who are a kind of intellectual elite in the French academic world (Bourdieu, 1964).

[29] Regarding this subordination of sociology, see Commaille (1983, 2007a); Israël (2008a); Soubiran-Paillet (2000).

[30] Like his predecessor in the role of editor of *L'Année sociologique*, Carbonnier was trained in the French Durkheimian school of sociology. However, unlike Gurvitch, whose studies in legal sociology had no impact on law schools, the writings of Carbonnier, especially his manuals, are still studied today.

[31] A similar project was created in Italy under the leadership of Renato Treves (Odorisio et al., 1970).

[32] For a critique of this subordination of sociology, see Commaille (1989); Commaille, Demoulin, & Robert (2010). For an interdisciplinary vision of the relation between law and social sciences, see Israël et al. (2005a, 2005b).

[33] The international reception of Carbonnier's ideas was also exceptional. See García-Villegas (2012b).

The fact that he was a great author of treatises on civil law before becoming a sociologist of law allowed him to evade the usual criticism leveled by jurists at legal sociologists, which was that sociologists lacked a sound knowledge of law. Additionally, he shared the conservative spirit of his colleagues, espousing an approach in which sociology was a sort of "handmaiden to law" – aimed at enhancing the capacity of legislation to affect social phenomena – with no autonomy or critical potential. According to Audren and Halpérin, Carbonnier was a "rigid defender of a French tradition that identifies the national legal culture with the cult of the law and with the Cartesian interpretations, in a refusal tinted with hostility towards the common law methods and free and creative jurisprudence" (2013, p. 262).[34]

The idea of legislative sociology was finally extinguished with the arrival of the conservative movement of the 1990s. Once again, law professors were able to consolidate legal doctrine and their own position in the legal field. With this victory, the triumph of formalists and positivists was affirmed, and, more importantly, the typically French division between civil law and public law professors was cemented.[35] This division separated two ways of interpreting the normative corpus: a formal and inflexible one (the civil law vision) and a social and flexible one (the publicist vision) (Milet, 2012).

The autonomy of law in relation to the social sciences was accentuated by a perception, rather significant in the 1970s, of law schools as right wing and of sociology departments as left wing. Carbonnier depreciated the work of sociologists of law working at the National Center for Scientific Research in the following terms: "[The sociology of law] gives an image, it must be said, of being quite politicized. This can be explained by the fact that, in France, many sociologists are

---

[34] For a similar critique, see Commaille (1983, 1989, 2003b). On the other hand, according to Francine Soubiran-Paillet, "professors of law, such as Carbonnier and Land, practice legal sociology to enhance their quality as experts to the legislature and become themselves, if appropriate, legislators" (1994, p. 141).

[35] Public law professors in France, as opposed to civil law professors, belong to a long legal academic tradition that is more open to the social sciences. During the first three decades of the twentieth century, there was an important debate in Germany and France around the Weimar Republic. Public law's protagonists in the debate (Herman Heller and Gustav Radbruch, in Germany; Maurice Hauriou and León Duguit in France) predicted a rapprochement between public law and the social sciences. See Blanquer & Millet (2015); for a general explanation of this cleavage among law professors, see Encinas de Muñagorri et al. (2016); Jouanjan (2016a).

located on the left side of the political map" (quoted in Arnaud & Andrini, 1995, p. 53).[36]

It is also important to add that within sociology, there were tensions between some of its leading figures – for example, between Gurvitch and Raymond Aron – which had an impact on the way law was seen in social theory (Lascoumes, 1991; Soubiran-Paillet, 2000, p. 134).[37] According to Francine Soubiran-Paillet, "the story of the relationship between lawyers and sociologists, over the last fifty years, is primarily one of a missed opportunity" (2000, p. 142).

Another phenomenon that contributed to the exclusion of the social sciences in law schools was the departure of political science from most law schools in 1968. In addition, in 1970 the *aggregation test*, which is the entrance examination to law school, was divided into two: one exam in public law and the other in political science.[38] Since then, public law professors have been forced to justify their field as an autonomous discipline, separate from political science. As a result of this disciplinary divide, two communities of public law experts have emerged in France: the traditional group, composed of lawyers graduated from law faculties and working as legal advisers or practicing law in the judicial system, and public law lawyers formed in Sciences Po (the Paris Institute of Political Studies) and working in public administration and even in the judicial system.[39] Not only did the two areas target different markets, but they had different conceptions of law and legal practice (Chevallier, 1997; Milet, 2001).

The privileged position of legal doctrine over the last two decades has begun to show signs of weakening. The process of conceiving of law as autonomous knowledge occurred alongside law schools' loss of influence in the training of French elites. In short, law professors have won the battle around law's autonomy, but at the cost of social and political influence. The crisis of the Paris Law School, at the center of doctrinal authority, illustrates this situation to a large extent. According to Halpérin, "The meritocratic endogamy in Paris has led

---

[36] A similar disdain is expressed by Legendre (1995).

[37] A great number of these disagreements still exist, as can be seen by the publication of two volumes of the *Droit et société* review dedicated to this topic (nos. 69/70 and 75).

[38] There are three types of *agrégation* in France: in public law, in private law, and in legal history.

[39] Those with a degree from Sciences Po can participate in some competitions for judicial appointments.

to an excessive respect for their 'masters' in spite of the new generation of professors" (2011a).[40]

French jurists have seen their symbolic capital reduced to legal and judicial circles. Nowadays, public administration frequently belongs to specialized schools (*grandes écoles*), especially the École Nationale d'Administration and Sciences Po. Today, most of the justices at the Council of State (France's highest administrative court) come from these specialized schools. The crisis of law and law schools in France is also associated with the decline of the university system vis-à-vis the National Center for Scientific Research and the *grandes écoles*. Whereas the university environment is characterized by poor working conditions, relatively low salaries, inflexible rules, and disciplinary tension, scholars at the National Center for Scientific Research work under conditions similar to middle-range universities in the United States.[41]

Additionally, the globalization of the economy, the constitutionalization of rights, the legalization of politics, and the rise of a European legal field, among other factors, have contributed to the emergence of a "new legal culture."[42] The crisis in the French legal profession has led lawyers to implement new strategies to regain their social position. Yves Dezalay and others have analyzed French lawyers' attempt to recover power by entering international business through law firms designed, organized, and managed by large American firms.[43]

This globalization is directly related to another major threat to the traditional French legal model. It comes from the option, created in 2007, allowing Sciences Po graduate students to take the bar exam without going to law school, which has broken the monopoly that law schools had enjoyed since the Middle Ages regarding access to the bar. In addition, business schools, through agreements with

---

[40] A group of more or less open and critical professors (Gény, Duguit, Hauriou, Louis Josserand, Paul Huvelin, and Lévy) worked from time to time in provincial law schools.

[41] According to Mouly & Atias (1993), the attraction of legal scholarship comes from the possibility of developing parallel activities without losing the security gained by the status of being a civil servant.

[42] See Hesselink (2001); Kagan (2001, 2007). For more information regarding the analysis of recent periods, see Garth & Dezalay (1996); Gessner & Budak (1998); Kennedy (2006); Nelken (2012); Trubek & Mosher (2003).

[43] In this regard, see Boigeol & Dezalay (1997); Dezalay (1993, 1992); Dezalay, Sarat, & Silbey (1989). See also Garapon (2007); Gessner & Nelken (2007).

universities, are increasingly able to train lawyers to pass the bar (Biland & Israël, 2011).

Not only have law schools lost their monopoly on the training of lawyers, but also – and even more importantly – the institutions involved in this training now have a much more pragmatic and inter-disciplinary conception of law, due largely to the influence of American legal culture. Some have criticized the fact that the formation of French elites is now driven by economic targets. According to Émilie Biland and Liora Israël, the more flexible and even more political conception of law that prevails at Sciences Po and business schools such as Haute Ecole de Commerce caters to large firms invested in protecting the interests of global financial capital.

Thus, in clear contrast with the triumphalist vision of Jamin (the dean of the Sciences Po Law School), Biland and Israël argue that "the legal system is conceived to serve the economy and therefore it helps legitimize a financial capitalism whose goals are rarely discussed" (2011, p. 651). I have a less pessimistic view of this influence: embracing social sciences can break the monopoly of legal doctrine in the interpretation of law, and possibly open the door to SLS.

Finally, the influence of legal positivism also affected the social sciences. Degrees in sociology were not available in France until 1958.[44] Thus, at the beginning of the twentieth century, sociologists struggled for the recognition of their discipline by sympathetic jurists. The work of Émile Durkheim, particularly his idea of law as an integration between law and sociology (Lascoumes, 1991), was very influential in the formation of these alliances between professors of the two disciplines.[45] As Daniel Pécaut (1996) explains, when the moment of separation arrived, the justification of an autonomous sociology ran counter to the Durkheimian tradition (represented above all in the work of Gurvitch). In fact, both Marxist visions (led by Georges Friedmann) and liberal views (led by Aron) tried to deflect from their interdisciplinary origins, particularly from the

---

[44] For more information, see Bowen & Bentaboulet (2002, p. 539); Cuin & Gresle (2002). It was not until 1913 that Durkheim was able to get the title of his course on the "sciences of education" in the Sorbonne changed to the "science of education and sociology."

[45] Duguit (1889) asserted that sociology consisted primarily of two elements: law and political economy.

Durkheimian idea of the relation between sociology and law (Pécaut, 1996; Soubiran-Paillet, 1994, 2000).[46]

THE LEGAL MARKET IN THE UNITED STATES

The Victory of Legal Realism

In the United States, unlike in France, legal antiformalism triumphed, resulting in legal realism's predominance. It brought about a profound transformation in fin-de-siècle American legal culture. The realist legal critique was "energetically pursued in the torrent of scholarship that poured out in the United States between 1927 and 1940" (Herget & Wallace, 1987). Even today, most law professors regard themselves as legal realists (Hutchinson, 2003).[47]

According to some experts on legal realism, the movement originated in the strategy of some liberal lawyers to confront the isolation of law and lawyers in an era in which the legal system did not seem to be well connected to the rapid social and economic changes of the times (Dworkin, 1985; Sarat & Silbey, 1988; Tomlins, 2000). The rise of realism was a response, explains Christopher Tomlins, "less to scholarly isolation than to the erosion of law's political authority" (2000, p. 94). New ideas and policies reflected in the New Deal and its regulatory-administrative state presented an opportunity for realists to strengthen the social and political influence of law. Legal realists "employed an imaginative, modern, experimental approach to problem solving and to expanding the role of the welfare state" (Kalman, 1996, p. 17). According to Edward Robinson, realists were able to impose the idea that it was necessary to turn lawyers into social engineers who could apply general social scientific methods to "a wide front in the practical solutions of urgent social problems" (1934, p. 266). In so doing, they "put their faith in the utility of social science" (ibid.) and adapted legal thought to a changing political environment in which the state came to assume a much more explicit role (Ackerman, 1984). According to this view, authors like Pound and Robinson wanted to use other forms of social knowledge to

---

[46] For more information, see Bowen & Bentaboulet (2002, p. 539).

[47] When American professors write history, they present legal realism as the theoretical division between the ancient order and modernity (Kelman, 1987; Minda, 1995).

maintain law's ascendancy.[48] While it is true that a critical and relativist tendency existed in legal realism, it turned out to be incompatible with the progressive view of law and policy that finally dominated within the movement (Dezalay et al., 1989, p. 110; Peller, 1985).

The realists' strategy for intervening in social issues and valorizing law had important implications for the conception of law and legal scholarship in the United States. First, the idea of law as a scientific and formalist knowledge – embraced, for example, by legal doctrine in France and Germany – was rendered useless and even suspicious. The analysis and resolution of social problems necessarily called for a flexible approach and a multidisciplinary perspective.[49] In this sense, law faculties were seen as professional schools, teaching a trade with immediate practical applicability (Riesenfeld, 1937, p. 51; Tamanaha, 2012).

Second, the integration that lawyers achieved between their legal competencies and their knowledge of other social sciences reinforced the authority of law and its capacity to provide solutions. Although lawyers' training in social sciences was, and continues to be, weak, their analytical skills rendered them disposed to communication with other social scientists and allowed them to take leadership roles in these interdisciplinary encounters (Calavita, 2002; Dezalay et al., 1989; Mertz, 2008; Tomlins, 2000; Trubek, 1990).

Third, unlike in France, the dynamics of law in the United States were determined by legal practice and depended more on lawyers and their organization than on the state.[50] This favored an instrumental conception of law. As Antoine Garapon notes, "The law [was] not designed as an abstract set of rules that refers to a certain ideal but as a toolkit to act" (2007, p. 78).[51] The law became an instrument for doing things (especially for making money) more than a set of principles and

---

[48] According to Dezalay et al. (1989), realists modernized the image of law and restored some of its legitimacy by dissociating it somewhat from the traders and barons of Wall Street, to whom they were too closely linked. They also succeeded in integrating Jewish lawyers – who until that point had been excluded from the WASP establishment – who opened new fields for legal practice.

[49] The realist critique of the distinction between public law and private law was born from this perspective (Kalman, 1996).

[50] According to Garapon, "in the common law culture, the universal motor is not law or central power, but a community of lawyers" (2007, p. 78).

[51] For a critique of American legal instrumentalism, see Tamanaha (2006).

rules of justice (Tamanaha, 2006). Principles and arguments may have had their place – what Lon Fuller (1964) calls the internal morality of law – but, as Garapon emphasizes, the ideal was in the procedure, and the procedure was a fight (2007, p. 78).

To summarize, just as legal positivism was seen as the appropriate legal theory for a legal field in which, as in France,[52] law professors focused on the creation and interpretation of legal doctrine and received symbolic credits for it, legal antiformalism was seen as the appropriate theory for a legal field in which lawyers obtained their material and symbolic capital from their connections to other social fields. Furthermore, whereas in France the difference between legal positivism and legal autonomy, on the one hand, and antiformalism and the social embeddedness of law, on the other, could explain the fact that most of the country's legal debate was reduced to technical and doctrinal matters, in the United States there was also a place for legal theory, legal sociology, and, generally, sociopolitical visions of law. Thus, in the United States, the fight against the autonomy of law crossed the entire political spectrum and was not seen merely as a progressive or leftist idea.

In the 1960s, the North American legal field experienced a second wave of interaction with the social sciences and public policy. Its most noteworthy academic expression was found in the law and society movement, which emerged "at the high noon of law as state action in both domestic and international realms" (Tomlins, 2000, p. 955).[53] It was a time of change – a time during which no one doubted that law and the social sciences would be useful for social progress. Liberal legal scholars designed large-scale projects with the national government that were aimed at enacting progressive welfare programs.[54] However,

---

[52] Legal positivism, however, is not always embraced within French legal culture, especially outside France. The best example is probably the school of Brussels, a school of thought initiated by Perelman (Perelman & Olbrechts-Tyteca, 1976) at the Free University of Brussels. On the other hand, at Saint-Louis University in Brussels, a new wave of legal theorists (trained in law), whose emblematic figures are Ost and Van de Kerchove, has continued the work of theorizing an antipositivistic law that is slightly different from Perelman's school of Brussels (Lenoble & Ost, 1980; Ost, 2013, 2016; Ost & Van de Kerchove, 1978, 1987, 1991; Van de Kerchove, 2013). In this regard, see the contributions to SLS of the *Revue interdisciplinaire d'etudes juridiques* (Bailleaux & Ost, 2013).

[53] For a detailed discussion of the law and society movement, see Chapter 5.

[54] The idea of making law more effective in solving social problems was particularly strong at the University of Wisconsin during the 1950s under the leadership of Professor Hurst (1956).

beginning in the 1980s, the rebirth of conservative ideologies and the consequent dismantling of social policy put an end to the alliance between the government and liberal scholarship. The legal field turned its eye toward economics and gave birth to the law and economics movement, perceived by many legal scholars as the "only sure route to promotion and tenure" (McCloskey, 1988, p. 765). Thanks to its political affinity with the new neoliberal and individualist times, law and economics have been able to capture the most important part of the legal market and utilize the "social engineering" force of law in favor of a conservative perspective.[55]

How has the socio-legal emphasis imposed by realists and their followers influenced positions and dispositions within the American legal field?

First, it is important to keep in mind that the phenomenon of "legal doctrine," as it is understood in France, has no place in the United States. The rejection of the continental perspective of Roman law – as the foundations of the absolutist state[56] – and the adoption of a conception of law linked to legal practice and to the authority of jurisprudence worked against the establishment of a sort of priestly body (as in France and Germany) composed of university professors and charged with maintaining the integrity of law.[57] In the United States, the symbolic capital of legal actors is derived largely from the fact that society considers them "social engineers, as persons specially equipped to perceive and attempt to solve social problems" (Merryman, 1975, p. 867).

The result is that the legal field in the United States is connected much more closely and directly with the market and the political system, which results in a transfer of competitive practices and flexibility from these two spheres (i.e., the market and the political system)

---

[55] See Posner (1975, 1995). There is a debate regarding whether law and economics are an heir of legal realism; for an affirmative answer, see Horwitz (1992, p. 270); against this idea, see Duxbury (1995, p. 307).

[56] Although English jurists of the seventeenth and eighteenth centuries rejected the fundamental categories of Roman law, they accepted its analytic, procedural, and antisystemic conception embodied in the Roman legal advisor, which gave meaning to legal practice (Jestaz & Jamin, 2004).

[57] See the special edition of the *Yale Law Journal* (no. 90, 1981) entitled "Yale Law Journal Symposium on Legal Scholarship: Its Nature and Purposes." See also Tunc (1994).

to the law.[58] Investments in the social sciences depend on their dividends. Most of the opportunities in the legal field are associated with the resources for the interpretation and manipulation of exterior reality (Garth & Sterling, 1998, p. 410). For this reason, competition and one's place in the hierarchy are frequently less important among judges, lawyers, and professors than they are *within* each of these groups[59] and among legal *institutions* (particularly law schools). It has even been suggested that the creation of the law and society movement can be explained by the need of some Midwestern universities – such as the University of Wisconsin – to challenge the legal paradigms coming from the Ivy League universities on the East Coast (Dezalay et al., 1989).

In short, the prestige of American law professors is linked less to their membership in a priestly caste – guardians of a body of knowledge strictly connected to republican ideals – than to their capacity to operate in a competitive and hierarchical market that produces legal understandings of and solutions to various problems. This social role, which took form with legal realism at the beginning of the twentieth century, remains in place today.

Universities and Markets in the Legal Field

The French academic system – conceived by Napoleon at the end of the First Republic in 1908 – is designed and directed by the state, the guardian of the republican idea of equality and universality in education. This notion has given rise to a highly centralized system featuring a strong separation between teaching and research, a sense of intellectual and financial self-sufficiency in research centers, and a weakly developed international perspective (Bowen & Bentaboulet, 2002).[60]

---

[58] We can also recall Weber's (1922) explanation on the sacredness of the legal profession in the Protestant environment, as opposed to the figure of the cleric in continental Europe.

[59] Merryman (1975) thinks that whereas meritocracy characterizes law schools in the United States, democracy characterizes them in Europe. In any case, American law schools and their members give a great deal of attention to their comparative standing among other law schools (Tomlins, 2000). Likewise, there is a clear hierarchy among lawyers and law firms (Galanter, 1974). For a recent critique of American law schools, see Tamanaha (2012).

[60] Nevertheless, there is a long-standing debate in France about the university system, in which references to the German and American systems are always present. A clear illustration of this for the end of the nineteenth century can be found in Brunetière (1897); Marchis (1914). For a more recent illustration, see Charle

Additionally, the design of the continental European university is predicated on classical disciplinary divisions that correspond to faculties and that translate into a strict adjudication of quotas for professors according to the subjects within each of these disciplines.[61] Quite frequently, regular and tenured professors who head research institutes in Europe cast the deciding ballot against interdisciplinary research in Europe (Charle, 2003).[62] This rigidity in the classification of knowledge leaves little room for maneuver among professors and students in law faculties who want to explore areas that are not doctrinal.

Arguments against interdisciplinary knowledge that are aired in European universities are based on a classical conceptualization of the university, founded on a position of respect for a tradition of academic rigor. That is the reason why many Europeans who dedicate themselves to the sociology of law, particularly the French, do not believe that they take a back seat to the Americans from a qualitative point of view, even if they might from a quantitative one. "I ask myself if foreigners do more legal sociology than the French," remarked Carbonnier at the end of his life. "Much more, certainly, in volume, but more in depth, I am not so sure" (quoted in Arnaud & Andrini, 1995, p. 43).

In the United States, by contrast, departmental organization offers more flexibility in terms of disciplinary boundaries and mobility for researchers. While it is true that in the United States, "law" is not a department within a university but rather a largely autonomous and

(2003). The university system in Germany is, in principle, decentralized, but conditioned by some state requirements: for example, the state organizes competitions for university posts. In Germany, strength in research skills gauged in terms of publications is privileged, while in France rhetoric and pedagogical learning are a preferred background for admittance into higher education (Becker, 1925; Charle, 2003; Von Humbolt, 1979).

[61] In France, this understanding of academic content originates in the close links between secondary education and universities. Until relatively recently, university professors taught classes for secondary students, and training in philosophy and the social sciences was understood to fall within the domain of high schools.

[62] In countries like Germany, France, and Italy, opportunities for those seeking a position as a university professor are substantially reduced when candidates present themselves as sociologists or political scientists of law. Therefore, professors do not encourage their students to pursue socio-legal arguments. A deficit of the institutionalization of the sociology of law is observed in Europe precisely because it is too rarely taught (Travers, 2001); in the civil law tradition, if a course is not taught, it is because its content does not exist. However, in Italy the situation may be a little different due to the influence of Treves. For the French case, see Arnaud & Andrini (1995). For Italy, see Bixio (1994).

separate school, law schools' faculty seats, as well as their personnel, are usually highly mobile. Positions and salaries are subject to labor market forces, with each law school negotiating individually with its academic staff (Tamanaha, 2012). Additionally, although law professors enter the faculty based on the commitment to teach a required and strictly legal course, they can also propose teaching other seminars almost without restriction. This is due in great part to the fact that in the United States, law is designed as a postgraduate program, which means not only more flexibility in the content of courses but also more interdisciplinary content.

Furthermore, the strong participation of philanthropic foundations in the financing of higher education must be mentioned.[63] The United States has developed a competitive system between universities, which are ranked according to their available resources. Well-endowed institutions possess resources that are unimaginable to practically any European university. In addition, the fact that American universities are well connected to the private sector and the market stimulates the production of goods aimed at facilitating research, such as databases – something that is possible only in a large economy such as that of the United States.[64]

In spite of these advantages, however, a debate has recently been taking place regarding the current situation of the American legal model and the role played by law schools. Brian Tamanaha, former president of the School of Law at Saint John's University in New York, argues that law schools are in a profound crisis. In recent years, he says, law schools have neglected their ethical responsibilities in the quest for economic benefits (Tamanaha, 2012). Law schools' search for profits,

---

[63] At the beginning of the twentieth century, as American sociology expanded, the pragmatic notion that knowledge and research should have an ameliorative function with respect to social problems was widely influential. The interest shown in the 1930s by private entities such as the Rockefeller Foundation, the Social Science Research Council, and the Institute for Social and Religious Research arose from that view. With respect to the sociology of law, a detailed explanation of the funding of the most significant research projects in the law and society movement is provided in Garth & Sterling (1998). This work dedicates special attention to the role of the Russell Sage Foundation.

[64] Widely used databases are available to professors and students of both sociology and law. These databases are designed by private firms that sell their products to universities and can do so thanks to the large market for these products. In Europe, national and linguistic divisions have not allowed for a substantial improvement in such resources.

the huge debts acquired by students to pay tuition, and the low contribution of teachers to the training of lawyers have all brought about, in general terms, the commercialization and degradation of law schools.

A final point is worth mentioning. The differences between France and the United States refer to the complex and difficult-to-resolve tension between universities whose primary mission is to be open, democratic, and inclusive and those whose primary function is to be meritocratic and competitive. For decades, the first model was embraced by universities in France, while the second model was adopted in the United States. Today, there is a growing influence of the American model in France based on the belief that it will help France improve the quality of its universities while also avoiding their commercialization.[65]

Beyond the questions raised by this goal, it is important to bear in mind that one of the hardest things to change in law is legal education, which remains deeply rooted in the culture of lawyers, seldom changing at the whim of reforms or with the addition of a few courses or seminars.[66]

CONCLUSION

In this chapter, I have tried to show the different developments within the French and American legal fields over the last century. The ratio of power between actors in the legal field (professors in one case, judges in the other) and the conceptions of popular sovereignty and fundamental rights, and the relative autonomy of legal knowledge vis-à-vis the social sciences (the two factors set up in Chapter 1 for the comparison), have intervened in the two countries' trajectories and have paved the path

---

[65] See, for example, the reforms initiated in 2008 at the University of Paris II (Panthéon-Assas), which gave rise to the "College of Law," with a design resembling American law schools and a focus on internationalization and economics. See Jamin (2012, p. 85). See also Audren & Halpérin (2013); Halpérin (2011b); Israël (2012b); Kagan (2007).

[66] This is related to the debate on "legal transfers" and the difficulty of importing models or norms; see, for example, Legrand (1999); Nelken (2001, 2012); Twining (2005); Watson (2000). A concrete example of this difficulty lies in the failure of the law and development movement to influence legal education in Latin American law schools.

for the development of different sociopolitical legal studies and different symbolic uses of law.

In the United States, legal realism triumphed over legal formalism. Despite the disturbing effects of the realist critique in the early twentieth century, the legal mainstream managed to limit its scope (by reworking the content and force of law with the help of the social sciences) and to preserve the needs of certainty and stability in the legal system (Duxbury, 1995). Thus, social sciences, and not abstract logic, provided important criteria for the definition of law, the process of judicial decision-making, and the idea of SLS, while also providing key elements for the establishment of the objectivity and stability of law in spite of the presence of antiformalist tenets (against legal autonomy and legal neutrality). This encouraged a rapprochement between law and social reality and promoted the symbolic uses of law not just by judges and public officials but also by social movements and leaders.

In France, on the other hand, legal doctrine was clearly separated from the social sciences, and the legal system preserved its autonomy and political neutrality. There, the more radical antiformalist critique did not have any lasting effects on legal doctrine.[67] It conceived legal doctrine as being too close to political power – and for this reason, it saw no possibility of social emancipation through law; political power had to change in order for law to change (Commaille, 2015; Miaille, 1976). The antiformalists were therefore placed outside the law to critique both the political system and the law. This external view has led them to a kind of discourse away from legal technique and closer to politics and philosophy. Antiformalists in France discouraged social movements' use of law because they believed that nothing good could come from the state, much less from judicial decisions.

According to Évelyne Serverin (2000), legal positivism in Europe, which prefers written rules over other sources of law, was never really challenged. Law professors, especially civil law professors, have rejected the influence of the social sciences in the debate on the interpretation of law and its truth (Audren & Halpérin, 2013; Jouanjan & Zoller, 2016). If, at some point, they had a certain respect for legal sociology,

---

[67] "While the European field has always focused on state affairs, the main feature of the modern United States is the institutional alliance between Wall Street law firms and law schools of the Ivy League" (Madsen & Dezalay, 2002, p. 197).

it was under conditions of the subordination and instrumentalization of sociology in relation to law (Commaille, 1983; Deflem, 2010; Travers, 1993).

Law schools in France have won the battle regarding the autonomy of law but have paid a high price for this victory: not only have they lost their monopoly over legal education and much of the influence they used to enjoy in elite education, but they have also lost the opportunity to participate in social and political debates prompted by the complexity of contemporary politico-legal phenomena (Israel & Vanneuville, 2017). While it is true that this situation has recently changed, it must be pointed out that the current sociopolitical debate on law is developed outside law schools, under the indifferent eyes of the professors who work there (see Chapter 6).

In the United States, on the other hand, the realist critique was focused on judges, who are the central political figures in the legal field. This critique denounced the interested and partial nature of judicial decisions. In contrast to what happened in France, in the United States the politicization of judicial decisions did not stop the interest in and debate regarding these decisions. On the contrary, it allowed for both a richer and more interdisciplinary debate, which used arguments based on the social sciences that made political dialogue within the law more sophisticated, and a broader and firmer conception of SLS.

Moreover, given the existence of a less interventionist and less visible state than in France, American lawyers, judges, and law professors did not feel the urge to differentiate themselves from political forces or the market. Not only have American lawyers and law professors relativized the significance of the borders between the market and political power, but they have also used the interstices between the law and the market to increase their symbolic power – seeing themselves as experts able to solve most social problems – and to strengthen the political uses of law.

But these differences should not lead us to idealize SLS or the critical dimension of law in the United States. For one, American legal antiformalism is not necessarily a progressive form of thought. In other words, the realistic idea of the connection between law and the social sciences is not necessarily a critique or progressive idea of law. Therefore, movements such as law and economics and law and society may present themselves as heirs of legal realism, even if they espouse different political visions. Second, the fact that American legal thought draws from the interstices between the market, power, and the law has problematic implications, not just in relation to the domestication of critical perspectives but also in relation to the commodification of law schools, which results in a loss of professors' autonomy vis-à-vis existing political and economic powers.[68] I will return to this question in Chapters 4 and 6.

[68] Even during the first half of the 1960s, when political radicalism was common in Europe and the United States, the most radical of the American critical legal studies texts, including a paper on rights by Mark Tushnet, were less virulent and radical than the writings of the *critique du droit* movement in France, such as those of Michel Miaille. One might even suggest that the American antiformalist criticism, which emphasizes the need to define the connections between law and society, was favorable to the legal field and conservative views. See Dezalay et al. (1989); Garth & Sterling (1998); Tamanaha (2012); Tomlins (2000).

CHAPTER FOUR

SOCIOPOLITICAL LEGAL STUDIES IN THE UNITED STATES

In the United States, the social dimension of law is always present, even among judges and lawyers. The 1908 case *Muller v. Oregon*[1] is an example of that. One of Oregon's attorneys, Louis Brandeis, who later became a US Supreme Court justice, presented a voluminous dossier in which he criticized women's interminable work hours at the beginning of the twentieth century and demonstrated their negative impact on women's health and well-being. Since then, empirical arguments, based on facts, and the intervention of the social sciences in judicial trials are considered not only normal but necessary. *Brown v. Board of Education*,[2] a landmark case on racial discrimination, is another example in which the sociological point of view played a fundamental role in illustrating discrimination. According to Michael Freeman, "One of the most characteristic features of twentieth-century jurisprudence was the development of sociological approaches to law. The social sciences had an influence almost comparable to that of religion in early periods. And legal thought has tended to reflect the trends to be found in sociology" (2001, p. 835).[3]

This closeness between legal practice and the social sciences has fostered the development of sociopolitical legal studies (SLS) in the United States. SLS is accepted, at least in academic circles, as a legitimate field of study. Even if technical and doctrinal approaches

---

[1] 208 U.S. 412 (1908).   [2] 347 U.S. 483 (1954).
[3] For a general vision of the relationship between law and the social sciences, see Mertz (2008).

continue to dominate within law schools, sociopolitical perspectives of law do not produce a negative reaction in the United States, as is often the case in France. Indeed, in the United States, saying that law is a social, or even a political, practice is a rather banal statement that does not raise many eyebrows in legal circles.

Sociopolitical visions of law in the United States extend across several disciplines and fields of study: not just sociology, anthropology, and economics but also legal theory and socio-legal studies. SLS is a broad and complex field of study whose unity derives from the political dimension adopted by each of these disciplines, as explained in Chapter 1.

Given the magnitude of SLS as a field, I will limit my presentation to three of its production sites: first, the political sociology of law as adopted by sociologists in departments of sociology (the sociology of law in the strictest sense); second, the legal theory produced in law schools by professors of philosophy and legal theory; and third, the socio-legal studies that result from interdisciplinary work undertaken by jurists or by sociologists who are often affiliated with law schools.[4] Most of this chapter will explore the different types of SLS associated with these last two sites of production. Today, in the United States, unlike in France, socio-legal studies and legal theory are more developed and dynamic than the sociology of law produced by sociologists. This can be explained, in general terms, by the enormous influence of legal realism in the American legal field and, in more concrete terms, by the relative success of two movements in American law schools since the end of the 1970s – namely, law and economics (L&E) and law and society (L&S), both intellectual heirs of legal realism. Therefore, the majority of this chapter will be devoted to SLS produced by professors of law and by academic groups (sometimes interdisciplinary) strongly connected with law schools.

This chapter is conceived of as a continuation of Chapter 3's comparative historical analysis of SLS in the United States and France. Its aim is less theoretical and more descriptive: instead of tracing the main historical features that influenced the development of SLS, it concentrates on describing the main forms of SLS and the main political uses of law that have emerged in the last fifty years.

---

[4] On the dominant position of law professors in the law and society movement, see Dezalay, Sarat, & Silbey (1989); Trubek (1990).

The chapter is divided into two parts. The first part discusses the sociology of law in the United States, while the longer second part seeks to describe the major tendencies, movements, and developments in socio-legal studies and studies of legal theory. This second part explores two periods: 1960–1990 and 1990–today. The separation of these two periods is not only chronological but also thematic to the extent that the main sociopolitical theories of law underwent an important transformation in the 1990s. The chapter ends with a brief conclusion drawn from the preceding analyses on antiformalism, the relation between law and social science, and the symbolic uses of law.

SOCIOLOGY OF LAW

The sociological debate on law in the United States was, at first, a continuation of the European discussion that had begun with Max Weber, Karl Marx, and Emile Durkheim. But it took until the end of the Second World War, with the work of Talcott Parsons (1954, 1962, 1968, 1977), to see the development of a properly American sociology.[5]

Drawing on functionalist social theory, Parsons's thought conceived of law as a mechanism that produces order (Turner & Maryanski, 1995). External forces, such as social contracts or repression exercised by the government, he argued, cannot explain society. The same holds true for law, which needs no external justification and produces its own rationality as well as its own conditions of validity.[6] Society, according to Parsons, is a system maintained by four essential functions: adaptation to the environment (*adaptation*), the pursuit of goals (*goal attainment*), the integration of different elements of the system (*integration*), and the maintenance of shared values (*latency*). These

---

[5] Other authors, such as English historian Henry S. Maine (1861) and jurists Albert V. Dicey (1905) and Oliver W. Holmes (1920), had a significant influence on the sociology of law from the 1850s onward. For a vision of the sociology of law from the point of view of sociologists, see Comack (2006); Cotterrell (1983, 1990); Deflem (2008); Emirbayer (1997); Travers (2001); Treviño (1996). For Durkheim's influence on the American sociology of law, see Greenhouse (2015).

[6] We can see here a precedent to the debate between Niklas Luhmann (1985), also a functionalist, with his idea of autopoiesis and the internal production of truth in the legal system, and Jürgen Habermas (1998), for whom law necessitates a justification in the communication procedures of democracy. For a comparison of the legal ideas of these authors, see Guibentif (2010).

functions are involved in four subsystems: economy, politics, community, and values. Integration, which constitutes the most important
function, is achieved through family and school. Law, according to
Parsons, also plays a fundamental role in social integration by resolving
problems concerning the solidarity and coordination of the four subsystems. Thus, for example, law is a key element in crime prevention,
particularly when the system of social values fails to maintain the
cohesion of the whole. Furthermore, he argued, lawyers are a powerful
mechanism of social control acting in the middle of the relationship
between legislative power, government, and society.[7]

Parsons's social theory is written in the tradition of social consensus
theory – as opposed to social conflict theory – according to which, in
every society, cohesion is assured by the fact that most individuals share
the same fundamental social and moral values (Collins, 1994). This
tradition has been especially important in the United States, and
Parsons is perhaps its most eminent representative. Other perspectives
in this tradition have also had a significant influence on law. Among
them is the normative sociology of Philip Selznick and Philippe Nonet
(1978),[8] also known as "old institutionalism," which seeks to understand the way in which organizations develop their own cultures and
values according to their environment, and how their objectives are
affected by it.[9] "New institutionalism" is linked with this tradition,
albeit with significant differences (especially with regard to Parsons's
ideas).[10] It is interested in the way in which individuals and organizations respond to their social and institutional environments in seeking
to influence or even modify them (Di-Maggio & Powell, 1991; March
& Olsen, 1989). Important contributions to new institutionalism have
been made in the domains of organizational sociology (Edelman, 1992;
Edelman & Suchman, 1997), police and social control (Hawkins,

---

[7] For an explanation of Parsons's contribution to sociology of law, see Deflem (2010);
Treviño (2001, 2007).

[8] For a detailed explanation, see Kagan, Krygier, & Winston (2002). William Evan
(1980) and Harry Bredemeier (1962) drew on these ideas.

[9] His best-known study is *TVA and the Grass Roots* (Selznick, 1949).

[10] Old institutionalism was founded on a normative vision of society that aimed for
conformity with values and norms (Nonet & Selznick, 1978; Selznick, 1996). New
institutionalism, on the other hand, has a more cognitive character and is based on
the idea that social reality depends on a constitutive relationship between institutions and the social contexts in which they integrate themselves (Berger &
Luckmann, 1966).

2003; Hutter, 1988; Johnston, 1992), and the legal profession (Freidson, 1984; Heinz & Laumann, 1982; Larson, 1977).

But Parsons's work generated significant criticism among adherents to confrontational and critical visions of society. One of these was Donald Black, whose book *The Behavior of Law* (1976) seeks to formulate a general theory of social control that excludes normative and legal elements. According to Black, law is observed in terms of quantity (more or less) and style (criminal law, therapeutic law, compensatory law, etc.). Law changes with stratification (strongly stratified societies develop more law), with social classes (there are more laws attached to wealth and status), and with culture (traditional societies possess fewer laws than modern societies).[11]

These critical visions also had an important influence on the study of the legal profession. Unlike Parsons, who looked on lawyers favorably, critical authors saw lawyers as representing a powerful professional group, essentially motivated by special interests, and as being associated with capitalist domination (Bankowski & Mungham, 1976). Critical studies showed the hierarchical and unequal character of the legal profession and the way in which it perpetuates the social order (Abel, 1989; Heinz & Laumann, 1982).

It is also important to mention the influence of interpretive sociology in the United States, particularly the school of "symbolic interactionism" directed by George H. Mead (1934).[12] According to this school, the key to social cohesion is intersubjective communication. Socialization is the result of a process that pushes individual actors to behave in conformity with their own representations of the way in which other actors perceive them. As a result, the symbolic dimension is fundamental to human communication, and the meaning of any social object results from a process of communicative interpretation. These ideas were subsequently developed by Herbert Blumer (1945, 1969) and Axel Honneth and Joas (1998), who influenced the schools of labeling theory and critical criminology (Baratta, 1986; Becker, 1963; Garland & Sparks, 2000), as well as some studies on the practice of law (Carlin, 1962; Flood, 1983; Paterson, 1982).

---

[11] See also Black (1972, 1995).

[12] This school was originally associated with Weber's (1978) ideas, whereby society cannot be understood without studying the way in which individuals interpret and give meaning to their actions and those of their fellow citizens. On the importance of this tradition, see Banakar & Travers (2002); Travers (2010).

Richard Quinney's work on criminology should be mentioned here. In 1970, he wrote *The Social Reality of Crime*, a breakdown in classical studies that viewed crime as a pathology.[13] Criminality is not determined by the nature of behavior, he explained, but is rather an artificial construct created by powerful interests in society and imposed by political agents such as police, legislators, judges, and so forth. In 1974, Quinney published *Critique of Legal Order*, in which he partially abandoned his constructivist and labeling approach perspectives and adopted what he called an "instrumental Marxism." He explained, "Criminal law is an instrument of the state and ruling class to maintain and perpetuate the existing social and economic order" (1974, p. 16). He connected his critique of legal order with the war in Vietnam. In the book's preface, he stated that "[t]he legal system at home and the military apparatus abroad are two sides of the same phenomenon; both perpetuate American capitalism, the American way of life."

Quinney's work was widely criticized twenty years ago. However, modern criminology has adopted most of his main ideas, such as the class definition of crime, dangerous classes, the crime control industry, crimes committed by corporations, and the political dimension of the war on drugs (Baum, 1997; Chambliss, 1999; Chomsky, 1993; Zinn, 1990, 2002).

To conclude this brief description of the sociology of law in the United States, it is important to discuss the tension that sometimes exists between sociologists of law who work in sociology departments and those who work elsewhere, especially in law schools. L&S was an important magnet for researchers educated in disciplines other than law (such as sociology, anthropology, and political science) who found a certain receptivity in law schools (Deflem, 2010, p. 2; Garth & Sterling, 1998). Sociologists of law who work in sociology departments often have a critical vision of the socio-legal work produced in law schools. According to Mathieu Deflem, for example, the dominant position of jurists and their interdisciplinary visions of law have created a sort of balkanization of the sociology of law. "The resulting situation," he writes, "is such that the sociology of law has, some exceptions notwithstanding, lost its distinct space in sociolegal studies as well as

---

[13] For an analysis of Quinney's work, see Shelden (2010); Treviño (2007).

in sociology" (2008, p. 2). This analysis leads him to advocate for a sociology of law with its own disciplinary identity.[14]

Further, interdisciplinarity has been considered to be the cause of important methodological and theoretical insufficiencies. According to Max Travers, "the sociology of law as currently taught in law schools, represented in textbooks, and published in socio-legal and law and society journals, can be criticized for being both theoretically and methodologically undeveloped from the standpoint of research and theorizing within mainstream sociology" (1993, p. 448). This type of critique has also been formulated, as we will see later in this chapter, within L&S in numerous exercises of reflexivity that have taken place in the movement's history (Abel, 2010; Calavita, 2002; Dezalay et al., 1989; Edelman, 2004; Friedman, 2005; Garth & Sterling, 1998; Handler, 1992; Sarat & Silbey, 1988; Tamanaha, 2001; Trubek, 1990).

To fill these gaps, some sociologists affirm, it is necessary to develop a type of sociology of law that is understood as a subdiscipline of sociology, in the same way that there is a sociology of health or education.[15] Some, like John Griffiths, go even further in proposing a sociology of law understood as the fundamental basis of sociology. Given that sociology is the study of human social life and social control is the constitutive element of every group, he argues, it follows that "the study of social control is the fundament on which the whole of sociology necessarily rests ... [T]his explains the key role of social control (law) in the work of classical sociologists like Weber, Durkheim, Malinowski and Homans" (Griffiths, 2006, p. 66).

Although there are notable divergences between the sociological and socio-legal gazes, it must be said that this contrast has been less marked in the United States and England than in other countries, especially those belonging to the civil law tradition, and particularly France in the latter half of the twentieth century.

Alan Hunt, for example, thinks that despite the divisions and tensions, "there has been a fundamental coherence, continuity and unity in these two currents" (1993, p. 194). There are multiple linkages

---

[14] It is perhaps useful to recall that the creation of a special section dedicated to the sociology of law in the American Sociological Association became possible only in 1993.

[15] Not all sociologists agree about the creation of a strictly sociological sociology of law. For this debate, see Banakar & Travers (2002); Comack (2006); Cotterrell (1992); Dingwall (2007).

and shared views among these disciplinary tendencies. Numerous jurists, for example, have taken interest in the classical themes of sociology – order, domination, social cohesion, and so on – and, for this reason, they not only address the classical debates in social theory but also take part in sociological debates between the different schools of social theory. Conversely, many sociologists and, more generally, social scientists have also sought to comprehend the work of jurists in order to better answer the fundamental questions of sociology.[16]

SOCIO-LEGAL STUDIES

In the middle of the twentieth century, two socio-legal movements appeared in the United States. The first, known as the law, science, and policy movement, sought to maintain the realist project by focusing, without any critical pretension, on public policies.[17] The second, known as the legal process school, tried to find an intermediary way between legal formalism and legal realism. Its most famous representative was Lon Fuller (1964), whose major contribution consisted of revealing the creative potential of judicial activity and the importance of social context in legal claims.[18]

The tragedy of the Second World War, and the necessity of affirming liberal values against totalitarianism, put an end to these critical movements. SLS would not reemerge until the 1970s, an era that bore witness to the creation of very important movements in American legal scholarship. All of these movements are, in one way or another, the heirs of legal realism.[19] As explained in Chapter 3, the realists fought

---

[16] Numerous legal sociology textbooks and socio-legal studies show the wealth and diversity of these perspectives. See Calavita (2010); Deflem (2010); Galligan (2007); Guibentif (2002); Pavlich (2011); Roach Anleu (2000); Sutton (2001); Travers (2010); Vago (2012). For collective volumes on the subject, see Freeman (2006); Mertz (2008); Seron (2006); Silbey (2008); Treviño (2007). For readers, see Abel (1995b); Sarat (2004a). A notable effort to encourage communication among the disciplinary perspectives of law can be found in Mertz (2008). See also Ewick, Kagan, & Sarat (1999).

[17] Legal realism originates in Lasswell & McDougal (1943).

[18] The heirs of this school were John Hart Ely and Alexander Bickel.

[19] This movement was strongly influenced by the pragmatic thinkers of the beginning of the twentieth century. Pragmatism is the North American philosophical current par excellence. Its origins are thought to go back to the end of the nineteenth century with the philosophy of Charles Peirce, but its full development did not occur until the beginning of the twentieth century, with thinkers like William

the dominant legal culture at the end of the nineteenth century and exposed the marginal, imprecise, and political character of law and legal practice.[20] They thus, on the one hand, used logical reasoning to show the lack of coherence of judicial decisions – a phenomenon called "debunking"[21] – and, on the other, argued for the use of the social sciences, particularly empirical research, as an instrument for the objective explanation of legal processes. In this way, the social sciences were perceived as an antidote to the political tendency of legal interpretation and as a guarantee for the production of legal norms connected to the social environment.[22] These legal realists sketched out a proposal that was at once critical, close to legal theory (and Karl Llewellyn), and scientific, close to political science (and Roscoe Pound).[23]

Still, this duality was not without problems. From the beginning, there was a tension between the raw relativism inherent to deconstructionist practice and the confidence in the objectivity of empirical research and public policy (Duxbury, 1995; Trubek, 1990; Trubek & Esser, 1989).[24]

From this tension emerged two divergent tendencies: one seeking to demonstrate the deficiencies and incoherencies of official law and the

James, John Dewey, and, later, Richard Rorty. Pragmatic philosophers, unlike their European colleagues, reclaim the necessity of evaluating ideas in light of their practical consequences for reality, and not simply in light of their internal construction.

[20] This dominant vision finds its origin in the vision proposed by Christopher Langdell of Harvard, known in the United States as legal formalism. Under this perspective, law is a coherent, determinant (i.e., it produces the practical effects that it establishes), and politically neutral system.

[21] At the end of the twentieth century, critical legal studies began to use the more sophisticated term of deconstruction, introduced by the French philosopher Jacques Derrida (1976, 2002).

[22] The positivist vision of the social sciences had a certain influence on the realist movement and can be found in the idea of a positive science of public policy. See Deflem (2008); Lasswell & McDougal (1943).

[23] This tension can be seen in Pound's article "Sociology of Law and Sociological Jurisprudence" (1943), which explains how the sociology of law goes from sociology toward law, while sociological jurisprudence goes from law toward sociology. For an analysis of this tension, see Deflem (2008, p. 106).

[24] In more general terms, these authors had to face the tension between the empirical analysis of social reality (knowledge) and the political evaluation of state institutions and law (critique). Edward White (1986, p. 825) explains this tension in terms of the fact/value dichotomy. See also Trubek & Esser (1989).

other seeking to show that legal understandings passed through the social sciences. During the second half of the twentieth century, these two tendencies grew into two academic movements: critical legal studies (CLS) and L&S. CLS concentrated on the political critique of law, while L&S emphasized the scientific treatment of law, based on the social sciences. In this same period (one of the most creative and dynamic in the history of the United States), two other movements, also associated with realist heritage, were born: L&E and law and development.[25]

This section will begin by exploring the evolution of these movements between 1960 and 1990, and will then discuss the contemporary debates that emerged around these movements from 1990 onward.

Reinventions of Law: 1960–1990
Law and Economics

The birth of L&E goes back to the publication of "Problems of Social Cost," an article written by Nobel laureate Ronald Coase (1960), and to the writings of Guido Calabresi (1970) on the economic analysis of legal responsibility.[26] This first generation of authors, ill at ease with the judicial activism of the Warren court and, in general, with the state's intervention in the market, sought to transform law into a neutral, predictable science by using the methods and rationality of economics, all under the idea that judges base their decisions on the efficiency of law and not on moral or political values (Calabresi, 2016; Posner, 1995, 2014).

Coase and his successors adopted some of the premises of the Chicago school, such as the principles of economic liberalism and the defense of the market economy (Becker, 1993b). For them, individuals are rational actors who maximize their interests through strategic calculations.[27] Applying this epistemological postulate in favor of the rational actor (and also the normative postulate in favor of economic liberalism) to law, they claimed that prisons deter criminals, that the costs of law are mostly opportunity costs, and that the best way to

---

[25] For an evaluation of these movements based on a quantitative analysis of their writings, see Ellickson (2000).

[26] A collection of classic texts is found in Coleman & Lange (1993). See also Harrison (2003).

[27] For a critique of this type of rationality in the economic world of law, see Sunstein (2000). See also generally Bourdieu (2000).

optimize transactions (i.e., to make them efficient) is through voluntary exchanges, among other things (Becker, 1993a).[28]

The practice of law, according to Coase, must be guided by the principle of efficiency. Judges must make their decisions based not on what seems most just to them but on what produces the most efficient result and, consequently, best protects everyone's rights. In other words, when there are no obstacles to economic transactions between parties (i.e., no transaction costs[29]), resources must be used efficiently, without regard for those who initially possessed the rights or for the legal norms regulating the relationship between the parties.

Coase wanted to build a model of economic efficiency capable of reducing externalities (the cost or benefit that affects a party who did not choose to incur that cost or benefit) to a minimum.[30] Thus, the famous "Coase theorem" stipulates that when transaction costs are minimal or nonexistent, legal intervention is useless, and the most efficient measure is to allow individuals to negotiate among themselves without interference from the state (Gjerdingen, 1983). For example, if a farmer's cattle crosses onto another farmer's property and ruins the second farmer's crops, the solution is not to impose legal responsibilities on the first farmer but to allow the two farmers to negotiate in conformity with the price that each of them accords to his right. In this way, the crop farmer will accord a price to his interest in preventing his neighbor's cattle from crossing onto his side, and the cattle farmer will accord one to his interest in keeping his cattle in an enclosed space.

Coase's ideas were particularly influential in the mid-1980s, in an epoch that favored conservative politics (MacCoun, 1993; MacKenzie, 2002; Tyler, 2006). A great number of federal judges (Richard Posner

---

[28] The question of the relative importance of these two postulates (epistemological and normative) is often debated; it is possible, as Lauren Edelman argues, that in recent years the normative postulate and the politically conservative character of the movement have lost the importance they once had (2004, p. 182); on this point, see also Minda (1995).

[29] This scenario is very uncommon. In this sense, L&E assumes the postulates of the neoclassical school of economics, according to which the market regulates itself without external intervention. But Coase also admits that negotiation almost always involves "transaction costs" – for example, hiring lawyers or consultants, getting to negotiation sites, taking time off work, and discovering information.

[30] In other words, these are the collateral economic effects of the actions of one individual on another not expressed by a price. An example of externality is the impact that an object's production has on the environment.

among them), and even some Supreme Court justices, explicitly adhered to this conservative tendency.

However, L&E was not a unified movement. So many years of intense intellectual production generated fractures and dispersion at its core. Nonetheless, Lewis Kornhauser maintains that the following four postulates were shared by all authors of the movement: (i) the law must be efficient; (ii) the common law is efficient; (iii) legal processes select for efficient rules; and (iv) economics furnishes a useful theory for predicting the behavior of individuals in relation to the law (Kornhauser, 2008; Shavell, 2004).

However, according to Gary Minda (1995), the movement was much more fractured than it seemed. The only truly shared postulate, he affirmed, is the fourth: the behaviorist postulate. An illustration of this lack of unity appears in Judge Posner's work, probably the most famous of the movement's authors. Even if his first writings advocated the founders' ideal of creating a hard science capable of predicting the way in which judges decide and how these decisions conform to the objectives of the market (Posner, 1977), his later books (Posner, 1990, 2014) are clearly less emphatic about the scientific postulate and much less optimistic about the benefits of the market. For him, the hard core of the movement is its pragmatic posture toward law.

The rise of L&E occurred during a time of political conservatism and economic liberalism in the United States. But the partial crisis of this economic model at the end of G. W. Bush's presidency, the failure of the war on drugs, and the rise to power of a new political elite with Barack Obama seem to have vindicated authors who were critical of the movement, which may bring about its reorientation.[31]

Law and Development
In 1960, the United States Agency for International Development, in collaboration with the Ford Foundation and other private institutions, undertook an ambitious project designed to introduce legal reforms

---

[31] For a critical vision of L&E, see Edelman (2004); Edelman & Stryker (2005); Fiss (1986); Kennedy (1998). See also what is called "behavioral law and economics" (Sunstein, 2000). Susan Rose-Ackerman (1988) proposes a type of progressive L&E linked to administrative law. In March 2002, several professors (Kent Greenfield, Jon Hanson, Morton Horwitz, Frank Michelman, and Joseph Singer) debated the possibility of a progressive L&E in a panel entitled "Progressive Law and Economics: An Oxymoron?"

(particularly in the domains of legal education, agrarian reform, and justice) in certain countries in Asia, Africa, and Latin America. The project was based on the premise that law is an essential tool for economic development. The idea was that once these legal reforms were in place, actors in the legal field – notably judges, law professors, and lawyers – could then act as "engineers" of social life and encourage a dynamic of development.[32]

The enthusiastic participation of North American professors (especially from the universities of Wisconsin, Yale, and Stanford) transformed the initial project into a veritable progressive intellectual movement.[33] A large part of these participants' intervention in the movement was intended to reform legal education and, more precisely, the understanding and interpretation of law. North American professors thought that it was necessary to reduce the traditional distance, in certain countries, between written law and social reality, which constituted an indispensable pragmatic demand to transform law into a tool of development. In order to attain this objective, these professors emphasized the importance of teaching law based on concrete cases (as in the common law) and of diminishing the dogmatic and abstract character of law (as in the civil law tradition). However, the objective of transferring American legal culture to countries like those of Latin America, which embraced a different legal culture, turned out to be far more difficult than planned – and consequently, truly successful educational experiments were rare (Gardner, 1980; Trubek, 1996; Trubek & Galanter, 1974).

The inefficiency of the legal reforms proposed at this time rapidly obscured the movement and diminished its prestige. Later analyses showed the complexity of the institutional reforms and the insufficiency of uniquely legal reformist proposals.

Three decades later, at the beginning of the 1990s, a second version of the law and development movement emerged. This time, the focus was not on agrarian reform or legal education but on justice (Rodríguez Garavito, 2001, 2006; Trubek & Galanter, 1974; Trubek & Santos, 2006). Nevertheless, the central idea of this second version was similar to the first: law, specifically the judicial system, constituted an essential

---

[32] For an introduction to this movement, see Trebilcock & Mota-Prado (2014).
[33] On this subject, see Carty (1992). For a critical evaluation, see Trubek & Galanter (1974).

element of development, and, consequently, judicial reforms were an inevitable condition for human progress.

This time, as in the past, the reforms were directed by the state – namely, through the United States Agency for International Development and the World Bank, which invested considerably in the former Iron Curtain countries and Latin America.[34]

Law and Society

The old realist idea that law is an object that can and must be studied by the social sciences was at the origin of the creation, in 1964, of the L&S movement.[35] Since then, this movement has continued to grow and to affect law not just in the United States but worldwide.[36] After L&E, this movement has enjoyed the most influence in US law schools and in interdisciplinary studies interested in law (Sarat, 2004a; Sarat & Ewick, 2015). Any non-American sociologist could be caught by surprise by the movement's vitality and by the apparent facility with which it draws in scholars from disciplines as diverse as law, political science, sociology, and anthropology.[37] One expression of L&S's vivacity is the amount of reflexive thinking that it produces – through publications, seminars, meetings, and so forth – about the movement, its evolution, its work, and its future.[38] Nevertheless, it should be said

---

[34] For a general vision, see Shihata (1995); Trubek (1996). A critical explanation of the movements is developed in Santos (2000b). An analysis of this phenomenon through political science is found in O'Donnell (1998).

[35] For a detailed explanation of this idea, see Ewick & Sarat (2015); Trubek (1990, p. 5). This idea was particularly strong in Pound's "Sociology of Law and Sociological Jurisprudence" (Pound, 1943).

[36] For the international impact of L&S, see Cotterrell (2012); Darian-Smith (2013); Friedman, Pérez-Perdomo, & Gómez (2011); Gessner & Nelken (2007a); Nelken (2002); Sarat (2004a).

[37] Almost 2,000 people attend each annual congress of the movement, where around 700 papers are presented. The 2008 congress, held in Denver, Colorado, featured more than 1,000 presentations. In 2014, L&S celebrated its fiftieth anniversary in the city of Minneapolis, Minnesota. Every four years, L&S organizes its annual conference outside the mainland United States; for example, in 2007 it was held in Berlin, and in 2011 in Hawai'i. In 2017, it was held in Mexico City.

[38] Among the publications that discuss this exercise of reflexivity are Abel (2010); Friedman (2005); Garth & Sterling (1998); Munger (1998); Sarat & Silbey (1988); Silbey (1987); Suchman & Mertz (2010); Trubek (1990). The annual speeches of the presidents of L&S present an occasion to rethink the movement; see, for example, Calavita (2002); Engel (1999); Erlanger (2005); Galanter (1985); Gómez (2012); Handler (1992); Lampert (2010); Macaulay (1987); Merry (1995); Sarat

that most law professors who are interested in socio-legal studies do not believe that L&S has been sufficiently influential. Indeed, they deplore the influence of legal doctrine and legal technique on law students and the rather marginal character of social sciences in the teaching of law (Mertz, 2007, 2008; Sarat, 2004b; Sarat & Ewick, 2015; Tamanaha, 2001). Despite this, comparatively, law in the United States is much closer to the social sciences than it is elsewhere, especially in France and Latin America.

L&S was initially created on the basis of four essential purposes[39]: (i) to study the way that law influences social reality (as opposed to studying the legal rules found in texts); (ii) to use the social sciences as a tool for capturing the reality of law; (iii) to adopt a progressive and reformist political conception intended to consolidate democratic, liberal, and egalitarian values; and (iv) to recognize the importance of the study of institutional processes, especially public policy, in order to arrive at the proposed political objectives of transformation.

These four purposes evoked a return to realist ideas, particularly the idea of constructing a type of empirical legal research that would be critical and useful for public policy.[40] The central preoccupation of the movement was the empirical study of institutional processes. At its beginnings, this concern manifested itself in three thematic domains: justice, the legal profession, and socio-legal theory. With regard to the first of these domains, Marc Galanter's (1974) text on justice and litigation in the United States is considered an icon of the movement.[41] As for the legal profession, a vast amount of publications address issues such as the organization of lawyers and professional practice (Abel, 1989; Carlin, 1962; Heinz & Laumann, 1982;

(2000); Silbey (1997). See also Abel (1995a); Calavita (2010); Clark (2012a); Cotterrell (1992); Darian-Smith (2013, 2015); Friedman et al. (2012), Gordon & Horwitz (2014). Several readers have been published: Abel (1995b, 2010); Sarat (2004a); Sarat & Ewick (2015). See also the two reviews associated with L&S: *Law and Society* and *Law and Social Inquiry*. For a comparison of empirical legal research see Holger (2015).

[39] According to Trubek (1990), the objectives of the movement maintained an implicit ambiguity toward their own object of study.

[40] For a detailed analysis of realist ideas and their legal heritage, see Schlegel (1984).

[41] A French version of this paper was published in *Droit et société* (no. 85); for a Spanish version, see García-Villegas (2001). This article gave rise to a large secondary literature; for a recent analysis, see Grossman, Kritzer, & Macaulay (2014); Heinz et al. (2014).

Macaulay, 1979), the political dimension of the profession (Auerbach, 1976; Scheingold, 1974), and legal education (Macaulay, 1987; Riesenfeld, 1937). Finally, the texts on socio-legal theory published by Boaventura de Sousa Santos (1977, 1987), Austin Sarat (1985), Susan Silbey (1987), and David Trubek (1972, 1990) are a good demonstration of the scope of the theoretical debate within the movement.[42]

The pursuit of this program (scientific, reformist, and progressive) involved a combination of tasks. L&S found its identity in the often difficult management of this combination: the quest for objectivity (science) and the defense of the marginalized (politics).[43] This difficulty sustained a certain rivalry between jurists and law schools on one side and social science professionals on the other. The rivalry entailed two theoretical debates.

The first debate concerned the autonomy of socio-legal studies in relation to law and the social sciences, as well as the question of the borders of the field – in other words, what (and who) is included and excluded. A good number of authors thought that socio-legal studies had acquired, over the years, an important degree of autonomy with the creation of programs of study and the professionalization of the teaching of these studies (Erlanger, 2005; Macaulay, Friedman, & Mertz, 2007). For Carroll Seron and Susan Silbey (2004), it was nevertheless a relative autonomy given the absence of a proper theoretical framework.

The question of borders goes back to the relationship between the professions that participated in the movement (Abel, 2010; Clark, 2012b; Dezalay et al., 1989; Tomlins, 2000). According to Bryant Garth and Joyce Sterling (1998), the tensions within L&S were partially pacified by the dominant position acquired by law professors in

---

[42] See Sarat & Silbey (1988); Silbey (1987). Nevertheless, the dependence vis-à-vis certain European authors within these debates, as well as the absence of general socio-legal theory, affected the continuity of these debates and led to the disaffection of certain authors (as, for example, was the case for Boaventura de Sousa Santos, who still produces a lot of critical sociology of law, but outside of L&S).

[43] The institutional arrangements that assured control of the production and development involved the support of two foundations – the Russell Sage Foundation and the Walter E. Meyer Research Institute of Law – as well as the University of California, Berkeley, and the University of Wisconsin–Madison. For a discussion of these institutions, see Garth & Sterling (1998); Schlegel (1995); Seron & Silbey (2004).

the first years of the movement.[44] And Dezalay et al. argue that jurists used the social sciences as intellectual subcontractors intended to reinforce the formalist view of the law (1989, p. 80). Trubek (1990), for his part, agrees with this judgment but believes that in L&S there is nevertheless enough room for the construction of critical visions against the perspective of jurists.

The identity of L&S depends heavily on the definition of borders to the extent that they determine the construction of a theoretical canon that lends a political and analytical unity to the movement (MacDonald, 2002b; Sarat, 2004b; Sarat & Ewick, 2015; Seron, 2006; Twining, 2009, p. 12). There is consensus neither on the theoretical foundations nor on the canonical list of authors who intellectually guide L&S.[45] But the simple fact that this discussion is always present attests to the sharing of theoretical and normative referents. In fact, part of the wealth of this movement resides, as stated earlier, in the importance that its members give to the exercise of critical reflexivity of the movement and its future.

The second debate emerged around the relationship between science and politics.[46] In other words, the movement's theoretical foundations were based on a conception of social science according to which there exists an objective reality, external to subjects, that can be known, evaluated, measured, and described, just as a natural fact.[47] This theoretical presupposition was accepted at one time (in the mid-1970s), when the relationship between the university world and state institutions was prospering in a context of relative harmony, allowing for the consolidation of a strong movement centered on research aimed at improving public policy and relatively uninterested in institutional critique. Over the course of the movement's first two decades, the critical spirit gradually declined because of the predominance of empiricism and especially because of the financial support of the state

---

[44] However, according to Suchman & Mertz (2010), the dominant theoretical orientations were traditionally proposed by sociologists. For an analysis of disciplines within L&S, see Silbey (2000).

[45] For this debate, see Munger (1998); Santos & Rodríguez-Garavito (2006); Seron, Coutin, & Meeusen (2013); Seron & Silbey (2004).

[46] According to the creators of the movement, empirical research (or empiricism) constitutes a remedy for the doctrinal distortions of law. With regard to the notion of empiricism, see Trubek (1984, p. 582); Trubek & Esser (1989).

[47] This idea, according to Trubek, was associated with a progressive political agenda; science was a tool for unmasking different forms of inequality (1990, p. 8).

for perfecting public policies. The proximity of the university to government policies resulted in an overestimation of the social impact of law and the state, which dismantled the relatively progressive agenda predicted at the beginning of the movement (Trubek, 1990, p. 28).[48] These two events (empiricism and proximity to the state) acted, as Sarat and Silbey (1988) have shown, against the maintenance of critical energies.

At the time of L&S's creation, it was thought that there existed a marked difference between politics and policy. Policy, unlike politics, was founded on an analysis of institutional reality, indifferent to all political evaluation and limited to technical questions around the means for realizing certain ends. The theme of law's inefficiency was central, to the degree that legal sociology was expected to resolve the technical problems of norms not attaining their intended goals. Studies that adopted this approach, characterized by an instrumental vision of law and known as "gap studies," were strongly criticized in the mid-1980s.[49] According to Sarat (1985), when it is supposed that the objectives of law can and must be attained, law becomes mythologized. On the other hand, by trying to make law more efficient, these studies make resistance to the law more difficult.[50] The realist idea, according to which law is a marginal, contradictory, and indeterminate phenomenon, loses its initial force and becomes a simple problem of dysfunction that can be resolved by the creation of better norms and by the perfecting of their application.[51] To these critiques was added, at

---

[48] According to Trubek, "because of the absence of any agency ready to offer financial support to an autonomous sociolegal discipline, its result was adjusted to serve the needs of governmental agencies and foundations" (1990, p. 29). For their part, Austin Sarat and Susan Silbey argue that "[t]he alliance between the sociolegal academy and the elite responsible for public policy within the liberal State is simultaneously strong and subtle, in such a way that apparently critical research ... paradoxically reinforces the essential premises of legal liberalism" (1988, p. 113).

[49] The essential critique of this perspective is that its reformist character leads to an acceptance of liberal values. See Abel (1980); Munger (1998, p. 40). For a less pessimistic vision, see Macaulay (1984).

[50] According to Gordon, these studies, which assume a harmony of interests in the satisfaction of social necessities, see conflicts as a dysfunction or imbalance (1984, p. 70).

[51] In the United States, this perspective is common in analyses of public policy; see, for example, Pressman & Wildavsky (1973). Concerning the European case, see Charboneau & Padioleau (1980); Dellay & Mader (1981).

the end of the 1970s, the creation of the CLS movement, which constituted a frontal attack on the essential theoretical presuppositions of L&S; it was an attack as much against empirical science as it was against L&S's institutional and reformist orientation.

L&S tried to construct its identity from these debates. It was an unstable identity that became increasingly evasive with the growth and inclusion of new perspectives within the movement. These debates, which continue today, are characterized by a reinforcement of the critical dimension to the detriment of the scientific one, as we will see later in this chapter.

Critical Legal Studies

CLS was created over the course of a conference on critical studies organized by David Trubek, Duncan Kennedy, and Mark Tushnet in 1976.[52] The ideas that gave rise to the movement were inspired largely by Marxist thought (Tomasic, 1985, p. 18) and provoked, in the intellectual milieu of North American law schools in the 1980s, a controversy that was both stimulating and antagonistic.[53] The movement as such disappeared in 1992, but its ideas are still present in legal literature, even if they have lost the vigor that they had in the 1980s (Stone, Wall, & Douzinas, 2014; Unger, 2015).[54]

CLS recharged the critical batteries that legal realism had installed against the liberal view of law during the first decades of the twentieth century. However, it was less a neorealism than a postrealism to the extent that the content of the critique, the political reach of its

---

[52] For more on this conference, see Schlegel (1984). For an explanation of the theoretical scope of the movement, see Kelman (1987); Unger (2015). For a selection of studies, see Hutchinson (1989). For a bibliographic guide, see Bauman (1996); Brown & Halley (2002); Campos, Schlag, & Smith (1996); Gordon (1984); Hutchinson (1989); Kelman (1987); Tomlins (2012); Trubek (1984); Ward (1998); White (1986). See also the classic compilation of Boyle (1985, p. 706). For a critique of critiques, see Waldron (1998).

[53] There is no lack of occasions where the movement provoked strong negative reactions. Paul Carrington, for example, dean of Duke University, affirmed in 1984 that his professors had nothing to do with these schools, given their nihilist position and their scorn for the legal profession (Friedrichs, 2006).

[54] The main academic centers for the critique of law are Harvard Law School, Georgetown University Law Center, Northeastern University, and the University at Buffalo. There is also an English CLS, sometimes more active than its American counterpart. It organizes an annual conference on the critique of law, which met for the first time at the University of Kent in 1984, under the direction of Alan Hunt.

postulates, and the theoretical baggage from which these postulates were conceived deflected from the theoretical and political heart of realism (Trubek, 1984). CLS's critique of dogmatic thought was founded less on a problem of language, as the realists thought,[55] than on a political problem involving two premises: first, legal interpretation is still, even in "easy" cases,[56] marked by tensions between opposite values that cannot be resolved in a coherent manner by the legal system; and second, faced with these dichotomies, judges customarily choose values compatible with the status quo (Kelman, 1987, p. 13). For this reason, CLS, in contrast with realism, sought neither to improve law and public policy nor to create a balance between opposing principles.

CLS did, however, come closer to realism to the extent that it was interested in law's role in society. This interest translated into three reflections: (i) on the internal contradictions of legal thought and the impossibility of resolving them; (ii) on the political function of legal legitimation in modern capitalist societies; and (iii) on the possible progressive transformation of society beginning with a leftist political conception of the legal system.

The internal contradictions of legal doctrine were treated by CLS with the help of concepts such as "trashing"[57] and "deconstruction."[58] The critiques were part of a legal-philosophical debate that attempted to solve the following question: What criteria do judges rely on when deciding "difficult" cases? In other words, faced with a problem of legal interpretations for which there are several possible legal solutions, what criteria does a judge use to decide?[59]

---

[55] In other words, on the impossibility of fixing the meaning of legal norms.

[56] Difficult cases are those in which the legal order does not offer a clear response to the problem at hand, whether because of difficulties in interpreting applicable norms, because of problems of the factuality of the case to be decided, or because of the conjunction of the two levels. See Dworkin (1977).

[57] For a deeper explanation, see Kelman (1987).

[58] This is a concept introduced by Derrida, consisting of reversing the order of analysis and evaluation of a discourse in order to show its random and arbitrary character. One example of this approach can be seen in Duncan Kennedy (1976).

[59] This problem is linked to the distinction between principles and legal rules, about which there is an intense debate. In simple terms, principles are general norms that do not envisage the factual hypothesis to which they are applied (e.g., the principle of equality), while rules are specific norms that are applied in cases that they predict (e.g., a norm that determines the speed limit). While rules are either applied or not applied, principles' application is a question of balancing – in other words, of

CLS answered the question with three observations: (i) difficult cases are not exceptional cases but ordinary ones, which generally means that the legal system does not provide clear answers for their interpretation or application; (ii) difficult cases are often the most important cases for a society; and (iii) judges decide in accordance with their own political opinions and not from preexisting legal rules.

Dominant legal doctrine supported the idea that there exist methods of interpretation and reasoning that guarantee the unity and coherence of interpretative practices. Conversely, CLS refused all possibility of rationality in this field and sent the explanation of decisions back to the political field: the choice between opposite values and principles depends not on law but on the political choice of the judge or public bureaucrat at the moment of interpretation or application. No legal doctrine can resolve such tensions, and the fact that liberal thought supported the contrary constituted an illusion, given that legal dogma constantly favored one of the values in the tension, leaving aside the non–politically correct one (the "dangerous complement"). Duncan Kennedy's work is particularly rich in this sense. In his book *A Critique of Adjudication* (1997), he opposes Ronald Dworkin's claim of finding correct answers in law. Critiquing the idea of "taking law seriously" (accepting law's normative, decisive character – in other words, the possibility that it can be used as an imperative for the regulation of human behavior), Kennedy instead proposes "taking ideology seriously" (1997, p. 70).

He also explains how the rules of private law can be interpreted either in an altruistic and antiformalist manner or in an individualistic and formalist manner; in practice, argues Kennedy, given that judges have a conservative political vision, they end up choosing the first option and not the second (1976).[60]

The problem of internal contradictions in law led to the second theme. The justification of legal interpretation not being tenable, what

---

equilibrium between principles that are frequently opposed to each other. Critics argue that there is no legal reasoning or interpretive technique that assures the result of this balancing. On this subject, see Alexy (1993); Zagrebelzki (1992).

[60] Roberto Unger, for example, argues that contract law is not coherent if it is viewed through the prism of contractual freedom and if the opposing principles that constitute it are excluded (1986, p. 561). In the same sense, for Gordon, every act intended to apply a contract implies supporting a particular regime of "free negoti-ation" against alternative regimes that could be applied in its place (1987, p. 215). See also David Kennedy (2002); Duncan Kennedy (1979, 1997).

role does legal doctrine thus play? According to CLS, dominant elites value the indeterminate character of normative postulates in order to impose an ideology centered on the presumed coherence, rationality, and neutrality of legal interpretation. Therefore, law obscures the way in which the powerful profit from a legal order that does everything except recognize their dominant position. The concept of hegemony was used to support this argument. An ideology is hegemonic when – as Robert Gordon affirms – its practical effect consists of closing the imagination to alternative orders. He adds that "law, like religion and television images, is one of the clusters of belief ... that serve to convince people that all the many hierarchical relations in which they live and work are natural and necessary" (1998, p. 648).

Here appeared the concept of "reification," according to which legal concepts are considered real things – in other words, natural phenomena independent of individuals.[61] The idea of reification was used to criticize the image of a world where every term of our language corresponds to a thing, a world where univocity is the rule (see Chapter 2). On the contrary, there is a *vision* of reality, made by the intermediation of language and whose nature is constructed, artificial, and political. Over the course of the process of legal reification – that is, during the conversion of something that is contingent into something permanent – critical legal scholars discovered an unavoidable mechanism of domination: official legal culture blocks the possibilities of imagining alternative visions of the world and accords legal institutions a solidity and permanence that they do not really possess (Kelman, 1987, p. 270).

Finally, the most constant characteristic of these critical authors was their progressive political position, opposed not only to conservative legal thought but also to liberal thought.[62] Tushnet, for example, refuses to consider any other aspect of critics aside from their political position: CLS, he says, adopts the political positions of a leftist group (1991, p. 1516). For Roberto Unger, one of the movement's leaders, the deconstructionist work of critics leads to the creation of alternative legal dogma that privileges values, like social equality,

---

[61] On this concept, see Bourdieu (1986); Ewick & Silbey (1998); J. Gabel (1975); P. Gabel (1980); Gordon (1998, p. 650).

[62] CLS, says Trubek, seeks not only to show the relationships between modern legal consciousness and capitalist domination but also to change this consciousness and these relationships (1984, p. 591).

generally excluded from the application of law (Gordon, 1998, p. 653; Unger, 1986).[63]

CLS was not a homogenous movement. Some even point out that the authors had a large thematic and conceptual diversity (Bauman, 1996; Boyle, 1985; Kelman, 1987), as well as a strong interdisciplinary imprint, because of the inclusion not only of sociological theory but also – and especially – of social theory, continental philosophy, and political science.

After intense internal debates, and following the arrival of postmodern ideas, the movement finished by breaking up into a series of dispersed studies. I will return to these later.

The Renewal of Socio-Legal Studies: 1990–2013

The Reinvention of Law and Society

L&S has experienced significant growth over the last twenty-five years (Ewick & Sarat, 2015; Friedrichs, 2006; Morril & Mayo, 2015; Sarat, 2004b; Seron, 2006). This is evident not only in the increasing number of publications, events, and attendance at annual meetings organized by the Law and Society Association but also in the growing number of topics discussed by members of the movement.[64] Due to space constraints, I will address just a few of the key issues and debates that have marked the trajectory of the movement in recent years.

The Amherst Seminar

Between 1980 and 1995, the city of Amherst, Massachusetts was the seat of a discussion group in socio-legal theory known as the Amherst Seminar on Legal Ideology and Legal Process. For more than a decade, some of the most distinguished intellectuals of law were invited to the seminar with the goal of helping construct a theoretical approach that

---

[63] This alternative dogma is a positive result of the deconstructionist method; see, for example, H. Collins (1986); Unger (1986).

[64] Certain topics linked to the globalization of law – such as the regulation of the environment, the protection of human rights, international markets, the weakening of the state, and transitional justice – are part of the movement's scholarly production; see, for instance, Conti (2014); Garth & Dezalay (1996); Duncan Kennedy (2006); Rajagopal (2005); Santos & Rodríguez-Garavito (2005); Silbey (1997). For an aggregate picture, see Calavita (2010); Darian-Smith (2013); Ewick & Sarat (2015); Larson & Schmidt (2014); Macaulay et al. (2007); Vago (2012).

was simultaneously empirical and critical.[65] The initial idea was that socio-legal research could provide new ways of grasping legal phenomena without making claims regarding objectivity or truth. The objectivist postulates typical of positivist social science were abandoned, but the conviction that empirical research must prevail was maintained. In this sense, the essence of the original L&S movement was preserved. Thus, the defenders of this perspective argued for a postempiricism that does not see science as an authoritative or incontrovertible knowledge but that, according to Sarat, "continues to keep alive the hope that science can serve as a tool of persuasion, albeit a limited one, in a world with 'a multitude of values, knowledge perspectives, and criteria'" (1990a, p. 165).

Three ideas underpin the reconceptualization proposed by the leaders of the Amherst seminar:

First, it is necessary to overcome both subjectivist and structuralist conceptions of the social. In accordance with the "cultural turn,"[66] the seminar adopted a constructivist social theory, based on the idea that social actors build social reality through their practices, and according to which neither subjects nor objects exist before this construction.

Second, in order to foster greater critical engagement, it is necessary to abandon the predominant instrumentalist position of L&S (i.e., *gap studies*), which is politically and epistemologically insufficient because of the importance that it gives to the institutional point of view and in favor of public policies.[67] Instead, the idea is to prioritize the indeterminate character of law (Villmoore, 1985) and the fact that legal norms give rise to multiple social practices, differentiated and changing, which can be understood only by empirically researching the way in which concrete social actors see law.

---

[65] In their analysis of the seminar, David Trubek and John Esser (1989) point out that despite the fact that the participants abandoned a determinist and structuralist vision of equality, they remained attached to the concept of an empirical social science, which generated significant theoretical problems.

[66] For a general explanation, see Laclau & Mouffe (1985). In L&S, Clifford Geertz is often cited as saying that law is a cultural resource that allows us to imagine the real (1983, p. 184); on this subject, see, for example, McCann (1994, p. 282). See also Ewick & Silbey (1998); Fitzpatrick (1992); Kahn (1999); Sarat & Simon (2003); Tyler (2009).

[67] For a critical explanation of instrumentalism in law, see Tamanaha (2006). See also Sarat & Silbey (1988).

Finally, it is necessary to defend the political interests of the marginal-ized (minorities, the underprivileged, and so on) and to create alternative social forums through the use of law (Bumiller, 1988; White, 1990). In this sense, it is important to recognize the possibil-ities of struggle against hegemony through law, without forgetting that law can also function, in certain cases, as an instrument of oppression (Villmoare, 1985).

Legal Consciousness Research

The Amherst seminar gave rise to a branch of studies known as legal consciousness research,[68] which combines essential elements of L&S and CLS.[69] From L&S, the movement adopts the idea that empirical research is essential for understanding the way law functions in society and the way it is used by social actors.[70] According to Susan Silbey and Egon Bittner, "The meaning of any specific law, and of law as a social institution, [can] be understood only by examining the ways it is actually used. What is important is not what law is but how it is used by people" (1982, p. 399). From the critical tradition, legal conscious-ness research not only rejects instrumentalism (the idea that reality and interpretation are inseparable) but also adopts the hope that socio-legal studies can reveal the mechanisms of political domination and, from there, contribute to societal transformation. Legal consciousness research attempts to explain law's long-lived institutional durability. Current events in our globalized world reveal the gap between law-in-books and law-in-action and maybe even belie law's claim to the legitimate monopoly of violence. In this light, the movement looks at what sustains this institution in spite of what legal domination is and the inability of the rule of law to fulfill its promises (Mertz, 2014; Silbey, 2005).

The movement entails a reorientation of L&S in three ways: (1) from a focus on legal rules and legal materials to one on ordinary people (i.e., nonofficials and nonprofessionals); (2) from a focus on measurable

---

[68] In their analysis of these studies, Michael McCann and Tracey March (1995, pp. 208–209) focus on the following authors: Ewick & Silbey (1992, 1998); Merry (1990); Sarat (1990b); White (1990); Yngvesson (1993). See also the group of socio-legal scholars under what Trubek and Esser call "cultural anthropology" (1989); Brigham (1996, 1998). For a more recent evaluation, see Silbey (2005).

[69] They follow the line indicated by Felstiner, Abel, & Sarat (1981) about the origin and transformations of disputes in society.

[70] For a collection of these texts, see Larson & Schmidt (2014).

behavior to one on interpretative communication among actors; and (3) from a focus on "law and society" to one on law as part of social life, which looks at how people make sense of legality.

From a theoretical point of view, legal consciousness research adopts a culturalist and constructivist conception of social reality in which the symbolic use of law is a central element, to such a degree that reality is perceived as constructed from social actors' representations and interpretations. This perspective highlights the rather cognitive aspect of the symbolic dimension of law (in contrast with the political dimension, as explored in Chapter 2), which explains the importance that the movement attributes to legal culture, understood as a complex collection of discourses and symbolic frameworks through which individuals give meaning to legal practices in everyday life (Calavita, 2001; Ewick & Silbey, 1992; McCann, 1994, p. 15; Silbey, 2005, p. 327).

In this microculturalist conception, legal representations are malleable, and their meaning is never static (Merry, 1985; 1990, p. 147; Silbey, 1998).[71] The concept of legal ideology is brought back to the level of daily practices and understood as a complex process through which meaning is produced and reproduced. Legal consciousness research's reconceptualization of culture, conscience, structure, and ideology supposes an erasing of the conceptual lines that typically divide these terms (García-Villegas, 2003a). The structures that, in conventional formulations, tend to be understood as material and external are presented here as linked to mental representations and as mental resources for social and political action (Ewick & Silbey, 1998, p. 225).[72]

Legal consciousness research offers a more complex and developed vision of the life of law. It also reveals a reality of law that is not simply

---

[71] According to Sarat, for example, disadvantaged citizens do not accept "the myth of rights," and because of that, they seem to be capable of resisting legal symbols (1990b, p. 374).

[72] Authors do not always agree about this apparent reduction of structure to consciousness. "I fear however," writes Silbey in an evaluation of the movement, "that recent efforts to track legal consciousness may have inadvertently contributed to the loss of the social, leaving us with studies of individual psychology and its accommodations to predefined policy goals" (2005, p. 359). For a perspective that is more sensitive to structural constraints within legal consciousness research, see McCann (1994); McCann & March (1995); Merry (1990); Silbey (2005). On the difficulties of formulating a cultural theory, see Alexander (1987, pp. 225, 302, 328). See also Burawoy et al. (1991); Fraser (1998); García-Villegas (2003b); Hall (1996, p. 41).

institutional, as jurists and political scientists would often have it. However, the movement's cultural emphasis provokes questions about the emancipatory possibility of law (Dudas, Goldberg-Hiller, & McCann, 2015; García-Villegas, 2003a; Handler, 1992; McCann, 1992; Munger, 2004). Its emphasis on the constitutive dimension of the social world seems to dissolve the distinction between the exterior and the interior of subjectivity in such a way that the critique loses its referent. More importantly, the movement overestimates the idea of consciousness (the psychological dimension of legality) as an expression of free will. This is because most compliance and noncompliance with rules is determined not by free will but by imitation or by habitus. Behavior is often the result of a logic of reciprocity in which people imitate other people's behavior. In other words, people comply when they see other people complying. Additionally, as explained by Bourdieu, action often happens somewhere on the spectrum between causality and free will. The concept of "habitus" – something that lies between causal constraint (physical world) and rules (legal world) – does a better job than consciousness of explaining behavior vis-à-vis rules (Bourdieu, 1977).

Nevertheless, it is also worth noting that legal consciousness research is not a monolithic movement, which is why we must also take into account a series of important authors opposed to the mainstream trend who warn against overemphasizing the constitutive dimension of social reality. Elizabeth Mertz (2014), for example, offers a constructivist social theory that is moderated by the fact that the theory is empirically rooted (Morril & Mayo, 2015, p. 24).

New Empiricist Movements

In the mid-1990s, two new movements were created with the goal of reinforcing the link between law and the social sciences: empirical legal studies and new legal realism.[73] In order to render socio-legal studies more scientific, these movements attempt to return to the social sciences the centrality they enjoyed at the beginning of the twentieth century, when legal realism dominated the study of law.[74] Both movements have

---

[73] Most of these publications appear in the *Journal of Empirical Legal Studies*, the *University of Illinois Law Review*, and the *Vanderbilt Law Review*. In 1996, Harvard created an empirical legal studies program.

[74] For a basic description of these movement, see Ellickson (2000); Heise (2002); Leiter (2003); Shaffer (2008); Suchman & Mertz (2010).

their roots in law schools and, in a certain way, compete among law professors with L&E, which is currently the most influential of these movements in law schools (Edelman, 2004). Empirical legal studies and new legal realism react against what they consider an excessive politicization (toward the left) and theorization (toward culturalism) of L&S that has been occurring since the end of the 1980s. In this sense, they can be seen as a reaction against the tendency established by the Amherst seminar, and especially against the critical influence of legal consciousness research in L&S.

Empirical legal studies is the best known of the two movements. It is also the most attuned toward quantitative empirical analyses of legal phenomena. According to Mark Suchman and Elizabeth Mertz (2010), empirical legal studies encourages a quantitative method in order to confirm (rather than to explore) in a contemporary (rather than historical) perspective.[75]

New legal realism's principal goal is to reintroduce the social sciences and pragmatism (Leiter, 2003) as originally proposed by legal realism. Its promoters – including Stewart Macaulay, Gregory Shaffer, and Howard Erlanger – feel close to the L&S movement and do not see their project as representing a rupture from it (Erlanger et al., 2005).

It is certain that new legal realism has many traits in common with empirical legal studies, although it is methodologically more flexible and more interested in exploring microsocial contexts to grasp what people think. All this has implications for the more flexible way in which new legal realism comprehends legal phenomena (Suchman & Mertz, 2010, p. 564).

In brief, despite their differences, empirical legal studies and new legal realism are an expression of the same impulse: to make more room for the social sciences and to reduce the place of politics in L&S.[76]

These two movements have been the object of a recurring critique from the social sciences, particularly sociology. According to this critique, the type of research that these new movements promote is of substandard quality due to the fact that lawyers are not trained in empirical research. Additionally, the legal journals in which they publish their research are student-edited law school journals whose articles are not peer reviewed (Deflem, 2010; Epstein & King, 2002).

---

[75] See also Chambliss (2008); Leiter (2003); Nourse & Shaffer (2009); Shaffer (2008).
[76] More important differences appear within other movements, such as CLS and L&E.

Furthermore, certain critics, such as Eve Darian-Smith, argue that empirical legal studies and new legal realism are united by the old instrumentalist perspective of gap studies, thus hindering the development of a critical perspective that is necessary for the construction of a global socio-legal field (2013, p. 18). Others scholars, like Richard Lempert (2010), believe that the creation of empirical legal studies and new legal realism is harmful and will weaken L&S.

Dissemination of the Critical Legal Movement

As stated before, in the middle of the 1990s, after intense debates triggered mostly by the arrival of postmodern ideas, CLS broke up into a series of dispersed groups and ideas. This section explores some of them.

Critical Race Theory[77]

The debate on "color-blind constitutionalism," embodied by *Brown v. Board of Education*, is at the origin of critical race theory.[78] The most well-known and communally accepted interpretation of the famous *Brown* decision claims to establish a version of the equal protection clause, contained in the Fourteenth Amendment of the US Constitution, whereby public authorities may not differentiate based on race when distributing benefits or imposing social charges. This principle, which operates as the foundation of liberal constitutionalism in matters of race, is summarized by the phrase "Our Constitution is color-blind," formulated by Justice Harlan in his dissent in *Plessy v. Ferguson*.[79]

Critical race theory comes from the work of a group of leftist academics (the majority of whom are black) who question the way in which racial power is constructed, represented, and perpetuated in American society, as well as the critical role that law plays in this dynamic (Crenshaw et al., 1995). The fundamental objective of this group is to call into doubt the antidiscriminatory impact of judicial decisions. Specifically, the movement aims to critically explore the

---

[77] This subsection and the following one (on feminism) are based heavily on García-Villegas, Jaramillo, & Restrepo (2007).

[78] For an introduction to these studies, see Crenshaw (2002, 1995); Delgado (1987); Delgado & Stefancic (2013); Haney López (1994). There are also critical perspectives on race in L&S; see, for example, Curry (2012); Moran (2010); Obasogie (2010). For the relation between race theory and social science see also Devon & Roithmayr (2014).

[79] 163 U.S. 537 (1896).

social dynamics favoring the presence of a white supremacy in the United States over time, how law plays a role in this process, and what to do in order to transform the relationship between law and racial power.

Its members do not have a homogenous methodology or line of doctrine. Nevertheless, they agree on two fundamental aspects. First, they seek to resolve the following questions: How did the regime of white supremacy establish and perpetuate itself in the United States, with the subordination of Afro-descendants as a consequence? How has law contributed to the preservation of this state of affairs? Second, they attempt to modify the existing relationship between the regime of racial subordination and the legal foundations that support it.

Critical race theory criticizes the formal and biological concept of race adopted by the US Supreme Court, which is based on liberal constitutionalism. For critical race theorists, the concept of race is a social and legal construction whose legal foundation constantly evolves according to historical, cultural, and social circumstances.[80]

For these authors, racism in the United States does not manifest itself in an isolated and occasional manner; rather, it constitutes a systemic phenomenon deeply rooted in culture and inscribed in a vast social and historical context in which the affirmation of white supremacy appears as a constant (Alexander, 2012). For this reason, the response must be just as vigorous – that is, it must constitute a project of social engineering that starts from the victim's perspective (Freeman, 1978).

Critical race theory presents itself, according to Kimberlé Crenshaw, as an intellectual current that seeks "a critical intervention in the liberal discourse on race and racial intervention in the critical discourse on law" (2002, p. 2). In this, racial critique appears in two domains of discussion.

The first domain rests on the confrontation with color-blind constitutionalism and, consequently, with American constitutional jurisprudence on matters of race. This critique articulates itself around three themes that, although linked, can be treated separately for the purpose of analysis: (1) the critique of the notions of race and racism on which liberal constitutionalism rests; (2) the analysis of the role played by constitutional jurisprudence in the preservation of white supremacy;

---

[80] See Haney López (1994). See also Butler (1990); Yoshino (2002).

and (3) the critique of the notion of race that emerges from this jurisprudence.

The movement's second domain of discussion goes back to its attempt to integrate a racial perspective into the critique of law by CLS. The racial critique of color-blind constitutionalism is largely a response to the critique of law developed by CLS. In the mid-1980s, a confrontation took place between the main representatives of CLS and the black professors who were attending their conferences. Even though these two groups shared the conviction that the legal system was reproducing the status quo in the United States and thus perpetuating an unjust social stratification, the black professors argued that critical legal theorists were failing to seriously reflect on how race and racism played a fundamental role in this process of preserving the status quo. For them, the absence of the racial thematic in CLS was revealing of the fact that the movement was reproducing the very racial power that it claimed to critique.

One of the fundamental points of controversy between these two movements is about, as highlighted earlier, the role of rights as vectors of social emancipation. According to CLS, the emancipatory struggle by way of rights is destined to fail (Gabel, 1984; Kennedy, 1981; Olsen, 1984; Tushnet, 1984; Uprimny & García-Villegas, 2003). Critical race theory rejects this devaluation of rights and affirms that legal struggles are useful and necessary for social emancipation – one reason for which, along with the feminist movement, critical race theorists ended up detaching themselves from CLS.

At the end of the 1990s, a theoretical current known as Lat Crit emerged from critical race theory with the aim of studying subordination as it is lived by the Latino community in the United States (Iglesias & Valdés, 2001). Its fundamental point of discussion resides in the will to overcome the binary black/white paradigm from which racial subjects and their legal treatment were conceived in the United States (Perea, 1997). According to the authors of Lat Crit, while Latino identity is of an ethnic character – that is, of a national, social, and cultural origin – the American paradigm is strictly racial and binary, which makes it a more closed model that excludes determinative aspects of Latino identity (Vélez et al., 2008).[81]

---

[81] For a more precise analysis of the movement, see Abrams (1991); Fineman (2015); Kay (1972); Krieger (1998); Littleton (1987); Siegel (1997); Smith (2000); Valdes (1995).

Legal Feminism

Feminist movements are probably the most progressive and influential in American society over the last five decades, and the legal academy has not been isolated from these transformations.[82] However, over the last decade, feminists have been less active and present in academic life, precisely because they won a good number of the battles they started in the 1970s.[83]

Legal feminism is based on the idea that law has played a fundamental role in women's historical subordination. Legal feminists denounce the way the law discriminates against women and seek to improve women's situation by reformulating the legal framework.[84]

Three types of legal feminism can be distinguished in the United States: liberal feminism, cultural feminism, and critical feminism. The first is characterized by its acceptance of liberal political and legal principles and, consequently, by the conviction that it is possible not only to understand women's subordination but also to eradicate it. The main argument of liberal feminism is that women are capable of the same rationality and morality as men, and should therefore enjoy the same rights and duties as men. For this reason, liberal feminists criticize the way in which legal norms use sex as a criterion of distinction. Their main tool in this struggle is the creation of a language of rights suited to equality (Jaggar, 1983).

Cultural feminism, for its part, tends to accept the traditional sharing of values for the sexes but believes that the problem lies in the hierarchical organization of these values and behaviors, which

---

[82] Legal feminism in the United States has more distant roots; see, for example, Crozier (1935); Kanowitz (1963). For a historical vision of women's legal struggles, see Strebeig (2009). Katharine Bartlett (2012), one of the movement's leading figures, recounts its intellectual history through a discussion of six articles published in the *California Law Review*: Abrams (1991); Kay (1972); Krieger (1998); Littleton (1987); Siegel (1997); Smith (2000); Valdes (1995). There are also feminist studies outside the critical movement, particularly in L&S; see, for instance, Merry (2014).

[83] However, feminists have not always won their battles; they lost the fight for the Equal Rights Amendment, have lost ground in the abortion rights struggle, and have not always succeeded in their defense of gay marriage; see Roach Anleu (2000, p. 170); Vago (2012, p. 65). In any case, a good portion of feminists have abandoned their political activism and have returned to academic work (Bartlett, 2012, p. 429).

[84] In that sense, there is a connection between critical race theory and legal feminism; see Gómez (2004).

privileges what is typically masculine.[85] Women's emancipation involves the destruction of this hierarchy in order to give more value to what is feminine. The main argument of cultural feminism consists of showing that women, because of their privileged access to the experience of maternity, share a perspective marked by the experience of connection, which gives them a greater empathy and a more sustained contextual conscience. This perspective implies that women prefer certain behaviors and make judgments based on different values from men (Gilligan, 1993). For this reason, cultural feminism's critique is devoted to revealing the mechanisms by which the "feminine" is made invisible and degraded. Its main tool is to blame the misfortunes of humanity on masculine culture; its sites of actions are those traditionally attributed to women, particularly "private" spaces. Probably the most important book in this perspective is Robin West's *Caring for Justice* (1997). According to West, the subordination (rather than discrimination) of women is such that their traits, experiences, and sensibilities are undervalued and result in women's inferior status in society.

Finally, critical feminism is just as much opposed to the idea that women's problem is one of equality (liberal feminism) or of difference from men (cultural feminism) as it is to the idea that law is neutral in matters of domination and that it can thus be a tool for social change.[86] For critical feminists, especially Catharine MacKinnon, the main representative of this line of thought, women's subordination should be framed not in terms of equality, a category created by the same oppressive masculine structures, but in terms of sexual oppression (MacKinnon, 1982, 1987, 1989, 1991).

More precisely, critical feminism sees two forms of manifestation of women's oppression: one repressive and the other creative. The first is linked to the possibility, for men, of obtaining sexual and reproductive satisfaction. The second is associated with the masculine possibility of representing women as simple objects of sexual satisfaction and as vehicles for reproduction. The central point of oppression thus resides in sex and reproduction. For these feminists, the political

---

[85] See also Chodorow (1989); Gilligan (1993); Tronto (1992); West (1987, 1988).

[86] A classic text in this regard is Shulamith Firestone's *The Dialectic of Sex: The Case for Feminist Revolution* (1970). See also Frug (1992); MacKinnon (1987, 1989); Olsen (1983, 1984).

struggle against discrimination must be attached to the fundamental problem of domination.

In situating the root of oppression in the relationship between the sexes and in reproduction, critical feminism not only explains oppression and its mechanisms but also demands that the political struggle combat the root of the problem and not merely its symptoms. With its battle cry "The personal is political," critical feminism reclaims abortion, marriage, rape, prostitution, pornography, and sexual harassment as spaces of political rather than moral contestation. Concerning the legal domain, critical feminists show how doctrinal and judicial representations produce and reproduce hierarchies of subordination. To demonstrate this, they point to the political character of law and to the strategic use of public/private and private/social dichotomies as justifications for masculine power; for these reasons, the struggle through law must happen individually in order to combat specific instances of oppression (MacKinnon, 1982).

The divisions within the legal feminist movement find their roots in two debates: one regarding the concept of equality and the other regarding the nature/culture distinction.

With regard to the first, as Katharine Bartlett indicates, feminists have a very complicated relationship with the concept of equality. Although for years feminists have called into doubt the possibility of achieving progress based on this concept, they almost always end up preferring equality to other alternatives.[87] According to Bartlett, "It is possible to explain, if not entirely reconcile, the love/hate relationship that feminist scholars appear to have with equality on the ground that feminist scholars are consistent in seeking equality, but what they seek is a continually redefined version thereof" (2012, p. 428).

The second debate concerns controversies between positions considered essentialist – that is, resistant to social transformation – and those that hold that all questions of gender and sex are historical, fashioned by culture, and, consequently, modifiable (Harris, 1990).[88] In cultural feminism, for example, one finds the idea of women's natural

---

[87] For example, they preferred equality of the sexes over the defense of privatization in the case of abortion and in the case of gay marriage.

[88] According to Angela Harris, "The notion that there is a monolithic 'women's experience' that can be described independent of other facets of experience like race, class, and sexual orientation is one I refer to in this essay as 'gender essentialism'" (1990, p. 588). See also Spelman (1988).

inclination toward empathy and maternity; other lines of thought, however, hold that these conditions are cultural and changing. Those who embrace the latter belief argue that the main question today is that of gender, not of sex. In this sense, the interests and preoccupations of the LGBT community align with those of feminists (Valdes, 1995).

The feminist movement reached its apogee in the 1980s and at the beginning of the 1990s. Today, a good part of feminist ideas have been adopted by other academic currents, such as postmodernism, postcolonial studies, and studies of race, oppression, and class. According to Laura Kessler, "[T]oday, masculinity, sexuality, and class are as important as gender and race in legal feminist analysis" (2011, p. 680).[89] This is why we can say, exaggerating slightly, that if today feminists seem a little outdated in certain contexts in Western countries, it is because they were right.

Debates on Rights
One of the most significant aspects of the legal debate in the United States concerns the evaluation of what is called, to use the phrase proposed by Charles Epp (1998), the "rights revolution" – in other words, the growing use of law, over the last four decades, in the political struggles of social movements (Dudas et al., 2015; Sarat, 2009; Stryker, 2007). There is no agreement on the scope of this social phenomenon, and even less on whether it has in fact produced a revolution. What are rights? Who benefits from them? These questions give rise to three different debates, each with its own theoretical references, audiences, authors, academic networks, and publications.

The first is a debate in legal theory between CLS and liberal legal theory regarding the concept of rights. The problem here is how to judge "difficult" cases, as explored earlier in the discussion on CLS. There is a similar debate in constitutional theory, where the critical position is defended by authors who belong to "popular constitutionalism," a movement that is opposed to the strong control of the constitutionality of laws as it exists in the United States.[90]

According to Jeremy Waldron, given that the interpretation of rights can evoke insurmountable conflicts (and it is impossible to find a legal

---

[89] See Bartlett (2012, p. 427). To understand the size of the extraordinary development of feminist studies, see Ellickson (2000).

[90] Among the main authors of this group are Kramer (2004); Tushnet (1999, 2015); Waldron (1999).

norm that solves all of them), the best way to resolve these divisions is through the democratic process, and not through the intervention of the Supreme Court. He argues, "Because there is disagreement about a given decision, the decision is to be made by a designated set of individuals ... using some designated decision procedure" (2006, p. 1387). From the perspective of L&S, Emily Zackin agrees with Waldron (and also Tushnet) when it comes to certain visible groups in the political debate – but with regard to less visible groups, the recourse to judges is a useful strategy (Zackin, 2014, p. 55).

In opposition to this idea, liberals argue that rights are not only objective realities that cannot be reduced to subjective interpretations but also embodiments of values that are indispensable to institutional and social organization. Dworkin (1977, 1985), for example, maintains that law brings clear responses to some difficult cases and that an enlightened judge (whom Dworkin calls "Judge Hercules") can always find the correct solution – that is, the solution predicted by law, and not the solution based on the judge's personal opinion.[91]

The second debate takes place within CLS regarding the political evaluation of progressive law, or rights intended to protect the interests of minorities, the marginalized, and the weak. This debate pivots around the evaluation of the legal struggles of social movements. What is the interest, for the political left, in a strategy that consistently encourages social movements to end in legal reforms? Is the law an effective tool for social emancipation? Critical authors tend to respond negatively: legal strategies are an illusion (Balbus, 1977). On the one hand, these strategies weaken the counterhegemonic political struggle by turning attention toward the process of legal reform; and, on the other, their collective efficacy is minimal because of the individualist character of rights. According to this point of view, the legal dimension of the "civil rights strategy" in the United States, instead of increasing the protection of individuals, weakened the civil rights movement and gave new legitimacy to institutions.

---

[91] According to Dworkin, a judge's job is to use principles to interpret the law in such a way as to make the best sense out of the legal system he or she has inherited. Deciding hard cases at law resembles a strange literary exercise in which each judge is like a novelist in the chain: "He or she must read through what other judges in the past have written not only to discover what these judges have said, or their state of mind when they said, but to reach an opinion about what these judges have collectively done, in the way that each of [the] novelists [forms] an opinion" (1985, p. 159).

This negative opinion of rights has continually provoked controversies. Certain critical authors, such as Gordon, argue that legal argumentation offers concrete resources for achieving social change (1998, p. 657). For Gordon, rights do not always benefit capitalists; they can, perhaps to a lesser degree, also benefit workers, women, the poor, and other marginalized groups, who can turn the finality of legal rhetoric to their own advantage. Trubek agrees, leaving open the possibility that legal structures can put progressive values into practice.[92]

The third debate, which takes place within L&S, was started in large part by the Amherst seminar and its attempt to reinforce the critical dimension of L&S. Two positions can be differentiated within the debate. On the one hand are authors who, drawing on a cultural vision, take an optimistic position toward the use of rights in political struggles. This position has been adopted, to a certain degree, by scholars of legal consciousness research. Sally Merry, for example, argues that "[t]he study of resistance within, by means of, and through law is of consequence for emancipatory projects" (1995, p. 23).[93]

On the other hand is a position that is skeptical of the postmodern and cultural vision of rights in legal consciousness research. According to Joel Handler, for example, rights are insufficient for overcoming the main structural obstacles of class that exist in society. "If postmodernism is to seriously challenge the ideological hegemony of liberal capitalism," he writes, "it must come up with an alternative vision, a vision of the economy and of the polity that will complement its vision of community" (1992, p. 727).[94]

This skepticism is shared by Gerald Rosenberg, sociologist and author of *The Hollow Hope* (1991), on the impact of the legal strategies

---

[92] See Trubek (1977, p. 554). This is what Trubek calls "new realism" – in other words, a program of empirical studies that shows how formal law can simultaneously promote and hinder equality and social justice. This subject, he argues, cannot be decided in advance by a theoretical generalization. The "new critics" of the 1990s agree with this opinion, believing that legal reforms on social rights and against discrimination can be a useful mechanism for political struggle. This position is generally supported by the defenders of minorities; see, for example, Crenshaw (1988); Minow (1987).

[93] For an alternative vision (more sensitive to social contexts) of practices of resistance and uses of law, see MacDonald (2002a). See also Felstiner (2005); Holston (2008).

[94] See also Handler & Hasenfeld (2007).

of civil rights leaders during the 1960s and 1970s. Rosenberg observes the potential limits of these strategies, indicating that

> American courts are not all-powerful institutions. They are designed with severe limitations and placed in a political system of divided powers. To ask them to produce significant social reform is to forget their history and ignore their constraints. It is to cloud our vision with a naïve and romantic belief in the triumph of rights over politics. (1991, p. 343)

The L&S movement also contains studies that show how, in some cases, judges' decisions can trigger perverse effects for social movements (the backlash thesis) while, in other cases, this effect does not exist (Keck, 2014).

The debate on rights has led to two research approaches. The first is devoted to the study of lawyers who defend social interests or public causes. These lawyers, known as "cause lawyers,"[95] conceive of legal strategies as one component within a broader political strategy. Michael McCann and Helena Silverstein (1998) show the creativity of cause lawyers in the pursuit of this strategy.[96]

The second line of research focuses on contexts in which legal strategies can be politically profitable. A number of studies within L&S try to overcome the optimism/pessimism dichotomy in the debates on rights by showing how the possibilities of the progressive use of law depend on the contexts in which social struggles arise. McCann (probably the most important representative of this movement) argues that when there is a coherent social movement, political opportunity structures, and adequate legal frameworks, the chances for the success of these legal struggles increase. In this sense, McCann (2004) has tried to link the political science literature on social movements with legal consciousness research in order to affirm that legal mobilization is a complex social phenomenon that should be studied empirically (Lovell, McCann, & Taylor, 2016). If it is true that recourse to law tends to reproduce social hierarchies and hierarchies

---

[95] This type of study is part of a long American tradition dedicated to researching the legal profession; see, for example, Abel (1985, 1989); Auerbach (1976); Felstiner & Sarat (1992); Gordon (1988); Heinz & Laumann (1982); Nelson, Trubek, & Solomon (1991); Parsons (1954).

[96] See also Coutin (2001). For an analysis of this debate, see Abel (1998); Etienne (1973); Krishnan (2006); Sarat & Scheingold (1998, 2005, 2008); Scheingold & Sarat (2004). On the incidence of this debate in France, see Israël (2001).

of power, it is just as true that, in certain contexts, rules and legal institutions "offer varying degrees of opportunity or space for creative challenges" (McCann, 1994, p. 9).

Robin Stryker, for her part, believes that the debate between those who have an optimistic vision of rights and those who have a pessimistic view is a "glass half-full or half-empty" debate. More important are analyses of the conditions under which legal struggles succeed. As she notes:

> Understanding how and under what conditions law undermines, reinforces, or extends social inequality requires examining multiple change mechanisms, from cost-benefit calculi in response to legal incentive structures, to cultural meaning making and institutional diffusion, to political mobilization and counter-mobilization. The greatest inequality reduction likely comes from substantive effects-oriented interpretation of welfare-oriented legislation, including both effects-oriented strategies of liability and effects-oriented remedies (2007, p. 91).

This type of analysis, sensitive to contexts, has been undertaken in other countries. In Colombia, for example, Cesar Rodríguez-Garavito (2011, 2014) shows how complex and controversial decisions of the Constitutional Court have a greater impact when they apply a dialogical process and establish strict control over the remedies they impose.[97]

Stryker describes similar results: "Maximizing real world inequality reduction through law requires combining a number of factors or conditions. Law interpretation and enforcement must be subject to sustained social movement pressure from below through a combination of litigation and mass political mobilization" (2007, p. 88).

Before closing this section, it is necessary to reiterate the importance of Stuart Scheingold's book *The Politics of Rights* (see Chapter 2), written in 1974, in which law is presented with a double face – one more suitable to political domination and passive acceptance of obligation imposed by the state (the myth of law), and the other more suitable for social struggles and social change (the politics of law). It is fair to recall here that his analysis opened the door for a more complex and nuanced vision of the political dimension of law.

---

[97] Uprimny and García-Villegas (2003), for their part, show how the success of a social movement's legal strategy depends on factors such as the type of social movement, the nature of the law evoked, and the relationship between the movement and public opinion. See also Gargarella (2014); Uprimny (2014).

Law and Postmodernism

During the last thirty years of the twentieth century, postmodern ideas flourished in all social disciplines and in daily life. In the field of law, the postmodern vision appeared as a reaction to the modernist conception. Two types of modern projects provoked the postmodern reaction within American law. The first was proposed by Christopher Langdell of Harvard Law School at the end of the nineteenth century. He sought to offer a scientific method for the knowledge and interpretation of law in an effort to overcome the shadows and ambiguities of the old system of common law. The second project was expressed by Oliver W. Holmes in his famous book *The Common Law* (1881), which was inspired by the pragmatic philosophy of William James and John Dewey to reject Langdell's logical conceptualism and to defend the idea that law is nothing but experience. The truth of law, according to Holmes, resides not in its postulates considered in an abstract way but in the use that judges make of them. His thought has a modern dimension to the extent that he believed in the existence of a science that can guide judges toward the best possible society in their decisions. Even if Langdell's formalism is opposed to Holmes's instrumentalism, the two visions share a confidence in the possibility of turning law into a social practice founded on universal and objective principles.

Each of these visions of law gave rise to a type of postmodern reaction. The first one, generally taken up by CLS, is opposed to the idea of law as a science (as initially proposed by Langdell) – that is, the idea of law as a systematic, objective knowledge endowed with principles that are neutral, decisive, and universal. It seeks to show the deficiencies of theories that view law as theoretical knowledge capable of giving sense and coherence to legal practice (Balkin, 1987). The second reaction, generally adopted by the cultural turn's perspective in L&S, and which is not incompatible with the first, is opposed to the modern vision of law as experience – initially proposed by Holmes and Pound – according to which it is possible to construct an empirical science of judicial decisions and their effects.

The first reaction can be called theoretical or legal-philosophical, while the second can be called socio-legal (but without implying that it is without theoretical pretensions). Between the two, there are multiple connections, as well as deficits in communication. Postmodern theorists oppose legal theories – whether liberal, conservative, or Marxist – with the idea that they lack foundation and do not hold up to critical analysis. As for socio-legal postmodernists, they deny the existence of a socio-legal science capable of producing social change through legal practices.[98]

It is worth mentioning here a particular postmodern approach that has had a significant influence on SLS not just in the United States but also in Europe and Latin America. This is the oppositional postmodernism of Boaventura de Sousa Santos.

Oppositional postmodernism is a critical theory that, while resembling postmodernism, distinguishes itself from traditional postmodernism's frequent resignation, despair, and even cynicism in relation to political struggles. Instead of adopting these attitudes, oppositional postmodernism calls for political struggle and the fight for emancipation. Santos rebelled against postmodern studies' lack of critical and emancipatory energy (Santos, 1987, p. 56; 1995a, 1995b, 1998a, 2000a).

Santos's critical thought begins with a deep questioning of the modernist paradigm.[99] Modernity is characterized by numerous broken promises – for example, the completion of a just and equitable society. Moreover, it has relentlessly pursued specific objectives, like the market, whose excessive enlargement has worked to the detriment of other modernist objectives. These broken promises and excesses of modernity, he explains, have gravely affected the delicate balance of the two fundamental pillars on which modernity rests: regulation and emancipation (1995b, p. 57). Modern regulation is the collection of norms, institutions, and practices confronting our present experiences and our future expectations. It materializes in the domains of the state, the market, and the community. Emancipation is the collection of practices of opposition that question the status quo,

---

[98] According to Patricia Ewick and Susan Silbey (1998), the way the law is felt and understood by ordinary citizens when they decide to invoke it, to avoid it, or to attack it is an essential part of the life of the law.

The distinction between these two groups is not always clear, which is why its interest is, above all, heuristic. There are two main reasons for this: first, they share theoretical referents in philosophy and sociology from a culturalist perspective, and, second, in the United States, the differences between legal theory and practice are not always very clear or very important (unlike in Europe). For a critical vision of the postmodern influence on law, see Hunt (1990); Travers (2010, p. 141).

[99] Santos's work can be regarded as an effort to construct a new critical theory. "Why is it so difficult, today, to construct a critical theory?" he wonders. An answer to this question can be found in Santos (2000a, p. 24).

norms, and institutions, with the goal of fostering experience toward broader perspectives.[100]

The insufficiencies and excesses of the modernist paradigm were originally conceived of as problems that could be resolved progressively through science and law. However, Santos explains, over time, science has lost the critical dimension that the Enlightenment had given it and has transformed into a hegemonic technique that favors the market. Its demands of methodological rigor and social utility are focused on productivity and approval of the existent (Santos, 1998b). Since then, it has reduced the lived world to a collection of "pertinent" experiences for regulation and the market; all other experience has been silenced and rendered invisible.

This leads to the defeat of emancipation and its absorption by regulation. The destructive alliance between science and the market has not only absorbed a large part of the regulatory energy of the state, pushed by the imperatives of capitalist globalization, but also crushed the emancipatory political energy of modernity.

Modern science has also colonized law through the exaltation of the principles of rationality, objectivity, and neutrality of the legal order. A large part of Santos's recent work critiques this modern conception of law, perfectly adapted to science and the market (Santos, 1995b, 2009a, 2010 2014, 2016; Santos & Grijalva, 2012). However, his opposition to modern legal thought originates less with the existence of a knowledge with scientific pretensions than with the fact that this knowledge has become a shield to stop the emancipatory energy of law, to depoliticize the legal domain, and to change it into an instrument that favors the domination of the capitalist market. It is for this reason that, according to Santos, postmodern legal movements, which he calls festive or "celebratory," are as insufficient as, or perhaps even worse than, modernity. He thus attempts to construct an independent way, simultaneously drawing from modern thought on law and from post-modernism. This way, which he calls "oppositional postmodernism," seeks to found theories and practices capable of reinventing social emancipation from the broken promises of modernity (2010). In short, Santos lays the foundations for a theory and practice of law that is

---

[100] These domains correspond to what Weber (1978) identified as the aesthetic-expressive rationality of the arts and literature, the cognitive-instrumental rationality of science and technology, and the moral-practical rationality of ethics and law.

opposed to almost all critical socio-legal and, obviously, conservative theoretical production written in the United States over the last four decades.

CONCLUSION

SLS in the United States constitutes an ample transversal field of study that bears witness to the American legal interest in both the political power and the nonformalist dimensions of law. The historical relationships between law and political power, on the one hand, and among protagonists of the legal field, on the other, have encouraged the law's connection to the social sciences and antiformalist critique (against the autonomy and neutrality of the law), which has given an important boost to SLS. Nowhere else in the world has the link between law, society, and political power led to such broad and deep reflections. Historically speaking, the fact that antiformalist positions were not abandoned after the Second World War (as was the case in most civil law countries, particularly France) contributed to the success of SLS in the United States. But, as shown in the first chapter, ideas alone are not enough to account for this relevance. The legal culture of the common law tradition, conceptions of political power and the federal state, and the link between social actors within the legal field are also important elements in explaining the relative success of these ideas in the United States.

Starting from this premise and from what I have discussed thus far, it is now time for me to outline some general characterizations of SLS in the United States.

First, the extraordinary facility with which new groups and intellectual movements are created in the United States deserves special mention. This was particularly evident in the 1990s, with the formation of a series of critical movements (e.g., legal feminism, critical race theory, Lat Crit, and postmodernism) and the rise of new tendencies within L&S (e.g., empirical legal studies, new legal realism, and legal consciousness research). In order to explain this proliferation, we must take into account the proximity that law (and law schools) has to society in the United States.[101] This phenomenon has two mutually reinforcing facets: on the one hand, law is close to social reality, which

---

[101] Furthermore, law is perceived not only as an object of regulation in the hands of state power but also as a collection of rights in the hands of citizens that can be used

is strongly determined by the market and economic dynamics. In this sense, as explained in Chapter 3, American lawyers are perceived as social engineers whose role is to find solutions to the problems that emerge in society. On the other hand, the legal field imitates the logic of the market: law professors are supposed to produce intellectual goods (e.g., conferences, journals, colloquia, and commentaries) that must be "sold" in the academic market. In this sense, the fragmentation of SLS also succumbs to the necessity of making these academic products more visible and more attractive in a competitive market.

Second, one consequence of this fragmented proliferation of SLS is the lack of communication between the new groups that are created. It is true that specialization serves to deepen the analysis of certain phenomena, in concentrating on increasingly specific aspects of legal reality. But because the sociopolitical reality of law is one reality, excessive specialization and a lack of communication between specializations obscure SLS and block an adequate explanation of legal phenomena. For an external observer, it is always surprising that there is not more academic exchange between, for example, CLS and L&S, or between L&E and L&S. Not only are the groups too focused (and too invested in their positions and scholarly productions) to communicate with other new groups, but, worse yet, they neglect to communicate even with the theoretical core of general disciplines, like political science or sociology. For instance, there is a general lack of academic exchange between the literature on social movements belonging to political science and the L&S literature on the political use of laws by these movements.[102] Moreover, there are cleavages between theory and practice and between theoretical analysis and empirical analysis, as is the case between the sociology of law and CLS. These cleavages prevent a precise comprehension of legal phenomena.

Third, SLS does not always have a progressive understanding of the law. Although, from the point of view of political practice, there is a long tradition of the progressive use of law (particularly during the civil rights movement and onward), over the last few decades, not only has this tradition been undermined by the lack of an encompassing critical legal theory, but the political right and conservatives have learned to use these same tools to defend their causes. This is why SLS from the

to defend their liberties against political power. This constructs a strong link between law, business, and citizenship.

[102] For a notable exception, see McCann (2004). See also (Levitsky, 2015).

right abounds. L&E proposes a clear defense of the market and of economic liberalism through a political interpretation of the legal system, intended to preserve a specific type of society and social relations.

Finally, while it is true that SLS constitutes a very dynamic transversal field of political practice and scholarship, its critical and transformative impact has been, especially over the last two decades, rather weak. There are several reasons for this phenomenon.

For one, it is difficult to sustain a progressive and critical project in a period of economic and political recession. As Mathew Arnold (1971) suggests, in periods of expansion, citizens are open to new ideas and ready to rise to new challenges. In periods of stagnation, however, citizens turn to the past for sources of stability and communal values.

But, to my understanding, there are also epistemological reasons for this lack of impact, at least regarding L&S. By these I mean that even though the "cultural turn" in SLS has contributed to the comprehension of the social reality of law, it has obscured the big picture and structural and class dimension of legal phenomena. It is impossible to see this large picture from the daily lives and legal consciousness of social actors.[103] This culturalist, often anthropological, and postmodern vision of law has produced an excessive reaction against the study of public policy and, in general, against the study of state institutions.

In American SLS, and particularly in L&S, actors' resistance is often overestimated.[104] It is not linked to social class, race, or workers' struggles. Resistance is embodied in the tactical maneuvers against judges, bureaucrats, mediators, administrators, and other functionaries of the state. Failing to consider the collective or contextual dimension (the institutional aspect included) of individual practices leads to a rather romantic and inoffensive concept of resistance.

In most legal consciousness research, for instance, practices of resistance are reduced to intentions of resistance that are represented as heroic but that are almost always revealed to be useless or temporary, even in terms of individual struggles (Sarat, 2000, p. 140). When actors' social and economic positions are not taken into account, domination and resistance seem equally possible. Each practice can be reduced to a dispute between actors who apparently have the same possibilities of winning. Only their world views – not their positions in

---

[103] For some exceptions, see Barclay, Jones, & Marshall (2011); Handler (1992); McCann (1994); Silbey (2005).

[104] For a detailed explanation of these critiques, see García-Villegas (2003a).

the social hierarchy – differ. It is a game where there is neither hierarchy nor violence. Even the state seems to be an actor among others. Each practice can be led back to a question of culture, or of meaning. Legal consciousness research's lack of interest in macrostructural analyses eclipses the underlying factors that determine the relative permanence of social hierarchy and domination. This perspective lends an image of openness, contingence, mobility, malleability, and indeterminacy to social relations that does not actually exist in the United States or anywhere else. One need not be opposed to the dynamic and omnipresent notion of power in Michel Foucault[105] to admit that a large part of power in society circulates through state institutions.

For someone who lives in another Western country, the culturalist reaction against institutions is difficult to understand: it exists only in the United States, where this idea of getting rid of state institutions in order to better understand the legal system (and resistance) is possible. But, in my opinion, L&S has paid a heavy price for abandoning an analysis of the state and its institutions.[106]

To avoid this effect, I have adopted here a notion of culture "rooted in social reality," which, as stated in the introduction, maintains a certain distance from the so-called cultural turn, or at least the more "micro" and psychological version of it.[107]

Moreover, it is perhaps necessary to adopt a more skeptical vision with regard to the "rights revolution" (Epp, 1998). In the United States, law is considered a weapon against abuses committed by the state. In Europe, the tradition is different. Politics has been the means by which people have tried to liberate themselves from oppressive legislation and unjust power (Dingwall, 2003, p. 317). The omnipresence of an overly optimistic vision of rights sometimes prevents us from seeing how the political use of law can also be a very powerful tool for

---

[105] In legal consciousness studies, and in L&S in general, there is a certain fascination with Foucault's concept of power; this attraction seems paradoxical to the degree that the opacity – even submission – of social actors with regard to power structures is a characteristic of Foucault's thought; see, for example, Buchanan (1994). Today, in the American sociology of law, Foucault's conception of power is often taken as something fluid, variable, and decentralized, when it is not. On the reception of Foucault in socio-legal studies, see Valverde (2010).

[106] For some exceptions, see Edelman & Suchman (1997); Ewick et al. (1999); Sarat (2010).

[107] For a similar analysis that compares economic knowledge in France, the United States, and England, see Fourcade (2009, p. 15).

exercising domination. In this sense, a vision of the symbolic efficacy of law that is more connected to economic structures and less dependent on the subjectivity of social actors could help us better understand the complexities and subtleties of political domination.

Finally, it is surprising to note how local and even parochial most of the SLS produced in the United States is, despite all that is published about the globalization of law and the internationalization of the sociology of law.[108] In practice, there are few real efforts to construct a more global academic knowledge, or at least a more global dialogue on SLS, as is the case in other countries. The vast majority of American authors are unable to read texts in a language other than their native language and adopt in this respect the wrong attitude in believing that everything that is interesting will be published in English (Wallerstein, 1999, p. 25).[109] I will come back to this point in the last chapter.

---

[108] Several notable exceptions include Darian-Smith (2013); Twining (2009); Santos (1989, 1995); Santos & Rodríguez-Garavito (2005). See also Friedman et al. (2012). For a similar critique, see Esquirol (2011).

[109] A similar attitude existed in France in the 1970s and 1980s, when social science works published in France were read almost all over the world.

CHAPTER FIVE

SOCIOPOLITICAL LEGAL STUDIES IN FRANCE*

Sociopolitical legal studies (SLS) are influenced by the historical conditions in which the legal field is constructed and, more precisely, by the relations among law, political power, and the state. In France, as the first chapters of this book have shown, the legal field took shape after the French Revolution, particularly during the period of codification at the beginning of the nineteenth century. At this time, the ideal of law (embodied in the Civil Code), understood as the expression of the general will (*volonté générale*) and as a founding myth of society, was consolidated.[1] Rights were seen as a manifestation of the democratic state expressing the will of the people, and the legal system, particularly legal science, was seen as independent from society, as well as politically neutral.

Across the Atlantic, in the United States, law and rights have been seen in the tradition of John Locke, as being not only an attribute of society but also an essential part of human dignity. In France, on the contrary, in the tradition of Jean-Jacques Rousseau, law and rights have been understood as attributes of democratic states – as a legal

---

* A previous version of this article was published in the *Revue interdisciplinaire d'etudes juridiques* in 2011 (García-Villegas & Lejeune, 2011).
[1] The idea of political power understood as the expression of the popular will came from Rousseau in the *Contrat social* and was adapted, during the French Revolution, by Sieyes (Pasquino, 1998). The school of exegesis played an important role in the process of consolidating this idea. On this subject, see Hespanha (2011); Jestaz & Jamin (2004). See also Cohen-Tanugi (2007); Garapon (2007); Garapon & Papadopoulos (2003).

expression of the popular will. For this reason, in France, law has long been regarded as independent from society and as a politically neutral instrument (Cohen-Tanugi, 2007; Garapon, 2007; Garapon & Papadopoulos, 2003).

However, this French conception of law is neither a monolithic and rigid legal culture nor a fixed and undisputed legal myth. It has evolved throughout history not only as a result of contextual factors (wars, institutional reforms, globalization, and so on) but also as a result of the different positions occupied by legal actors (such as judges, lawyers, teachers, and legislators) throughout French history. It is therefore a living culture that originated in the French Revolution (with strong roots in the *ancien régime*), was consolidated during the first half of the twentieth century, and began to lose strength after the Algerian liberation war. Moreover, the idea of identity between the law (assembled in the legal code) and the general will, which is the heart of French classical legal culture, is a myth that has had many detractors.[2] Although it has been strong in circles of legal doctrine and legal theory driven by professors of civil law, it has faded among public law professors and other professional legal circles, especially among lawyers and judges who have promoted alternative conceptions of law (and of rights), as shown by a recent book on French legal culture written by Frédéric Audren and Jean-Louis Halpérin (2013).

But we should not exaggerate the unfixed character of French legal culture. The revolutionary myth of the identity between the law and the general will, seen as a founding principle of the nation, has been more than a passing political idea defended by nostalgic lawyers and conservative law professors. Comparison with other cultures and traditions demonstrates that classical French legal culture, though partial and disputed, is still in place, at least in law schools and among private law professors.[3] Something similar happens with American legal culture, which in spite of permanent variations and internal contradictions and disputes, has some sociological trends that differentiate it from other legal cultures (Duxbury, 1995; Fletcher, 1998; Friedman, 1985; Minda, 1995). Anyway, my interest in this chapter (and in

---

[2] The notion of identity between the popular will and the legal code has had important consequences for the history of constitutionalism (Ackerman & Rosenkrantz, 1991; Blanco Valdés, 1998; Zagrebelzki, 1992).

[3] See Beaud (2006); Biland and Vanneuville (2012); France & Vauchez, (2017); Halpérin (2015); Israel & Vanneuville (2017); Le Beguec (2003); Vauchez (2012).

this book) is less in the analysis of the contemporary features of the legal field in France and the United States, and more in understanding how those features were shaped in the past, throughout the twentieth century.

This chapter aims to demonstrate a double hypothesis. First, this conception of law as a founding myth of society, autonomous from society and politically neutral, has largely hindered the development of sociopolitical visions of law in France.[4] French SLS has been caught in the tension between, on the one hand, a mythical and dogmatic vision of law that neglects its social and political dimensions and, on the other, a critical vision that reduces law to political domination and underestimates the internal rationality of the legal system. French SLS struggled to grow amid two visions of law: one overly confident in the law and another too critical of it.

The weakness of the theoretical and sociopolitical visions of law in France, compared to other legal traditions and cultures, is related to the strength of French classical legal culture in law schools, particularly among professors of civil law (Caillose, 1996). The reason is this: the more the law is seen as rational, complete, and autonomous from society, the more the social sciences and the political dimension of law are neglected. It is certain that alternative legal cultures, based for instance on the idea of human rights or the Europeanization of the French legal system, have gained importance during the last three decades (France & Vauchez, 2017; Audren & Halpérin, 2013). But this has happened within professional circles mostly outside of law schools and away from legal scholarship.

The second hypothesis is that French classical legal culture has faded over the last three decades. Several factors have caused this weakness: the globalization of law, the Europeanization of French law, the increasing power of judges, the crisis of political representation, the political uses of law by social movements, and the reciprocal influence among legal traditions (common law and civil law), among others (France & Vauchez, 2017; Delpeuch, Dumoulin, & De Galembert, 2014; Dezalay, 1992; Jamin, 2012). The new political struggles for (and with) rights throughout the political spectrum have particularly contributed to renewing social scientists' interest in the sociopolitical

---

[4] Even today, compared with the United States, France's political sociology of law is weakly institutionalized. See Abel (2010); Clark (2012a, 2012b); Friedman (2005); Israël (2013).

dimension of law (Arnaud & Fariñas Dulce, 2012; Commaille, 2012, 2015; Darian-Smith, 2013; Israël, 2008a, 2008b, 2009a).

Today, we are witnessing a renewal of SLS in France, which has led to interrogations of the fundamental (and founding) questions of legal sociology – namely, the question of the neutrality and autonomy of law. In discussing this renewed interest in French SLS, this chapter explores not only how new SLS scholarship explores an intermediary path between the veneration of the law and its pure and simple condemnation but also how new symbolic uses of law have emerged as part of France's daily political life (Israël, 2009a).

I pay particular attention to the historical, social, and political context in which these studies were developed. My objective is not to present French SLS in an exhaustive way but rather to highlight a series of works that reveal key issues in French sociopolitical visions of law.

The chapter is divided into two parts. The first part contains a brief historical explanation of the French legal tradition, and the second analyzes the groups, currents, and tendencies that presently constitute the political sociology of law.[5]

MYTH AND DEPRECIATION OF THE LAW

In France, the extraordinary strength of the myth of law has inhibited the development of SLS and of the political use of law (Jouanjan & Zoller, 2016; Muñagorri et al., 2016). Paradoxically, the myth of law in France works as a source of social impairment and inferiority of law in relation to political power and public administration. This social diminishing of law is the result of the autonomy of law in relation to society. I hope to clarify this idea in what follows.

The French Revolution of 1789 reacted against the excess of norms and the disproportionate power of judges and bureaucrats who interpreted the law in the *ancien régime*. According to Jean Carbonnier, the revolution "was persuaded that the abundance of laws was the mark of a corrupt civilization, and that a return to a golden age could be made

---

[5] Mine is not the first attempt to undertake such an aim; other attempts to reconstruct the French sociology of law have been made by Arnaud (1989, 1991, 1998); Commaille (1989); Commaille & Duran (2009); Delpeuch et al. (2014); Israël (2009b, 2013); Noreau & Arnaud (1998); Soubiran-Paillet (1994, 2000); Vauchez (2001).

by a legal dismantling in society" (2001, p. 10). The revolution, and especially the codification, sought to attain this ideal of non-law – or at the very least, the ideal of a simple law, autonomous in relation to society and applied in a technical and mechanical manner. One can see here the underlying vision of Rousseau, according to which a stable and democratic society does not question its law: "the conflict of men and laws, which puts the state in permanent internal struggle, is the worst of all political states" (1915, p. 160). The way judicial decisions are framed in France is a manifestation of this ideal of "non-law": they are written in an extremely simple manner, short and general, with no dissenting opinions, which differentiates them from the judicial rulings of most Western countries, whose analysis of facts is often exhaustive (Muir-Watt, 2000, p. 508). One could say that in France there is a judicial tradition that aims to dispel the political reality and the social facts from decisions made by judges. While in the United States the questioning of law is often perceived as a right, in France it is perceived as a sign of opposition to state institutions.

The revolution resulted in more than the social depreciation of the law. As discussed in the first two chapters, it also brought about a depoliticization of citizens' rights, triggered by the reduction of rights to the text of the legal code. The origin of this is article 6 of the Declaration of the Rights of Man and the Citizen of August 26, 1789, according to which "the law is the expression of the General Will"; the declaration thus established the ideal of law as a perfect expression of the general will.[6] This ideal contrasts with the English tradition of separation between rights and the popular will expressed by the parliamentary majority (Locke, 1946). In the English legal conception of the eighteenth century, rights preceded political action and thus allowed citizens to control governmental action. In France, on the other hand, rights were conceived as the product (not the cause) of politics and became codified (sacralized) and untouchable.[7] The result is the French paradox of a law that is very close to politics at the stage of its creation

---

[6] This norm came from Emmanuel Joseph Sieyès's adaptation of Rousseau's ideas as expressed in the *Social Contract*. For more on this adaptation, see Pasquino (1998).

[7] The revolutionary myth of a politically neutral law (one that cannot be interpreted or questioned) has impregnated not only the French institutional dynamic but also the country's culture, media, and entire political life. Hence, for instance, for an external observer, it may be surprising to see that during demonstrations against gay marriage that took place in Paris in 2012 and 2013, protestors brandished copies of the Civil Code to demand respect for human rights. When the same type of event

but that, once promulgated and codified, emerges politically petrified, untouchable, attached to public administration, and separated from citizenship (Blanco Valdés, 1998; Cohen-Tanugi, 2007; Matteucci, 1988; Zagrebelzki, 1992).

In the French classical legal tradition, the political dimension of law is then reduced to the process of the creation of law and to the political debate leading to the promulgation of norms. The process of interpretation and application, by contrast, is conceived as a technical and objective matter that belongs to judges and public administration. The French tradition sought to realize, through the law, the ideal of all power: to make it seem as though the exercise of political power is the result not of politics but of a mythological entity, transcendent and immutable (the popular will).

This tradition sees the production of law as a superior task, assigned to legislators (the representatives of the people), while its application is seen as a secondary task, assigned to obedient bureaucrats. If in the English tradition the judge and the citizen (assisted by a lawyer) are the protagonists of the production and development of law, in the French tradition the legislature and the public administration are the main actors. In England and the United States, the supreme courts produce the ultimate definition of law; in France, this definition comes out rather from the Assemblée Nationale and the professors of law in charge of legal doctrine. While it is true that there is a strong political dimension to the law in both traditions, this dimension intervenes at different moments in the life of a law: at the moment of application of legal rules (by judges) in England and the United States, and at the moment of the creation of a law (by legislators) in France. Schematically, in France, political debate occurs primarily during the production of a law and lessens after its promulgation; in the United States, on the other hand, this debate transcends Congress and passes through the courts, public administration, and civil society.[8]

This theoretical depoliticization of law leads to its practical subordination to public administration and lawyers, which hides the political

---

occurs in the rest of the Western world, people generally rely on the constitution, not the civil law.

[8] This distinction needs to be nuanced: there are some works that highlight the political dimension of law and rights throughout the process of its application. See the classical texts of Morand (1993); Perelman (1984); more recently, see Baudot & Revillard (2014).

dimension of the application of law under an apparently technical and neutral interpretation (Cohen-Tanugi, 2007, pp. 66–67; Commaille, 2015, p. 102). In other words, the depoliticization of law – its reduction to a technique – brings about, paradoxically, the subordination of law to politics. Indeed, given that the interpretation and application of norms are an inevitably political task, the lack of awareness of this political dimension of law does not occlude its existence, instead making it more effective and pervasive to the point that it is neither recognized nor controlled.[9]

The French classical legal tradition is a good example of what Stuart Scheingold calls the myth of rights (Bourdieu, 1986, p. 14; Scheingold, 1974). As explained in previous chapters, Scheingold distinguishes two conceptions of rights (and of law). The first one sees rights as the founding myth of the nation and the state (the myth of rights), while the second sees them as resources for political mobilization (the politics of rights). The first approach conceives of rights as untouchable real-ities, independent and separate from society, while the second envis-ages them as citizens' resources for their defense against political power.

As noted earlier, the mystification of the law has weakened in France in recent decades (Audren & Halpérin, 2013). This has resulted from different phenomena, such as the crisis of law schools as centers of elite formation, the Algerian colonial war, the judicialization of French political life, the influence of common law on French law, the political uses of law by groups and social movements, the victory of the Socialist Party in 1981, the reinforcement of constitutional control by the Constitutional Council, the Europeanization of French law, and the strengthening of human rights discourses, among others. As a result of the decline of the classic tradition the center of legal culture has partially shifted from the areas of legal doctrine (law schools) to professional arenas, such as the judiciary and law firms, as well as to the media and social movements. These changes also involve variations in the production of SLS. In law schools, both critical legal perspectives and socio-legal studies have stagnated, while sociology departments have become important centers of production of SLS.

However, despite this tradition's weakening, a good portion of the French classic legal culture persists and maintains its power in univer-sities, particularly within civil law circles. Additionally, the strong link

---

[9] This is what Bourdieu calls the "effect of normalization" (1986, p. 18).

between law, power, and society – which was very important in French classical social sciences, particularly in sociology (Durkheim, 1963) – has not been recovered, whether by sociologists or political scientists (Brunet, 2015; Commaille, 2015, p. 21). In spite of the fact that classic legal culture sees the law as the science of government (Legendre, 1974), political science mostly disregards legality and law as relevant phenomena (Commaille, 2015, p. 53)

OVERVIEW OF FRENCH SOCIOPOLITICAL LEGAL STUDIES

This section aims to present a panorama of SLS in France by focusing on the evolution of and debates on the sociology of law (among sociologists) and socio-legal studies (among jurists). There is undoubtedly a margin of arbitrariness in the distribution of authors, networks, groups, and schools of legal thought presented in this chapter.[10] Nevertheless, it is justified to the extent that my goal is to illustrate the main currents within SLS today in France.[11]

This chapter focuses on the political sociology of law developed by social scientists, particularly sociologists, as the main producers of SLS in France (Delpeuch et al., 2014).

Between the 1960s and 1980s, jurists largely dominated French sociology of law. Today, in contrast, sociologists are the protagonists

---

[10] Furthermore, I could have included certain authors, such as Michel Foucault, in the discussion that follows, though I did not. Despite the fact that Foucault did not develop a comprehensive vision of law as such, he is probably the French author who has most influenced SLS outside of France, especially in the United States. See, for example, Burchell (1991); Dean (2009); Garland (1990); Golder & Fitzpatrick (2009); Hunt (1994); Merry (2001); Valverde (2010); Wickham & Pavlich (2001). In France, see the book published by Márcio Alves de Fonseca (2013a). There are other notable absences of scholarly works from the fields of anthropology and legal history – and more specifically, legal criminology – particularly the works of Louis Assier-Andrieu (1996, 2011).

[11] Sociopolitical visions of law are dispersed both for disciplinary (sociology of law, socio-legal studies, legal anthropology, etc.) and institutional (research centers, law schools, colleges, etc.) reasons. This dispersion is accentuated by the absence of a strong tradition of thinking in this field of research: compared to the North American tradition, there are relatively few French texts conceiving of the sociology of law or socio-legal studies as a specific field of study: Arnaud (1998b); Arnaud & Fariñas Dulce (1998, 2012); Commaille & Duran (2009); Delpeuch et al. (2014); García-Villegas & Lejeune (2011); Israël (2009a, 2013); Lejeune (2011a); Noreau & Arnaud (1998); Soubiran-Paillet (1994, 2000); Vauchez & White (2013).

in the construction of this field of research. At the time of Carbonnier, a French classical author on the sociology of law, the cultural capital of socio-legal authors was largely influenced by their technical capacity to interpret law and by their relations with the state. Today, by contrast, the fate of socio-legal thought is dependent largely on academic and scientific networks. This change illustrates not only the disciplinary debate's evolution but also a profound transformation of the institutional conditions for the production of sociopolitical legal knowledge, especially the power relations between actors in the legal field (see Chapter 3).

More specifically, four determining factors boosted the current development of French SLS, particularly French sociology of law.

First, a good portion of sociologists have rediscovered law as an essential element of social cohesion. For a long time, between the end of the Second World War and the 1970s, sociopolitical visions of law were translated into the development of critical visions, especially Marxist visions, which reduced law to an instrument of domination.[12] Today, even within the left, there is an increasing interest in the role played by law in society.

Second, the North American law and society movement strongly influenced the recent developments of French sociology of law. These works were imported into Europe by social scientists such as Antoine Vauchez, Liora Israël, Thierry Delpeuch, Yves Dezalay, Anne Boigeol, and Lucien Karpik.

Third, law schools, traditionally dominated by legal positivism, have rejected all critical, interdisciplinary, and even theoretical perspectives of law for a long time. However, today, socio-legal studies are increasingly becoming more multidisciplinary, integrating knowledge and methodologies from different social sciences.[13]

Last but not least, the recent rise of SLS is partially the product of the work of several key authors in the academic world, including

---

[12] This underestimation of law is not a French peculiarity: every country has seen such an evolution, especially those that belong to the civil law tradition, where legal criticism historically acquired particularly radical forms. See Saffón & García-Villegas (2011).

[13] There are some efforts in law schools to promote socio-legal research. At Paris II Panthéon-Assas, for instance, there is the Laboratory for Legal Sociology, led by Dominique Fenouillet, Nicolas Molfessis, and Mustapha Mekki. See Heurtin & Molfessis (2006); Mekki (2013); Théry (2010). At Paris I Panthéon-Sorbonne, see Brunet (2014, 2015).

André-Jean Arnaud and Jacques Commaille. These two professors (of law and sociology, respectively) founded the journal *Droit et société* in 1968, contributed to the creation of the European Network on Law and Society and the International Institute of Legal Sociology in Oñati, Spain, and are today key figures in the sociopolitical vision of law in France.

Next, I offer a classification of SLS. It is important to bear in mind, however, that given the dispersion of works and sites of production that exist in France, it is always difficult to set up a satisfactory classification. The criterion used here comes from the two fundamental concepts of legal antiformalism: embeddedness (against legal autonomy) and domination (against legal neutrality). As explained in Chapter 1, these two concepts sit at the heart of SLS. Based on this idea, I have differentiated three categories of SLS: (i) the pioneers of the sociology of law who have contributed to the emergence of a sociopolitical dimension of law by criticizing both legal autonomy and legal neutrality; (ii) the authors who participate in the radicalized debate on legal neutrality; and (iii) movements that seek an intermediate position between the attack against legal autonomy and the reaction against legal neutrality.

Importantly, this division does not correspond to a chronological view of authors and movements. Indeed, some of the authors who radicalized their positions against legal autonomy and legal neutrality are contemporaries of those who seek conciliation between embeddedness and domination. These two positions distinguish themselves through their approaches: the first (the radical position against autonomy and neutrality) views the relationships between law and society in a binary way, either in terms of autonomy/embeddedness or in terms of neutrality/domination, while the second (the intermediate position) rejects these binaries and seeks to position itself halfway between the two elements of this polarity.

The Pioneers of Legal Sociology
Law in the Eyes of the Founding Fathers of Sociology
French socio-legal thinking goes back to the time of the founding fathers of sociology, especially Montesquieu and Alexis de Tocqueville (Lascoumes & Serverin, 1986). Montesquieu (1689–1755) wanted to understand the unity of the nation (what he called the "spirit of the nation") that allows for maintaining the unity of laws (what he called the "spirit of law"). A century later, Tocqueville (1805–1859), a historian and political scientist influenced by Montesquieu's work,

proposed some reflections on the relationship between law and society. Although his work is not always recognized in the sociology of law, his comparative study of democracy in America and France led him to analyze the role played by law and lawyers in the reestablishment of social cohesion and in the permanence of the democratic political regime. Unlike Montesquieu, who conceived of laws as variables dependent on the social world, Tocqueville envisaged them as independent variables and was therefore interested in their influence on the political system and democracy (Rocher, 1996, p. 157).

By the end of the nineteenth century, when the school of exegesis was exerting a quasi-hegemonic influence over the legal field and when non-dogmatic visions of law were relatively rare, Gabriel Tarde (1843–1904) proposed a new understanding of law. A French lawyer, sociologist, and philosopher, Tarde wanted to apply the "law of imitation," which hailed from criminology and sociology, to the legal domain.[14] His work was not received favorably among jurists. Similarly to Italian positivist criminologists, such as Enrico Ferri and Raffaele Garófalo, Tarde focused on the criminal approach, which uses an individualist or even biological point of view instead of focusing on social structures or legal and institutional dimensions.[15] Furthermore, Tarde's work passed relatively unnoticed in a context in which Durkheim enjoyed unequaled prestige in the academic world.

Emile Durkheim, Law, and Jurists (Late 1800s–1930)
Emile Durkheim (1858–1917) is considered by many as the founding father not only of French sociology of law but also of general sociology (Chazel, 1991). The son of a religious Jewish family, whose father was a rabbi, Durkheim decided to lead a secular life. However, his thought is marked by the idea that religion plays a determining social function. Durkheim lived through a period of great social, political, and economic change: capitalism extended its reach, industrial revolutions modified the relations of production, and individuals migrated toward cities. This unstable environment triggered a feeling of uncertainty for many. Like a great number of his contemporaries, Durkheim wanted to

---

[14] Society, according to Tarde (1993), is a level of reality that is run by imitation.

[15] According to Carbonnier, this is a reason to consider this type of approach as criminal sociology and not legal sociology (1978, pp. 107–109). Even so, nineteenth-century criminology was an important reference for the French sociology of law (1978, p. 106).

understand how the traditional mechanisms of social organization – such as religion – were affected and transformed in these times of change. He argued that a society can bloom only when there is a strong sense of solidarity and interdependence between the individuals who live within that society. Social groups thus organize themselves around rules derived from this sentiment of solidarity. Just as there is an individual consciousness, there is a collective one, and social harmony is obtained when collective consciousness engenders a strong consensus about fundamental values.

In his project to create an autonomous sociology, Durkheim affirmed that social phenomena must be considered outside of mental representations of reality and, consequently, must be analyzed as an "external and objective thing."[16] In order to objectively analyze social phenomena, he proposed a method based on the idea that the law is a social fact that embodies the solidarity of the community (Durkheim, 1899). Solidarity – one of the central concepts of his works – is a form of social organization produced by the encounter of two forces: integration (the existence of shared practices and beliefs) and regulation (which limits human behaviors) (Newburn, 2007, p. 173). Durkheim distinguished two forms of solidarity. The first is *mechanical*, belonging to simple and primitive societies characterized by a weak social division of labor, uniformity in customs and practices, and a relative equality and similarity among individuals. As the name indicates, social relations are organized in a quasi-mechanical fashion, and the function of law in these societies is to preserve uniformity. The second form of solidarity is *organic*, belonging to complex and advanced societies characterized by a strong social division of labor. Here, the apparent uniformity disappears to make way for difference and social diversity. The function of law is limited to the regulation of difference (Durkheim, 1993).

Durkheim considered law as "an indicator of the state of the collective conscious" (Lascoumes, 1991, pp. 39–97). In *Les règles de la méthode sociologique*, he differentiates between two types of solidarity. Each type of solidarity, mechanical and organic, corresponds not only to a type of

---

[16] This external view regarding law was crucial in the further development of French sociology of law; it allows for the production of approaches to law outside the traditional dogmatic vision. For example, Commaille & Perrin (1985) indicate that this external approximation does not question law but, on the contrary, reaffirms and reinforces its authority. For Carbonnier (1978), this input is essential to the sociology of law because jurists tend not to separate law from its representations.

society but also to a type of law. Mechanical solidarity, belonging to traditional societies and founded on religious values, would go hand in hand with a repressive type of law – namely, criminal law. Organic solidarity, belonging to modern societies, is founded on economic relationships and rests on the development of civil or commercial law (Durkheim, 1993).

Durkheim also wished to bring dogmatic legal studies closer to the social sciences, especially sociology (Lascoumes, 1991, p. 43). For him, the sociology of law should be seen as a specialized branch of general sociology (ibid., p. 39).[17] Since law is a central and constitutive element of social solidarity, it has to be analyzed from the social sciences. He thus contributed to the institutionalization of sociology of law in his time. One of his most important contributions was the foundation of the journal *L'Année sociologique* in 1898.[18]

Durkheim's ideas served as the foundation for most socio-legal traditions in France for more than three decades. Concepts such as "collective consciousness," "legal institution," and "social pressure" began to be integrated into the discourse of jurists (Carbonnier, 1978, p. 9; Noguera, 2006, p. 5). For the first two decades of the twentieth century, Emmanuelle Lévy, René Hubert, and Léon Duguit were among the jurists who, influenced by Durkheim's work, sought to construct a sociological theory of law outside of the dogmatic approach.[19] Duguit (1889), for example, thought that sociological rules existed prior to law and that all positive norms created by the legislature must conform to these rules.[20] He advocated harmonizing the production of legal norms with social reality and envisioning sociology as a science in the service of the production of legal norms.

---

[17] In Commaille's terms, sociology must be to law "what psychology [is] to medicine" (1989, p. 21).

[18] Since then, this journal has become one of the most prestigious publications in social sciences worldwide. Little by little, its doors have opened to jurists; in fact, in 1949, some jurists were part of the journal's editorial committee (Soubiran-Paillet, 2000, p. 21). See issues 59(1) and 59(2) of 2009, which are dedicated to the political sociology of law and coordinated by Commaille and Duran.

[19] At this time, in Europe, Eugen Ehrlich and the school of free law were very influential. Ehrlich believed that only legal sociology could be the real science of law. He was the first to propose the idea of a "living law," which differed perceptibly from the official law of the state.

[20] He founded, with Hans Kelsen and other academics, the *Revue internationale de théorie du droit*. This provided national and international visibility to French legal sociology (Arnaud, 1981).

Georges Gurvitch and Henri Lévy-Bruhl: Two Alternative Approaches (1930–1960)

Despite the influence of Durkheim's work, during the early twentieth century, the great majority of law schools were indifferent or even hostile to sociological and non-dogmatic visions of law. The sociology of law was not part of the university curricula. At most, it was the object of debate as an interdisciplinary curiosity (Carbonnier, 1978, pp. 114–115). Furthermore, because socio-legal studies of the time were mainly theoretical, interest in empirical work was practically nonexistent. The sociology of law (not just in France but throughout continental Europe) placed more emphasis on legal theory because it was closer to the philosophy of law than to the social sciences (Arnaud, 1988, p. 383). Nevertheless, Durkheim's ideas on law continued to play a decisive role in sociology beyond the Second World War. Between the 1940s and 1960s, a period characterized by an intense professionalization and institutionalization of research, his ideas allowed a favorable climate to develop regarding the independence and autonomy of scientific communities (Commaille, 1989, p. 23; Soubiran-Paillet, 2000, p. 137). In this context, several journals of sociology of law and research centers emerged.

Two academics played fundamental roles in shaping SLS during this time. The first, Georges Gurvitch (1894–1965), was a French sociologist of Russian origin who lived almost his entire life in France, where he carried out most of his academic and scientific career. In his work *Elements of Legal Sociology* (1940), he argued that alongside state law are rules based on "forms of association" – that is, masses, unions, or even churches, which rest on a social law (Serverin, 2000, p. 50). His distinction between state law and social law was an important contribution to the development of legal pluralism in socio-legal studies in Europe.[21] According to Gurvitch, the sociology of law aimed to discover the rules that exist in all of society, not just state institutions. "The mission given to sociology of law consists of collecting these rules so that a 'polyhedric democracy' can be established ... This type of democracy must oppose state law and individual law, which are promoted by both the state sociology of sociologists and the legal dogmatism of jurists" (1935, p. 225).[22] Through this project, in which he

---

[21] This was, in part, thanks to the influence of his professor, Léon Petrazycki. See Carbonnier (1978, p. 112); Romano (1946); Treves (1966).

[22] Cited in Serverin (2000, p. 51).

criticized the state, he also opposed Durkheim, whom he viewed as giving disproportionate importance to jurists (Gurvitch, 1940).

Gurvitch's contemporaries considered his works a threat to the state monopoly on law – a threat that was unacceptable in the eyes of French lawyers, especially law professors. His work was thus widely criticized and passed almost unnoticed within the sociological community. Despite this critical reception, Gurvitch strongly defended legal sociology, especially legal pluralism (Cramer, 1986). In addition to writing, he founded the journal *Cahiers internationaux de sociologie*. Furthermore, under his leadership, the Center for Sociological Studies, which was created under the direction of the National Centre for Scientific Research, began to acquire prestige and renown (Soubiran-Paillet, 2000, p. 127).

The other striking figure of this period is Henri Lévy-Bruhl (1884–1964), a jurist and historian who worked at the Center for Sociological Studies beside Gurvitch and Gabriel Le Bras.[23] Lévy-Bruhl was an editor of *Cahiers internationaux de sociologie* and *L'Année sociologique* and collaborated with the new *Revue française de sociologie*. He also founded the Laboratory of Criminal Sociology. In addition to being a professor at the University of Paris, Lévy-Bruhl was the director of research of a division of the École Pratique des Hautes Études, where he began, in 1948, to teach legal sociology. Lévy-Bruhl distanced himself from Gurvitch and returned to the Durkheimian model. "Law," he wrote, "is a social fact *par excellence* . . . It reveals the intimate nature of the group" (Soubiran-Paillet, 2000, p. 127). He argued that all legal phenomena have social causes and can be the object of scientific observation (Lévy-Bruhl, 1955). Because law is the manifestation of groups and not individuals, Lévy-Bruhl regarded it as an objective field that could (and even should) be the object of specific investigation (Commaille, 1989, p. 21). He therefore thought that it was possible to attain an empirical social science of law, which he named *juristique* – a science applied to institutions, concerned with the study of legal facts, and integrated into the heart of sociology and the history of law (Lévy-Bruhl, 1955; Soubiran-Paillet, 2000).

The Stand on Legal Neutrality

The second half of the twentieth century saw the emergence of several sociopolitical visions of law, each of which positioned themselves

[23] Regarding Le Bras's work, see Soubiran-Paillet (2000).

within the debate on legal autonomy and legal neutrality. Four of these visions of law are highlighted here: (1) Carbonnier and his analysis of sociology in service of the law; (2) the critical legal movement (*critique du droit*), which considered law an instrument of political domination; (3) Pierre Bourdieu and his theorization of the legal field; and, lastly, (4) Bruno Latour, who envisages the processes of construction and of transfers of law. Carbonnier's and Latour's visions accept the idea of law's neutrality, whereas the visions of *critique du droit* and Bourdieu focus on law as domination.

Jean Carbonnier's Sociology in Service of the Law (1960–1970)
After the Second World War, sociology underwent a long process of specialization. As a result, several currents of sociology emerged, motiv- ated by the fact that the social sciences were then considered to be useful knowledge for public policies and social development.

At the beginning of the Fifth Republic (1958), French law schools' reputations were diminishing, as they were considered to produce an archaic legal culture, distanced from reality (Dulong, 1997; François, 1996). Meanwhile, the Durkheimian tradition was also the object of recurring critiques, and its prestige was continually diminishing (Carbonnier, 1978; Chazel, 1991; Cotterrell, 1991). In this atmosphere of legal discredit, in the 1970s the Ministry of Justice supported a project designed to give more visibility to the law and to law schools. This project, led by law professor Carbonnier (1908–2003), aimed to use empirical research to reform current legislation in order to improve the law's impact on society. Like his predecessors, Carbonnier was educated in the French school of Durkheimian sociology. In opposition to Gurvitch's definition of legal pluralism, in which many sources of rules coexist (state, social, etc.), Carbonnier proposed a definition of pluralism in which one rule can be applied in several ways (Severin, 2000, p. 63). While Gurvitch's legal sociology did not garner much attention in law schools, the writings of Carbonnier were well received. In particular, his famous textbook *Sociologie juridique*, published in 1972, is still used and studied today in many law schools.

In the 1960s and 1970s, Carbonnier collaborated closely with several ministers of justice. According to Antoine Vauchez, he significantly influenced civil legislation, which allowed him not only "to change the *Code Civil*, ... but also to reinvent and adapt legal expertise to the frames of legitimacy imposed by the new political regime" (Vauchez, 2009, p. 106). Carbonnier defended "all the ways that legal sociology had of putting itself at the service of the Legislator ... not only to create new laws, but also, once created, to help the population accept those new laws" (Carbonnier, 2007, p. 394). This model of sociology to the service of law was called "legislative sociology" and sought to improve the production of law (Arnaud, 1998b; Commaille, 2007a).

In this sense, Carbonnier's project is close to Roscoe Pound's idea of using the social sciences at the moment of creating and applying law, which is explained in his *Sociological Jurisprudence* (1912). However, the differences between the two projects stem from the fact that Carbonnier did not specifically develop a critical approach. Indeed, his legislative sociology supports political decisions to the degree that it speaks for the content of the law. It is not, however, a normative sociology, interested in the meaning and the opportunity of the law. In his legislative sociology, social analysis assumes an auxiliary role compared to that of legislation. Moreover, according to Carbonnier, sociology can contribute to the creation of legislation but cannot, in any case, be confused with it (Papachristos, 1988, p. 388). Conversely, in Pound's *Sociological Jurisprudence*, the social sciences play a prescriptive role – that is, they have the authority to formulate or impose directives on governments in order to improve political decisions (Troper & Michaut, 1997, p. 381).

Despite the revival of socio-legal interest in France after the Second World War, this period was also the height of fragmentation between different centers and research institutions, which confined law professors to their faculties (Soubiran-Paillet, 2000, p. 135). During this time, coursework on legal sociology began to shift from social science centers to law schools, although such instruction was still marginal and was inscribed within the legislative sociology lineage. The emergence of the sociology of law in law schools can be explained largely by Carbonnier himself and his prestige in the domain of civil law. This allowed him to avoid jurists' common critiques of sociologists of law – namely, that they lack the necessary legal knowledge to give their opinion on law.

The welcoming of the sociology of law into law schools thus occurred in the context of the conservative spirit of the aftermath of the Second War World, exalting French legal doctrine against German jurisprudence (Audren & Halpérin, 2013). Sociology was therefore considered the "servant of law" and was intended only to valorize the power and impact of legislation (Commaille, 1983). In this way, sociology was stripped of all autonomy and of all critical stance (Commaille, 1983, 1989, 2003a). According to Jean Guy Belley, with

Carbonnier, the sociology of law became "empirical and an auxiliary of post-liberal law. Sociology of law [became] institutionalized as applied sociology of the state legal norm" (Belley, 1986, p. 19).

The Critical Legal Movement
The critical legal movement was born in 1974, when social protests were flourishing throughout Europe, sustained in large part by Marxist thought. The movement went against both the legal doctrine and the legal sociology proposed by Carbonnier (Dupré de Boulois & Kaluszynski, 2011). Founded by Jean-Jacques Gleizal, Philippe Dujardin, Claude Journès, and Jacques Michel, among others, it was developed in particular by Michel Miaille (1976) and Antoine Jeammaud (1987). Many of the ideas supported by these scholars were published in the journal *Procès, Cahiers d'analyse politique et juridique.*

The critical legal movement intended to fulfill several objectives. The most ambitious of these was to create a new science of law, opposed to legal doctrine and traditional law professors. According to the first issue of the journal *Procès*, this new science located its foundations in the historical materialism of Marx and Engels and thus showed that, from these theories, a new way of thinking about law could be constructed to replace the legal positivism dominating law schools. With this idea in mind, Miaille (1976) published *Une introduction critique au droit* (*A Critical Introduction to Law*), which became the most widely disseminated and influential text in the critical legal movement. The movement's legal critique had three supplementary objectives: transforming the dogmatic teaching of law into a critical and reflexive learning, overcoming the distinction between legal theory and legal practice, and demystifying the study of law (Dupré de Boulois & Kaluszynski, 2011).

The movement was marked by two distinct phases. The first and more radical phase, which began in 1978 and lasted until 1980, was driven by the publication of the movement's manifesto; in this document, the critics seated the theoretical bases of their postulates and dedicated themselves to denouncing law and the state as products of class struggle (notably through the critique of the public/private and individual/collective dichotomies). The second period, from 1980 to 1984, was less radical and was marked by a slowdown in the authors' activity, most of whom were dedicated to studying the functioning of liberal bourgeois law (Arnaud, 1988, p. 85). From the mid-1980s onward, the movement began to lose its vigor, disappearing at the end of the decade. The impact of these critiques on French law schools remains very weak, if not nonexistent. This can be explained by the fact that unlike their counterparts in the United States (who belonged to the critical legal studies movement), the French critics were not interested in legal doctrine.[24] Therefore, they were never able to establish a critical dialogue with traditional law professors, who considered them to be idealists who sought to destroy law rather than transform it.

This critical movement is not exclusive to France, although it developed differently in each country. As explained before, the critical movement attained a certain breadth in the United States; conversely, in France, it remained relatively marginal. Across the Atlantic, for instance, critical authors have developed specific subfields of research, such as feminist legal studies. In France, the situation is different: feminist works on law are relatively marginal and poorly institutionalized, which is explained by the fact that feminism has been built more *against* law than *within* law (Revillard et al., 2009, p. 6).

Pierre Bourdieu's Legal Field

Bourdieu regrets not having dedicated more time to the study of the legal field. Nevertheless, his analyses on law, though few, have exerted a great influence on SLS, not only in France but in the United States and Latin America.[25]

Bourdieu aims to construct a sociological explanation of law consistent with his theory of social fields.[26] For that reason, he distances himself not only from visions of law that emphasize the production of legal thinking but also from those that view law as a simple product of material conditions. His position is an attempt to overcome the

[24] Without inscribing himself explicitly within the framework of the critical legal movement, Arnaud wrote at the time his *Essai d'analyse structurale du Code civil français* (1973), which constituted a unique attempt to deepen dogmatic analyses of law. In this sense, it can be related to the works of the critical legal studies movement that were published in the United States around the same time.

[25] For Bourdieu's influence on sociology in the United States, see Lamont (2012); Sallaz (2007). For his influence on law, see García-Villegas (2004). Bourdieu's ideas have been developed by Dezalay (Garth & Dezalay, 1996; Madsen & Dezalay, 2002); Lenoir (2003); Pinto (1989).

[26] A field is a social space. The position of agents in the social field is a result of interaction between the specific rules of the field, agents' *habitus*, and agents' economic and social capital (Bourdieu, 1980, 1994; Bourdieu & Wacquant, 1992, p. 117).

dichotomy between *internalist* and *externalist* visions of legal knowledge. The first refers to the legal science as conceived by jurists who regard law as "a closed and autonomous system" (Bourdieu, 1986, p. 6). The second analyzes law as a reflection of existing social forces – that is, as the product of economic determinations and the interests of those who are in power (Bourdieu, 1986, p. 3). Bourdieu also argues that idealist and materialist visions of law must be overcome by a theory that explains law as a social field in which different actors participate in a struggle to define the law. Law is a particular social field because of its proximity to the political field and the state. This thereby explains the symbolic capital that is at stake and the importance that legal actors accord to the (very unequal) distribution of this symbolic capital.

According to Bourdieu, law is a social field in which professors, judges, and legislators struggle for the appropriation of the symbolic power implicit in legal texts (1986, p. 4). Given the possibilities that actors in the legal field have to create institutions and new historical and political realities, law becomes a privileged form of symbolic power and symbolic violence. For this reason, it is natural that the internal dynamic of the legal field is linked to the question of domination. Law's potential to establish classifications, such as legal/illegal, just/unjust, and true/false, provides certain legal actors with great political power. As a result, the symbolic use of law is an intrinsically violent practice to the degree that it is capable of imposing meanings on social relations, so that economic and political power lose their original arbitrary character and appear to be normal and acceptable.[27]

But law cannot be reduced to a tool of political domination, as is done by the authors of the critical legal movement. To understand its symbolic force and its legitimating effect, says Bourdieu, we must avoid the materialist explanation that views law only as economic power relationships, as well as the idealist visions that see only universal values. It is no longer possible to wonder if power comes from above or from below, as Bourdieu explains in reference to the debate between critical and doctrinal explanations of law. He is opposed to materialist explanations and, for this reason, recognizes the existence of an autonomous social field capable of reproducing itself thanks to its specific logic of functioning – in other words, a legal body relatively independent from external limitations. However, Bourdieu also recognizes

---

[27] This is what Bourdieu describes as a normalization effect (1986, p. 16).

that the legal field has a lesser degree of autonomy than other social fields, such as literary or artistic fields, because of its proximity to the political field.

Bourdieu's structural theory of practice, in which he attempts to connect culture, structure, and practice, results in a negative view of rules and norms. He regards norms as obstacles to real knowledge of social practices or as obstacles to knowledge of the "immanent principle of practice" – that is, the *habitus*. Further, he views norms' meaning and scope to be generally monopolized by jurists, owners par excellence of the symbolic violence in society, through the so-called science of law. Bourdieu thus views lawyers more negatively than, say, athletes or painters (Bourdieu, 1986, p. 18; 1991).

However, as explained previously, Bourdieu is careful not to overly condemn the legal sphere: the reaction against legalism (*juridisme*) in its overt or covert forms, he argues, "must not lead us to make the *habitus* the exclusive principle of all practice" (even if it is certain that there exists no practice without the *habitus* as principle) (1977, p. 20). For him, law cannot be reduced to a question of interests, just as interests cannot be reduced to the law. In other words, the legal field has a certain degree of autonomy vis-à-vis the political field. Thus, in the first lines of "La force du droit,"[28] he attempts to construct a relatively autonomous legal sphere, halfway between Hans Kelsen's positivist formalism, in which the subjective vision dominates, and Louis Althusser's materialism, in which the objective perspective prevails.

Bourdieu aims to construct a theory of legal practices that transcends the subject/object dichotomy:

> An entire social universe which is in practice relatively independent of external determinations and pressures, at the interior of which legal authority, a form *par excellence* of legitimate symbolic violence, is produced and exerted, the monopoly of which belongs to the State and which can avail itself of the use of physical force (1986, p. 3).

However, in the last few pages of "La force du droit," Bourdieu tends to reduce law to a simple phenomenon of political domination linked to economic structure:

> The closeness of interests, and, above all, the parallelism of habitus, arising from similar family and educational backgrounds, fosters kindred

---

[28] For the version in English, see Bourdieu (1987).

world-views. Consequently, the choices which those in the legal realm must constantly make between differing or antagonistic interests, values, and world-views are unlikely to disadvantage the dominant forces. For the ethos of legal practitioners, which is at the origin of these choices, and the immanent logic of the legal texts, which are called upon to justify as well as to determine them, are strongly in harmony with the interests, values, and world-views of these dominant forces (1986, p. 14).

This leads, according to Bourdieu, to a probable failure of critical legal perspectives and progressive uses of law at the heart of the legal field. This overly critical view of law seems to be in tension with the theory advanced at the beginning of "La force du droit," particularly regarding the recognition of law's internal perspective. Indeed, this critical approach to law implies an underestimation of the political complexity of the legal phenomenon in contemporary society and, in particular, of the ambiguous nature of rights as tools of political struggle and even of social emancipation (see Chapter 2). Although the symbolic efficacy generally works to reinforce the legitimacy of the state, it can also potentially be used as a political weapon against hegemonic power (García-Villegas, 2014). Bourdieu's failure to recognize this possibility is probably linked to the historical role that magistrates and law professors play vis-à-vis the state and politics (1990, 1997, 2012). In other words, Bourdieu overestimates the impact of French classical legal culture, and symbolic violence's influence, in France at the end of the twentieth century (Bourdieu, 1986, 1991, 2012).[29]

Several contemporary scholars draw on Bourdieu's legal theory to study law and legal practices. Yves Dezalay (1992), for example, studies struggles within the international market of business law. With Anne Boigeol, Dezalay also analyses the fusion of the legal profession with works councils and the business world in France, which originated as a means for lawyers to gain control in the field of commerce (1997). Furthermore, Dezalay is among the French sociologists of law who currently work in France and in the United States at the heart of the law and society movement.[30] In my opinion, his interpretation of Bourdieu's ideas on law is overly focused on Bourdieu's general theory of domination and does not sufficiently take into account Bourdieu's specific analysis of law, which is mostly found in the text "La force

---

[29] For a debate on Bourdieu's sociology of law, see issue 56–57 of *Droit et société*, particularly Caillosse (2004); García-Villegas (2004); Roussel (2004).
[30] See his text with Madsen (2002).

du droit." This implies some underestimation by Dezalay of the logic and complexity of the internal rationality of law, which is taken into account by Bourdieu in his analysis of the legal field.

Other French sociologists draw on Bourdieu's social theory in their analyses of the legal field.[31] One of them is Alain Bancaud (1993), who studies the social origin of judges in France's high courts to show the links between these judges and the political elites. There is also Anne Boigeol (2007), who has researched gender in the legal profession, and Laurent Willemez, who has analyzed the organization of the French legal profession, particularly in the area of labor law (2003). In *Robes noires, années sombres* (*Black Robes, Dark Years*), Liora Israël (2005) uses the sociology of collective action and a vast analysis of public and private archives to analyze lawyers' political engagement in the Resistance. Frédéric Ocqueteau (2006) studies police and security in France and, with Daniel Warfman (2011), security in France. Finally, using inquiries into immigration agencies, administrative jurisdictions, and tax administration, Alexis Spire (2008, 2012) studies inequality among citizens resulting from the application of law.[32]

Bruno Latour: Law as Language

A sociologist, anthropologist, and philosopher (a specialist in the sociology of sciences and knowledge), Latour works at the Center for the Sociology of Innovations at Mines ParisTech. Latour wanted to go beyond the critical program that was celebrated during the 1970s in the French social sciences. He accomplished this task with an exploration in the field of the sociology of science. In *Laboratory Life*, released in 1979 and written in collaboration with Steve Woolgar (1986), Latour implemented an ethnographic approach to describe a neuroendocrinology research laboratory in detail, with the actions, interactions, and especially the registrations taking place there.

More generally, Latour seeks to build an approach that takes into account the capacity of players to adjust to different situations of social

---

[31] Dezalay's approach denying any law's autonomy is also opposed to the vision of lawyers developed by Lucien Karpik in his book *Les Avocats* (1995), in which he defends the existence of a legal profession that is economically disinterested and politically allied to liberalism. See also Karpik (1989); Karpik, Halliday, & Feeley (2007). For a critical assessment, see Commaille & Duran (2009); see also Assier-Andrieu (2011), Bessy (2015), Vauchez (2012b).

[32] See also Lascoumes & Le Bourhis (1996); Roussel (2004).

life. This is the purpose of what is called pragmatic sociology. Rather than drawing attention to the gaps between a collection of practices and the formal rules that are supposed to regulate them, pragmatic sociology adopts a descriptive and comprehensive posture toward these practices and considers them as themselves, and for themselves (Boltanski, 1990; Dupret, 2010; Thévenot, 1992, 2006). Judicial reasoning is thus a type of reasoning among many others (Delpeuch et al., 2014, p. 75). In relation to the legal field, this implies an interest in the concrete processes of construction of legal truth (Latour, 2004).

In line with his sociology of science, Latour proposes a new way of understanding the relationship between law and society by focusing on how law is constructed. In an ethnographic study, Latour (2004) explores how law is constructed within the State Council, the highest French administrative jurisdiction.[33] Since the members of the council belong to a community, argues Latour, which has its own rules and norms, their actions can be analyzed as if they were members of a tribe. When an anthropologist places him or herself outside the object of study, "such an attitude would only lead to that detestable form of exoticism that we might call occidentalism. In associating the study with this distance, the ethnographer of contemporary societies is only reproducing the sins of old anthropology which could only study other peoples if they were at a distance" (2004, p. 262). He instead proposes an ethnographic methodology that is attentive to the construction of law. Unlike Durkheim, Latour defends an idea of sociology of law constructed from the law itself, not from an external perspective. In this sense, he believes that a sociologist cannot explain the law without transforming him or herself into a lawyer, because "in order to convincingly describe the law, one must be, once and for all, within the law" (2004, p. 274). Rather than paying attention to the law and its norms, advocates of a pragmatic approach to the law propose a detailed study of law "in its making." In this vein, Baudouin Dupret suggests a redefinition of socio-legal studies – one that would not "take law seriously" but "take legal practices seriously," evoking Ronald Dworkin's famous expression.[34] Understanding

---

[33] For the version in English, see Latour (2010).

[34] According to Dupret (2006), the ambition is therefore not to *gloss*, based on the law, on this or that deep sociological truth but rather to describe the law in its most accurate phenomenological reality. This conception opposes not only sociological visions of law à la Bourdieu but also philosophical approaches, such as that of Dworkin (1977) and Luhmann (1985). See also De Sutter & Gutwirth (2004, p. 273).

law not as an entity filled with morals, politics, or religion but as a link or a joint allows us, according to Latour, to reestablish law in its place and take notice of its specificity.

Latour's idea of law can be considered the opposite of the one developed by Bourdieu. For Bourdieu, legal practices can be understood only if they are integrated into the legal field, traversed by power relations that grow as a result of the legal field's close connections with other social fields in which power is a central element (i.e., the economic and political field). Latour, on the other hand, believes that legal practices are autonomous; their existence is independent of the world in which they are deployed, and hence they exist independently of the world of power. Law thus appears as a transparent language. According to Israël, Latour proposes a "conception of law 'as a vehicle' in which it is defined as a form of 'association', a mode of enunciation which connects facts, people, and things, and which defines itself less as a substance than as a type of textual link ceaselessly recreated between times, humans, places, goods, and decrees" (2012a, p. 137). Latour's sociological depoliticization of law, which parallels that undertaken by legal doctrine and legal formalism, seems to conform less to a liberation of law from society and power, and more to a capturing of society by law, which manifests itself as pure, scientific, and neutral knowledge. The idea of legal neutrality here, as in legal formalism, is part of the political dimension of law.[35]

The Quest for a Middle Way

Next to these scholars who take a radical position on the debate over the autonomy and neutrality of law, other academic movements have sought a more nuanced view of both legal embeddedness and legal domination. These movements are (1) legal pluralism; (2) the sociology of organizations and of power; (3) the Droit et Société project; and (4) the political sociology of law.

Legal Pluralism

Some authors from the first half of the twentieth century – including Eugene Ehrlich, Georges Gurvitch, and Santi Romano – argue that in

---

[35] For a critical vision of his work, see Commaille, Dumoulin, & Robert (2010, p. 213); De Sutter & Gutwirth (2004); Israël (2012a). De Sutter and Gutwirth, for instance, question three points of Latour's work on law: the choice of the French Council of State as the first field survey; the restriction of the scope of legal practice to the practice of jurisdiction; and the insertion of the fabric of law in Latour's "systematic anthropology of forms veridiction."

society, there is more than one legal system (the law of the state). Instead, there are many, which leads to the existence of what is called "legal pluralism." This idea was important among some critical legal thinkers but had very little impact in the French legal field, where the unity and efficacy of the state (which was associated with the idea of sovereignty) were seen almost as an indisputable postulate. In the second half of the twentieth century, when legal positivism secured its place within law schools, legal pluralism encountered even more difficulties.

Despite the little recognition accorded to it, legal pluralism has some followers in France, especially among anthropologists, such as Norbert Rouland, who has written extensively on this theme. Jean-Pierre Bonafé-Schmitt and Etienne Le Roy also deserve to be mentioned here. Bonafé-Schmitt (1992) is interested in the analysis of alternative modes of conflict resolution, while Le Roy – who was previously the director of the Laboratory of Legal Anthropology in Paris – is interested in legal pluralism in colonial societies (Arnaud, 1998a; Arnaud & Fariñas Dulce, 1998; Le Roy, 1978).

French jurist André-Jean Arnaud developed a sociology of the production of norms that involves the recognition of the plurality of levels of legality and of normative sources.[36] In his analysis, he adopts a critical perspective that opposes the idea of legal neutrality, though he does not deny the internal logic of law – in other words, his analysis does not eliminate legal autonomy. The distinction that he makes between the legal system (as conceived and lived) and the law (as imposed) is an important manifestation of the thesis of legal pluralism. His research on the theory of legal systems (1993) and on the definition of law as an "open game" in postmodern society also presupposes the existence of legal pluralism (1991). More recently, Arnaud has highlighted the complexity of contemporary law and the plurality of normative sources. His current works on globalization, European law, and the "new legal reason" of postmodern law are also headed in this direction (1998a, 2014).[37]

The Sociology of Organizations and of Power
Some sociologists and political scientists of law in France consider law to be not only a collection of rules establishing duties and rights but

---

[36] Professor Arnaud died on December 25, 2015.
[37] On this subject, see Vauchez (2013, 2014).

also a collection of rules that create opportunities for social actors to take action. For example, in his 1990 article "Legal Norms and the Implementation of Public Policies," Pierre Lascoumes explains that French analysis of public policies does not accord great weight to the legal dimension (1990, p. 43). Keeping this in mind, he is interested in the power games and strategies that play a role in the definition and application of laws. He thus emphasizes the manner in which actors mobilize law by adopting two points of view: the first envisions law as an instrument of action (a "strategic" perspective), while the second thinks that law not only imposes itself but also offers opportunities to define situations and actions (an "interactive" perspective) (1990, pp. 53–54). His work has been welcomed by French sociologists of public policy, who currently view norms as both constraints and resources for action.[38]

Two movements can be differentiated within this field. The first is linked to the sociology of organizations, which is encouraged by scholars at the Center for the Sociology of Organizations at the Paris Institute of Political Studies, notably Werner Ackermann, Christian Mouhanna, and Benoît Bastard. This approach focuses on analyzing the judiciary, which is conceived, under the influence of Michel Crozier, as an organization (Bastard & Ackerman, 1993; Bastard & Mouhanna, 2007). These scholars study different models of management and decision-making by social actors who participate in the judiciary's daily functioning and its processes of rationalization and innovation, among other issues (Noreau & Arnaud, 1998, p. 266). As they argue, formal legal rules do not explain how courts, prisons, or the judiciary function. Instead, sociologists must analyze the informal rules and negotiations between actors. Thus, "the legal edifice, as solemn and formalist as it may be, is only habitable if one includes in it an informal part – the tacit understandings and agreements negotiated in order to resolve possible divergences and to assure in practice the good proceedings of judiciary activity" (Bastard & Ackerman, 1993, p. 60). These works have given rise to literature on the managerialization of the

---

[38] This approach saw great success in the domain of penal law and criminology not only in France but also in Brazil, notably through the works of Wanda de Lemos Capeller (2009), who sought to construct a sociology of penal control. Capeller's work focuses on the application of penal law in different political contexts, as well as the relation between criminality and techniques of control and repression through penal norms. See also Noreau & Arnaud (1998, p. 273).

judiciary (Kuty & Schoenaers, 2010; Schoenaers, 2003; Vigour, 2007) and on the international transfer of judicial reforms (Delpeuch & Vassileva, 2009).

The second movement, which is close to the sociology of organizations and of power, is led by Lascoumes. He pays particular attention to the power games and opportunities for action arising from the law itself. From a political science perspective, Lascoumes defines law not only as a space of power but also as a mechanism of control. He believes that the dominant legal forms coexist with other forms of social control and that these create power relationships between the actors involved in creating and implementing norms and public policies. His work on environmental policies demonstrates ambiguities in the implementation of legal standards and in local actors' involvement in the construction of the law as it is applied (1995).[39] In a recent work on crime, with Carla Nagels (2014), they examine the sociology of delinquent elites, asking why deviancy and delinquency of elites are not perceived as having the same gravity as those affecting people and property, nor do they evoke the same social reaction.

Contrary to certain sociologists in the United States and England (Banakar & Travers, 2002; Deflem, 2010) who suggest that the sociology of law should free itself from the point of view of jurists and become a subdiscipline controlled by sociologists, the sociological visions in France on informal rules tend to develop a less radical point of view and are more receptive to law.[40] Basing themselves on the comprehensive sociology of Max Weber, French authors think that a sociology of law freed from all forms of instrumentalization by the law must not neglect the rationality of legal actors (Delpeuch et al., 2014).

The Droit et Société Project
There have always been tensions between sociologists and lawyers, as well as a sort of reciprocal mistrust. Each group analyzes society differently: while the former observes society from below, from the perspective of social practices, communities, individuals, and social movements, the latter regards it from above, by analyzing institutions. This division entails a certain scorn for what is normative in the case of sociologists, and a certain disdain for social norms in the case of jurists.

---

[39] See also his text with Galès (2005) about instruments of public action.
[40] For these Anglo-Saxon visions, see Banakar (2003); Deflem (2010); Travers (1993).

This divergence of positions also leads numerous sociologists to express sympathy for social and progressive positions, while many jurists adopt a more conservative stand. As Arnaud (1998b) writes, French jurists accuse sociologists of not recognizing the superiority of law's normativity over social norms. For this reason, these jurists find it unacceptable that some sociological approximations (like that of Gurvitch) cast doubt on the state's monopoly on the production of legal norms. Some jurists equate this with questioning popular sovereignty. Many jurists also think that sociologists do not understand the internal nature and specificity of the law, which leads sociologists to reduce the normative to a simple expression of power relations.[41] Conversely, many sociologists believe that jurists are so attached to dogmatism ("willingly caught in the gloomy shadows of theory," as Rudolf von Ihering used to say) that they ignore the law's practical and social aspects. Furthermore, sociologists believe that jurists' lack of training in social sciences prevents them from understanding the social reality of law.[42]

Despite the great mistrust between disciplines, the middle of the 1970s saw the creation of a project championed by both jurists and sociologists. At this time, the results of a survey on teaching and research in the sociology of law were published in the *Revue trimestrielle du droit civil*. This publication facilitated the creation of the Circle of Sociology and Legal Nomology, an internationally renowned and very active interdisciplinary research center.

In 1985, scholars at this new research center organized a global congress of legal sociology that invited professors from around the world. This congress resulted in the publication of several collections of works, as well as the launch of the journal *Droit et société*, which celebrated its thirtieth anniversary in 2015. The review, which is open to all social sciences, conceives of the sociology of law as an

---

[41] According to Carbonnier, the internal and authentic logic of law would be accessible only to jurists. The sociologist's external regard to analyze the law is, for him, merely an *appearance* (1978, p. 17). See also Legendre (1995).

[42] Bourdieu said that each time jurists tried to understand this reality, they remained locked in what he called *juridisme* (legalism) (1980, pp. 249 et seq.). In France, the legal sociology produced by lawyers is so different from that produced by sociologists that Renato Treves observes the coexistence of two sociologies of law, each with its own publications, public, and research topics. In spite of efforts to overcome this dichotomy, the sociology of law has still not managed to free itself from law schools to become an independent discipline located "halfway" between law and sociology (Commaille, 2010; Delpeuch et al., 2014; Soubiran-Paillet, 2000, p. 113).

"interdisciplinary specialization."[43] This joint work gave rise to the European Droit et Société network, which today is the most dynamic and productive manifestation of French sociology of law. The foundation of a long series of publications in the Droit et Société collection, as well as the journal's achievements, attest to the movement's success.

At the same time, in "Le modèle de Janus de la sociologie du droit" ("The Model of Janus in the Sociology of Law"), Jacques Commaille and Jean-François Perrin, a sociologist and a jurist, respectively, conclude that the combination of jurists' and sociologists' knowledge and methods could enable the sociology of law to analyze the "specificity of the legal phenomenon, stopping before the production of prescription" (Commaille & Perrin, 1985, p. 133). They argue that the quarrel between jurists and sociologists results less from theoretical or methodological disagreements and more from institutional and disciplinary foundations.[44]

Commaille has developed these ideas in a recent book called *A quoi nous sert le droit* (*What Is the Law Good For?*). He sees law as a concept in tension between, on the one hand, the ideas of reason, representation, and myth and, on the other, the ideas of practice, resources, and politics. He speaks then of law as a dual legality (2015, p. 94). According to Commaille, most of the problems of French sociology of law emerge from the denial of one of these two sides.

In the same vein, Arnaud, former director of the International Institute of Legal Sociology in Oñati, undertakes the important task of promoting the specificities of the sociology of law. In his books *Critique of Legal Reason* (1981) and *Law Betrayed by the Sociologist* (1998b), he analyzes legal sociology's position in France and, more generally, in Europe. According to Arnaud, legal sociology's lack of identity stems from the fact that neither jurists nor sociologists have come to an agreement on the concept of law itself. In order to solve this problem, Arnaud advocates distinguishing between the law as a normative system with its own dynamics and characteristics and law as a social phenomenon. He proposes leaving the

---

[43] See the manifesto published by *Droit et societé* (2015). For a better explanation of the different approaches that converge in *Droit et société*, see Arnaud (1998, pp. 90–92).

[44] Others have also adopted an intermediary model of "moderate intrusion," which takes a point of view external to the law while taking into account the internal rationality of jurists (Ost & Van de Kerchove, 2001).

first to the jurists and opening the second to an interdisciplinary investigation (1998b, pp. 96–97).[45]

Despite the traditional difficulties in creating interdisciplinary studies in France, many stimulating conversations between sociologists, political scientists, and jurists have emerged in recent decades. Some authors posit that there has been a decline in the differences between these three fields and their methods (Israël et al., 2005b). Two recent issues of *Droit et société* attest to the timeliness of these debates between sociologists and jurists. The first issue, coordinated by Liora Israël and Martine Kaluszynski (no. 69–70, 2009), a sociologist and a historian, respectively, proposes complementing legal and judicial analysis with better research methods, particularly with ethnographic surveys and the use of databases on judicial statistics. The second issue, coordinated by Pierre Brunet and Michel Van de Kerchove (no. 75, 2010), responds to the first issue, offering the jurists' viewpoint on this debate about methods. They warn of the dangers of neglecting the specificities of legal knowledge and reducing it to a social sciences perspective.

Political Sociology of Law
In France, politics and law are analyzed as two distinct and well-differentiated fields. As discussed at the beginning of this chapter, this separation stems from the French Revolution and the belief that although the law originates from the political will of majorities, it is free from politics and, once promulgated, acquires its own rationality. In this sense, this conception is different from the North American – and more broadly, Anglo-Saxon – legal tradition, in which law is never completely separate from politics.

Conscious of the artificial and inappropriate nature of this separation, Commaille proposes a political sociology of law "dedicated to the analysis of the relations between the legal and the political, the place of the legal in the construction of the political, and the role of the legal as indicative of the political" (2010, p. 36). In this sense, he suggests reuniting, on the one hand, reflections on the sociology of law and, on

---

[45] Arnaud's works are also dedicated to the study of classic legal authors such as Renato Treves, Jean Carbonnier, and Michel Villay (Arnaud, 2009; Arnaud & Andrini, 1995) and to the production of an interdisciplinary dictionary of legal theory and sociology (Arnaud, 1988).

the other, analyses of political science and public policy (2015, p. 21). According to Commaille, these two movements use similar analytical frameworks that highlight the top-down institutional construction of law and of public policies (2003a, 2003b, 2013). Furthermore, they both reveal the French state's loss of regulatory power, not just in relation to law but also in relation to public policies.[46]

This sociopolitical vision of law is also structured around critiques of the specific character of the sociology of law and, more fundamentally, of the question of the autonomy of law in relation to society and politics.[47] In the first issues of L'Année sociologique, Durkheim encouraged the development of the sociology of law as a branch of general sociology that conceives of law as any other social issue. Thus, based on Durkheim's idea that law is the organization of social life, Commaille suggests that the study of law lays the groundwork for issues of general sociology. He aims to widen reflections on law in such a way that the study of law passes from a specialized sociology to a general sociology.[48] As he and Patrice Duran argue, the political sociology of law is "a movement oriented toward a return to general sociology, manifesting notably through a reestablishment of the link with the great founding figures of sociology and a correlative account taken of the political dimension of the legal question" (2009, p. 12). Law becomes, as the founding fathers of sociology thought, an indicator of the production and use of sociological knowledge (Commaille, 2015, p. 67).

However, it must be taken into account that Durkheim's vision dissolves law in social reality and therefore law loses its autonomy from society. "As an epiphenomenon of the collective consciousness," says Pierre Lascoumes in this respect, "product or projection of it, the law appears therefore as having no special autonomy" (1991, p. 47). Aware of this loss of the specificity of law, Commaille offers a type of sociology that, without being fooled by the logic of legal discourse, examines the

---

[46] For the development of the relationship between law and public policies, see Duran (1993, 1999).

[47] This question has always been very important in North American sociology of law. See, for example, the reflection proposed by Nonet and Selznick (1978) on the evolution of the relation between law and politics in the tradition of law and society.

[48] Lascoumes and Severin also opened the way with their paper on Max Weber's legal sociology (Nonet & Selznick, 1978).

symbolic and actual construction of law and observes its arrangements, principles, and effects over social reality (2010, p. 20; 2015, p. 402).

Furthermore, Commaille is critical of disciplinary struggles around law, especially in France, that have led to the reduction, and even the annihilation, of one discipline for the benefit of another. This occurs in Carbonnier's legislative sociology, as described previously, which proposes the reduction of sociology at the service of law. This is also the case in the reduction of politics to law (which Commaille calls the *juridiste* vision of politics) according to which law is nothing but the science of politics (Commaille, 2010; Legendre, 1995). One can also not reduce law to politics (Commaille calls this vision the *politiste* vision of law), as often occurs when political science professors who are aiming to differentiate their discipline from law end up neglecting it.

Commaille thus proposes a "permanent disciplinary opening" between law and social, political, and cultural processes (2013, p. 3), and a critical vision of disciplinary fences. He argues:

> The mutual ignorance of the reciprocal constitution of knowledge and of the surprisingly parallel evolution of the findings and analysis in the field of public policy and that of the sociology of law perfectly illustrates these disadvantages of the division between academic territories and, in this case, their blurring effect on the study of the relationship between politics and law (2010, p. 39).

Bourdieu also champions the non-reduction of law to political power and domination. Nevertheless, Commaille defends this principle more consistently than Bourdieu. One can see the difference between these two authors in relation to the importance they give to the political uses of law in society. According to Bourdieu, actors in the legal field – especially professors, lawyers, and judges – use the law as a political tool, and they use it in order to increase their symbolic and material capital and to perpetuate the structure of political domination. Commaille's conception, on the contrary, extends the political use of law – what Commaille calls taking law as a political resource (2015, p. 65) – to large sectors of civil society. To that extent, his political conception of law is broader and more dynamic than Bourdieu's vision.

In this way, Commaille's (2015) ideas have opened the way to a closer dialogue with the North American sociology of law, in which the idea of the political uses of law is widespread. The sociology of law in the United States has been largely interested in the political uses of law.[49] Law is considered both a product and producer of society – as a constitutive element of social life. Rather than envisaging it as an entity that exists before society, numerous authors have analyzed it as a reality that exists only if individuals grasp it and use it (McCann, 1994; McCann & March, 1995). These analyses, born in North America and linked to what is called the "cultural turn," have been introduced into the landscape of Francophone sociology, framed as analyses of "social and political uses of law" (Baudot & Revillard, 2014; Colliot-Thélène, 2009; Israël, 2001; Vauchez, 2001, Delpeuch et al., 2014). According to Israël et al.:

> [T]his attention to uses made way for a shift in interrogations about the social reach of law, which thus definitively freed them from long-dominant problematic in terms of norm/application, of law-in-the-book/law-in-action, efficacy/inefficacy, which we can say were perpetuating, in the guise of a critique of legal formalism, a positivist reading of the norm of law as a univocal and coherent text (2005a, p. 3).

The term "political uses of law" makes it possible to highlight the multiple ways in which lawyers, bureaucrats, and citizens utilize the law in order to produce social and political effects. This idea of political uses of law has had an important impact on current French SLS in at least two main respects.

The first is a special attention to the functioning of the judiciary. In France, justice has long been considered a technical legal subject, belonging to the world of the state and of law. As a state institution, with prerogatives belonging to public power, justice is seen as an institution that cannot cause debate or provoke reflections on the part of sociologists or political commentators. As Anne Wyvekens (2000) explains, neither penal justice nor the police constitute a privileged object of study for sociology or political science. This "invisibility" is born of the fact that these institutions are perceived as apolitical entities, subject to legislation and executive power. Furthermore, French political science has tried to distance itself from law schools and judicial practice. It is for this reason that Jacques Caillosse affirms

---

[49] Concerning the idea of the political uses of law, the classic text belongs to Stuart Scheingold (1974); among the numerous publications that followed, see Abel (2010); Calavita (2002, 2010); Darian-Smith (2013); Handler (1992); McCann (1994); McCann & March (1995); Merry (1990, 1995); Sarat (1990b); Sarat & Scheingold (1998, 2008); Silbey (1987).

that "the institutionalization of political science was done by pushing away legal thought" (2011).[50]

Nevertheless, this tendency has been changing over the past 20 years, to such a point that the major interest in judicial institutions today is one of the specificities of French sociopolitical visions of law.[51] Certain sociologists and political scientists have highlighted the organizational structure of the courts and the links that they share with their environment (Bastard & Ackerman, 1993; Schoenaers, 2003); others have highlighted the reforms that traverse this institution (Vauchez & Willemez, 2007; Vigour, 2007, 2008); and still others have examined European courts (Cohen & Vauchez, 2011; Vauchez & Witte, 2013), and the transformation, and increasing power, of globalized law firms, working in France and Europe (Vanneuuville, 2013; Israel & Vanneuville, 2017; France & Vauchez, 2017). Testifying to the growing interest in justice, the thematic network of legal sociology of the French Sociological Association was rechristened "Sociology of Law and Justice" in 2005. The first textbook to systematically cover the collection of works of political sociology of law is entitled *Political Sociology of Law and Justice* (Delpeuch et al., 2014).

The second aspect is the influence of the American law and society movement within French sociology of law and the construction of an epistemological and theoretical reflection on the conditions of importing these works to continental Europe. A large part of the power relations within legal sociology in France depends on the accumulation of a cultural capital that comes from researchers' capacity to dialogue with actors in this North American movement.

Two movements have played a particularly important role in the recent developments in France: cause lawyering and legal consciousness studies. Cause lawyering is born of collective works directed by Austin Sarat and Stuart Scheingold (2008) and examines the role of law professionals as political actors (Marshall & Crocker Hale, 2014). Israël has contributed to the dissemination of studies of the American law and society movement in France, and particularly to the diffusion of cause lawyering studies.[52] Eric Agrikoliansky (2003) also studies

---

[50] See also Commaille & Duran (2009); Vauchez (2006).

[51] For an explanation of this transformation, see Commaille (2007b); Delpeuch et al. (2014); Garapon (1996, 2010).

[52] A good portion of her work, written from a perspective of the political sociology of history, examines French lawyers and magistrates who resisted during the Second World War (Israël, 2001, 2005, 2009b).

activist uses of the law, reflecting on the links between law and social movements. Anne Revillard et al. (2009) investigate judicial and legislative strategies through which social movements frequently seek recourse, particularly on behalf of the rights of women or people with disabilities. Laure Bereni (2009) analyzes the appropriation of law by different actors, notably the entrepreneurs of diversity at the heart of businesses. Aude Lejeune (2011b) compares the mobilization of law by citizens in Europe and the United States. From a historical perspective, Laurent Willemez (2003) studies the political engagement of French lawyers and, more specifically, the relationship between lawyers specializing in labor law and activism. Violaine Roussel (2002, 2003) examines the links between the magistrature and the political world within the framework of politico-financial scandals in France in the 1990s. The second trend, which has influenced recent studies on the social and political mobilization of the law, is called legal consciousness studies. Patricia Ewick and Susan Silbey's *The Common Place of Law* (1998) is an indispensable reference for this North American current that examines the place of law in the daily life of ordinary actors. Jérôme Pelisse (2003) applies the concept of "legal consciousness," born of North American literature,[53] to the link that workers maintain with the law in the case of the debate on working hours in France and reflects, from a political sociological perspective, on how these works have been exported outside of North American borders. Israël (2009a) has been one of the main importers of this literature in the sociology of law in France.[54] Arnaud Vincent Chappe (2010) focuses on the use of the law by the victims of discrimination in France.

All these authors seek to substitute reflections on law as such with examinations of its social, political, and activist effects. They consider it not only as a framework of action but as an opportunity for action.

Finally, it is important to bear in mind that Commaille has also been a great entrepreneur of the political sociology of law. In 1984, with the support of the National Center for Scientific Research and the Ministry of Justice, Commaille reunited numerous scholars of the sociology of law and created the Vaucresson Center for Interdisciplinary Research in Paris. Later, as director of the Public Policy Analysis Group at the

---

[53] In particular, this concept comes from Ewick & Silbey (1998); Merry (1990); Silbey (1987).

[54] See also Israël & Pelisse (2004); Kourilsky (1998); Pelisse (2003, 2005).

École Normale Supérieure of Cachan, he undertook a study of the relations between law and politics. His analysis of the phenomenon of the juridization of politics is the fruit of this effort. It gave rise to different publications, among them the collective work of Jacques Commaille, Laurence Dumoulin, and Cecile Robert (2000) entitled *La juridicisation du politique: Leçons scientifiques* (*The Increased Litigiousness of the Political: Scientific Lessons*)[55] and, more recently, the textbook *La sociologie du droit et de la justice* (*Sociology of Law and of Justice*) by Thierry Delpeuch et al. (2014).

CONCLUSION

French SLS, in contrast with the American version, is characterized by the wide dispersion of trends, movements, academic works, publications, networks, and collective research. This dispersion cannot be explained solely by theoretical or ideological cleavages. It is also the result of structural conditions in the French legal field, particularly the conception of the state and its relation to the legal system and the relative position of power among legal actors (law professors, lawyers, judges, and legislators) in this legal field. The classical legal culture (in which legal autonomy from the social sciences is a doctrinal principle) emerging from this structural condition has hampered the evolution of SLS, which has developed in a legal field dominated by the legal technique and legal positivism within law schools and the legal profession. The lack of a social dimension of law among jurists (Chevallier, 2006; Garapon & Papadopoulos, 2003; Jamin, 2012) has contributed to the formation of a socio-legal field dominated by law professors who are close to the state, and committed to defending the autonomy of la in relation to social science.

This may help explain the fact that radical oppositions – not only within law schools but also in sociology departments – have long dominated the French sociopolitical debate about law. In law schools, two socio-legal perspectives are opposed. On one side, certain authors who question the autonomy of the law, without questioning its political neutrality, use the social sciences as an instrument in the service of the internalist point of view of law, as does Carbonnier and the defenders of gap studies in the United States. On the other side, the critical legal

[55] A second edition of this book was published in 2010.

movement neglects both the autonomy and the neutrality of the law from the point of view of political science.[56] In sociology departments, on the other hand, there has been a similar tension between scholars, particularly when it comes to understanding the relation between law and political power. On one side are authors such as Latour, who are not interested in questioning legal neutrality. For an outside observer, it is always surprising to note that some of the most renowned French sociologists and political scientists do not seek to question the aforementioned idea of legal neutrality in areas like civil law and constitutional law.[57] On the other side are authors such as Bourdieu, who put an almost exclusive accent on power and domination when explaining the social reality of law.

In this regard, it is surprising to see the poor reception by French sociology of law of theories that do not fit within this radical polarization. This is the case of the work of Tocqueville, who defended legal autonomy against the idea of identity between law and the general will that dominated during the French Revolution (Cohen-Tanugi, 2007, 2015; Schleifer, 2012). Tocqueville's legal ideas, as is the case for most authors who wanted to introduce Anglo-Saxon conceptions of law and politics in France (Montesquieu, for instance), are often perceived by radical sociologists of law as too liberal, too sociological or too closely connected to American civil society. This might help explain why the progressive dimension of rights, or even their emancipatory dimension, has been largely underestimated in legal circles until now (Champy & Israël, 2009; Delpeuch et al., 2014; Israël, 2001, 2009a; Israël et al., 2005a; Lejeune, 2011a).

Nevertheless, it is also important to bear in mind that this disciplinary polarization has been weakened over the last two decades. Currently, several significant changes in both legal scholarship and social sciences have weakened the conception of law as a founding myth of society. The legalization of politics, the partial Americanization of French law, the political uses of law by social movements, the strengthening of judicial review by the Constitutional Council

---

[56] Nevertheless, it must be said that radical positions have not always advocated the total rejection of law. See, for instance, Dupré de Boulois & Kaluszynski (2011); Herrera (2002, 2003a, 2003b); Israël (2009b).

[57] This is the impression that non-European readers of legal sociology get when they read the work of great French authors such as Latour (2004); Schnapper (2010); Supiot (2005, 2010).

(Epp, 1998),[58] and the internationalization of a large number of sociologists of law have challenged this view of the law by providing new sociopolitical insights on the social reality of law.

Because of these changes, there is a growing interest in both sociology and law schools on sociopolitical visions of law. As the second part of this chapter has shown, there is a proliferation of research on justice, legal professions, the political uses of law, and even the internationalization of law.[59] Many of these recent works seek to overcome the traditional gap between jurists and sociologists by adopting an intermediary point of view, more complex and less ideological, between the disqualification of the law as an instrument of political domination and the celebration of law as a founding myth of the nation and the state. The Droit et Société project, for instance, seeks to develop a transdisciplinary position between law and sociology, without subordinating either one of them. North American legal sociology's influence has played a large role in the development of a new SLS with an intermediate perspective, to such a degree that Francophone authors sometimes have a tendency to neglect the development of a more nuanced or critical perspective, faced with this corpus of North American literature.

Recent works on political sociology aim to overcome the aporiae of classic debates about legal autonomy and legal neutrality. Based on fieldwork, the defenders of this intermediary position, even if they recognize the existence of a certain internal rationality of the law, do not reduce legal knowledge to an instrument of political domination. They propose an approach that is attentive to the political dimensions of law without reducing it to an instrument of political domination (Commaille, 2015). Following these works, recent research on the political uses of law seeks to show the multiple ways in which social actors utilize the law in order to produce political and social effects. The political question and the disciplinary question thus become intimately linked and interdependent.

---

[58] See also Commaille (2007b).
[59] On this subject, see Commaille's text on the French judicial map (2000). See also Commaille & Kaluszynski (2007); De Galembert (2008); Delpeuch et al. (2014); Demoulin & Licoppe (2011).

CHAPTER SIX

CONCLUSION

The Present and Future of Sociopolitical Legal Studies

In this book, I have compared sociopolitical ideas in France and the United States. The comparison is not only transnational but also transdisciplinary: it includes the sociology of law, critical legal theory, socio-legal studies, and, more generally, an analysis that takes into account the political dimension as the central element of the law. The dialogue between these approaches is often scarce, even in the United States, where the sociopolitical dimension of law has been recognized in legal doctrine for more than a century. Such a lack of communication diminishes the understanding of legal phenomena and hinders the purpose of legal comparison. This book is designed to improve dialogue between these disciplines, not only within each of the countries but also globally.

In order to give meaning to such a large transdisciplinary comparison, I have proposed, in Chapter 1, the concept of sociopolitical legal studies (SLS). The inclusive character of this concept allows for a comparison between diverse perspectives and practices that generally do not communicate well with one another, as is often the case between the critical theory of law of jurists and the legal sociology of sociologists.

The central element of SLS is the symbolic dimension of law, explained in detail in Chapter 2. The words of law carry symbols associated with fundamental values of society (justice, fairness, order, respect, rights, protection, and so on) whose meaning is determined by social and institutional actors, frequently in dispute and equipped with generally unequal economic and cultural capital. These actors seek to settle the meaning of legal language so that it favors their interests. This symbolic function of law opens up the possibilities of political uses of law and feeds the practice and scholarship of SLS. The concept of symbolic efficacy helps us understand the legal field as a social space in construction, where different actors, endowed with different social and cultural capital, struggle to define the meaning of legal texts. These struggles take place in a social field that is often hierarchical and dominated by certain actors or institutions.

In this concluding chapter, I would like to do two things. First, I would like to propose a classification of sociopolitical visions of law and, second, I would like to address the question of the future of SLS in our globalized world.

COMPARATIVE OVERVIEW OF SOCIOPOLITICAL LEGAL STUDIES

The different conceptions of SLS described in this book can be analyzed in terms of the stand they take vis-à-vis legal autonomy and legal neutrality.

The closer law is to political power and the state (France), the more the autonomy of juridical doctrine will be proclaimed and, as a consequence, the weaker the connection between law and the social sciences will be, and the more radical legal critique will be. Conversely, the closer law is to society and the market (United States), the weaker the autonomy of legal doctrine will be and the stronger the connection between law and the social sciences will be.[1] Let me explain this in more detail.

SLS may adopt a critical position in regard to legal autonomy, legal neutrality, or both. Therefore, it is possible, in principle, to differentiate

---

[1] American legal antiformalism is not necessarily a progressive form of thought. Movements such as law and economics and law and society may present themselves as heirs of legal realism, even if they espouse different political visions. Additionally, the fact that American legal thought draws from the interstices of the market, power, and the law has problematic implications – not just in relation to the domestication of critical perspectives but also in relation to the commodification of law schools, which results in a loss of professors' autonomy vis-à-vis existing political and economic powers. One might even suggest that the American antiformalist criticism, which emphasizes the need to define the connections between law and society, was favorable to the legal field and conservative views. See Dezalay, Sarat, & Silbey (1989); Garth & Sterling (1998); Tamanaha (2012); Tomlins (2000).

between forms of SLS according to the critical target at which they take aim. We can then separate those forms that contest the autonomy of law from those that contest the political neutrality of law.

SLS can also be classified according to the point of view it adopts in relation to law. To that extent, there are, on the one hand, internal forms of SLS that view things from inside the legal system and, on the other hand, external forms of SLS that view things from outside the law. Internal perspectives, usually embraced by lawyers, envisage law from within the legal discipline, whereas external perspectives, usually embraced by social scientists, consider legal norms from the social sciences.[2]

From the combination of these two points of view (the critical target and the position with respect to the law), four types of SLS emerge. The first two are internal to the law (one against legal autonomy and one against legal neutrality), and the latter two are external to the law (one against legal autonomy and one against legal neutrality). I first consider the internal, or legal, positions and then the external critiques of law.

INTERNAL VISIONS

The first position combines the internal vision with the critique of legal autonomy. We often find this vision in the work of law professors and jurists who are unsatisfied with the doctrinal conception of law taught in law schools. Their objective is to show the relative dependence of the law on social reality, but without dismissing the legal system's internal rationality (imperfect though it may be). For them, it is about adapting law to social reality (against the idea of autonomy) to improve either its internal logic or its social efficacy. This type of SLS was particularly important in law schools, first in the United States during the beginning of the twentieth century and more recently with empirical legal studies, and second in France with the sociology of legislation (Jean Carbonnier) during the 1970s. Because the ultimate goal of these authors is to improve the law and the legal system, the critical potential of their theories is thus often limited.

The second position results from the combination of the internal point of view and the critique of legal neutrality. Legal norms are

---

[2] Hart (1961, p. 89) developed this distinction in his famous book, *The Concept of Law*; see also Ost & Van de Kerchove (1991).

perceived here as instruments designed and used for political domin-ation. The goal of authors who adopt this perspective is to deconstruct legal rationality and show the gaps and inconsistencies of the law to prove that law is and functions like a political instrument intended to dominate subaltern classes and minorities. Critical legal theories – such as critical legal studies,[3] critical race theory,[4] and legal feminism[5] in the United States – provide the best examples of this perspective. This perspective has prospered in law schools in the United States since the early 1970s.

EXTERNAL VISIONS

The third position results from the connection between the external point of view and the critique of the autonomy of law. The external perspective can originate in sociology, anthropology, political science, or another social discipline. The types of SLS located in this position attempt to demonstrate that law has no autonomy from social reality – that is, legal truth is not provided by the legal system itself. Their critique relies on the idea of mutual dependency between law and society, without being interested in the political character of law and its practice. This point of view has a long academic tradition, especially in sociology, which goes back to the writings of Montesquieu, Georges Gurvitch (1935, 1942), Léon Petrazycki (1955), Juan Bautista Alberdi (1981), and Eugen Ehrlich (1922, 1936), among others, and closer to us, to authors such as Mathieu Deflem (2010) and, sometimes, Roger Cotterrell (1983, 2004, 2012) and anthropologists in legal conscious-ness studies (Ewick & Silbey, 1998; Merry, 1988; Silbey, 2005). This

---

[3] For a general explanation, see Kelman (1987); Unger (2015). For a selection of studies, see Hutchinson (1989). For a bibliographic guide, see Bauman (1996); Brown & Halley (2002); Campos, Schlag, & Smith (1996); Gordon (1984); Kelman (1987); Tomlins (2012); Trubek (1984); Ward (1998); White (1986). See also the classic compilation of Boyle (1985, p. 706). For a critique of critiques, see Waldron (1998).

[4] For an introduction to these studies, see Crenshaw (2002); Crenshaw et al. (1995); Delgado (1987); Delgado & Stefancic (2013); Haney López (1994). There are also critical perspectives on race in law and society; see, for example, Curry (2012); Moran (2010); Obasogie (2010).

[5] See Butler (1992); MacKinnon (1982, 1989); West (1988, 1997); for a closer assessment, see Kessler (2011).

TABLE 2   Typology of sociopolitical legal studies

	Against legal autonomy (embeddedness)	Against legal neutrality (domination)
Internal (law)	(a) Legal improvement	(b) Legal deconstruction
External (social sciences)	(c) Sociological explanation of law	(d) Political admonition of law

perspective has prospered in social science departments in France and the United States in recent decades.

Finally, the fourth position results from the combination of an external view of law and a critique of law's political neutrality. From this position, law is seen as domination, and its rationality and technique can emerge only from outside the legal system. The authors from this group are frequently the most radical: the fact that they do not recognize or are not interested in the internal rationality of law drives them to adopt an attitude of radical disqualification of the legal system. This is the case of the French critics in the *critique du droit*[6] movement and of some Latin American authors influenced by Marxist thought on law (Correas, 1993; De la Torre, 2006; Rojas & Moncayo, 1978; Wolkmer, 1995). This type succeeded in law schools in France, especially during the 1970s and 1980s. Table 2 presents the typology established here.

The differences between these ideal types have important implications for the social and political scope of SLS. Indeed, as a general rule, internal critiques are more moderate than external visions, for the simple reason that recognizing the internal rationality of law involves, in principle, a certain acceptance of the legal system. External visions, however, tend to neglect not only legal rationality but also any possibility of redemption for existing law. This is particularly obvious for the critical authors of the 1970s in France (Miaille, 1976).

Furthermore, the types of SLS opposed to legal autonomy are usually less radical than those opposed to legal neutrality. The former kind point out how the law is socially dependent but admit that this can be addressed through institutional engineering and socio-legal reforms.

---

[6] See Jeammaud (1987); Miaille (1976, 1985). For a general view, see Dupré de Boulois & Kaluszynski (2011); García-Villegas & Saffón (2011).

By contrast, visions that conceive of law as a mechanism of domination tend to see no outcome other than a radical social change or revolution.

Overall, the evolution of SLS in the United States has favored the b and c positions outlined in Table 2 – that is, a moderate position against neutrality (legal deconstruction) and a radical position against autonomy (sociological explanation of law). In France, by contrast, these same studies have privileged positions a and d – that is, visions that range between the most moderate position against autonomy (legal improvement) and the most radical position against neutrality (political admonition of law).

The symbolic use of law has prospered in positions b (legal deconstruction) and c (sociological explanation of law), where the possibility of the political success of symbolic use appears more clearly. In the other types, this is not the case: in a (legal improvement), the political dimension is weak given that the emphasis is on impact, and in d (political admonition of law), the political dimension is too strong, which leads to a disregard for the possibility of legal strategies being successful in the political arena.

Finally, and even more importantly, it is necessary to highlight that the types of SLS that are against legal autonomy and against legal neutrality are not mutually exclusive. In fact, almost all the radical versions against neutrality are also strongly opposed to autonomy. Thus, although the typology is useful for explaining the historical diversity of SLS, it does not sufficiently take into account all the possible movements that have existed. This is the case of Max Weber's (1922) and Pierre Bourdieu's (1986) sociologies of law: although they adopt an external point of view, they also recognize the internal point of view. Moreover, the legal theory of François Ost and Michel Van de Kerchove, which adopts an internal and critical legal point of view, does not ignore the external point of view (Ost & Van de Kerchove, 1987; Ost, 2016)

Furthermore, for at least the past two decades, most forms of SLS, even those developed in France, have drawn on a constructionist social theory, which leads them to oppose both legal autonomy and legal neutrality without reducing legal phenomena to the social or the political (McCann, 1992, 1994; Scheingold, 1974). This constructionist approach is more sensitive to the complexity of legal phenomena and to the refinements of oppression, and it is often defended by the authors of the law and society movement, which has had a considerable influence in France and Latin America (Commaille, 2015; García-Villegas, 2015, 2010; Rodríguez-Garavito, 2014).

THE FUTURE OF SOCIOPOLITICAL LEGAL STUDIES IN A GLOBALIZED WORLD

Since the discovery of America, we Westerners have lived with the illusion of being the protagonists of a civilizing process that does not stop. This illusion, however, has begun to disappear in recent decades, in Europe and more recently in the United States. The inconsistencies and evils of the West, more visible today than ever before, may have contributed to this disillusion. The kind of inverted colonization of Europe by the East and the South, with all of the good and bad that it implies, has also played a role. I say this not just because of the massive immigration that we are seeing today in Europe, which seems to me, in principle, something positive, but also because of other less desirable phenomena, such as the increase in labor informality, the loss of the state's regulatory capacity, and the increase in inequality and violence.

All this is happening in the midst of a great international disorder, created in large measure by developed countries in the context of globalization, which has gradually reduced the economic maneuver of states, delegating their power to corporations and weakening the international legal system.

In 1962, Marshall McLuhan coined the idea of a "global village" to suggest that, thanks to advances in communications, the world was smaller and more manageable. The metaphor of the village was then reinforced by the advance of economic globalization at the end of the last century. Over the last two decades, we have witnessed further evidence of the compactness of the world, this time provided by nature. The facts are overwhelming: winds blowing in the Sahara raise tiny desert sands and take them across the Atlantic to the Amazon to feed, with their microscopic nutrients, the trees of the forest; but these trees are being cut by the millions, and this deforestation is destroying water in southern Latin America. The current drought in São Paulo stems from the weakening of the giant clouds that are formed in the Amazon and that travel, like flying rivers, to spray southern Brazil. According to NASA, air pollution in China is affecting food production in the western states of the United States (Scauzillo, 2015). While these states previously managed to reduce their ozone production by 21 percent, this reduction ended up being overturned by the rarefied air coming from

China. The Brahmaputra River, which originates in Tibet and ends in Bangladesh, passing through a part of India, has been increasingly diminished because of a dam built by the government of China in the upper reaches of the river. But perhaps the clearest evidence of the planetary unit is the increase in temperature caused by carbon dioxide emissions coming from fossil fuel consumption. All (or almost all) the world's scientists agree that more than two degrees of warming will bring catastrophic consequences for the planet.

While natural disorders affect everyone on the planet (actually, they disproportionately affect poor countries), developed countries (with the United States in the lead) and new industrial powers such as China, India, and Russia have contributed the most to this disorder and therefore bear greater responsibility. In fact, it is estimated that 63 percent of gas emissions are produced by fewer than a hundred commercial companies, each supported by a country that benefits from their business.

An overwhelmed capitalism has filled up almost the entire planet. This fact has hampered not only democracy but also the rule of law – so much so that we may be returning to the type of political order that prevailed at the end of the nineteenth century. According to Joseph Stiglitz (2013), the economic architecture that produces globalization has also driven the backlash against it. More specifically, Thomas Piketty (2013) has performed judicious empirical research on more than two centuries, from which he questions the capitalist postulate that economic growth is in line with the reduction of inequality. What has happened in the last 40 years, he argues, is just the opposite. Current levels of inequality are very similar to the levels that existed in the holding companies of the late nineteenth century. Economists Joseph Stiglitz and Paul Krugman have supported Piketty's findings. In 2016, Oxfam published the brief *An Economy for the 1 percent*, showing that the concentration of wealth is getting worse, to the point that in 2015, a mere 62 people controlled half of the world's wealth. This fact threatens democratic stability everywhere and diminishes the efficacy of international law (Sachs, 1998). Economic globalization not only has become the main factor in the current destruction of nature and democratic stability but is also weakening national states and international organizations, which have become almost irrelevant when it comes to providing solutions to problems like wars in the Middle East, global warming, arms trafficking, and world migration (Escalante, 2017; Stark, 2015).

The problems of globalization are, in good measure, regulatory problems derived from the institutional inability to penetrate, through legal norms, the social and economic tissue; national and international law are unable to control the major economic and political powers that dominate today's globalized world. In short, regressive legal pluralism, the spread of violence, and the rule of global lawless powers are the by-products of weak states and weak international law in the current global arena (Lemaitre, 2015). Two or three decades ago, these were the typical problems of the Third World. Today, the developed world is mimicking the Third World.

Almost four centuries ago, the Westphalian model of nations was designed to bring order and peace to a world threatened by enemies and international wars. But today's world is less a world of enemies (although they exist) than a world of risks and dangers, especially the danger of self-destruction. If a century ago armies were needed to defend countries, what is needed today are political agreements and new rules that can guarantee the lives of future generations. Tzvetan Todorov (2002) has suggested that rather than tyranny, the greatest evil is anarchy, a lawless world. The current logic of protecting the national interest is a suicidal model whereby each country, through its selfishness, will, paradoxically, eventually dig the grave where all countries will perish (Harari, 2015).

As the world becomes more interdependent, new and challenging problems arise for which the solutions are increasingly scarce. One way out is to find a new type of global model able to regulate our interdependent world. As Peter Singer puts it, "[T]he twenty-first century faces the task of developing a suitable form of government for the single world" (2004, p. 201). We must reinvent both political power and legal practices. I believe that we can achieve this only by recovering the old ideals of cosmopolitanism that were proposed by the Stoics of ancient Greece. Or maybe we do not have to go that far. Maybe we just need to take seriously, once and for all, the ideal of human dignity – a value that was proclaimed during the French and English Enlightenment (Nussbaum, 2014; Waldron, 2012) and that is above not only races, beliefs, and societies but also countries, borders, and nations. For many centuries, cosmopolitanism was no more than a humanist thinking founded on ethical grounds. Today, it still is, with the difference that these ethical reasons have joined a long series of practical reasons related to the sustainability of the planet.

What are the implications of these for the future of SLS? The weakening of the nation-state, with all its ramifications (the decline of sovereignty, the democratic deficit, the loss of universal values, the rise of illegal powers, the deficit of regulation, legal pluralism, and so on), is a big challenge for those who think about the sociopolitical dimension of law, and particularly the political and symbolic uses of law.

SLS is still too local and too dependent on conceptual categories belonging to the nation-state (such as sovereignty, codification, legal territoriality and legal spatiality, popular will, and international law). Globalization, on the other hand, has limited the legal cultures and legal traditions that have differentiated the French and American legal fields over the last century.

It is true that globalization has become a relevant subject today, particularly in the United States (Sarat & Ewick, 2015). But the way it is treated is very local, very restricted to global expressions of the national. It is also very conservative, since it does not question the world system, whose unity is the nation-state. SLS is not taking globalization and cosmopolitanization seriously (Darian-Smith, 2013; Krygier, 2016). Despite the fact that the world is more interconnected, SLS continues to think of both justice and democracy in terms of national jurisdictions. We need to be aware of the fact that most of the big problems we face today – such as climate change, economic globalization, illegal drug trafficking, migration, war, nuclear risks, the judgment of crimes against humanity, the consequences of artificial intelligence, and the weakening of the nation-state – are, problems of collective action (Ostrom, 1990) that are also problems of regulation (i.e., sociopolitical legal problems). Our contemporary tragedy is the lack of solutions in today's legal and political frameworks.

In order to understand the interconnection between law, society, and power in today's world, we need to enlarge our idea of time and space. A more global approach is essential to imagine and implement the legal strategies that can tackle the challenges, risks, and demands of the contemporary world. In this sense, perhaps we need to imagine new symbolic (political) uses of law – uses that are more efficient, more transnational, and maybe more radical. It is likely that the emancipatory struggles of the future will take place in globalized arenas that connect citizens from around the world. These struggles will undoubtedly embrace a legal dimension, to which SLS will be no stranger.

Our world is legally divided into nation-states and politically legitimized by the general will of national peoples. But these are formal and discursive patterns. In reality, we live in an interdependent world, dominated mostly by the powerful interests of a few nations, whose domination is both hidden and strengthened behind the fetishism of legal forms and political discourses. If the nation-state has always enacted limits to the effectiveness of rights and to the protection of human dignity, these limits are fortified in our globalized world: rights depend today on passports, as they depended on race or social class two centuries ago. The chasm between legal forms and sociopolitical realities has increased during this time of globalization. This is why the "myth of law," which is the myth of national laws, was never so fictional and so mythical as it is today. The political burden of these myths and forms (their symbolic violence) prevents us from understanding the current relationship between law, societies, and politics in the global arena and therefore precludes us from addressing global problems in democratic, humanitarian, and cosmopolitan ways.

We live in a world that believes it can solve its problems through technological innovation, markets, and repression. Science, markets, and war seem to be the only keys to defining the future of humanity. Law, global democracy, public goods, and international institutions have a marginal and diminishing role in defining and solving these problems, when everything indicates that they should play a leading role in such issues.

For these reasons, we need to reconsider SLS in a world that is losing the regulatory power of states – a world that is witness not just to new and more subtle forms of domination that go beyond geographical and political borders but also to new forms of social and political struggles that go beyond the framework of national borders. What are the implications of these changes in terms of rights and democracy? This is a crucial question for the future of SLS.

REFERENCES

Abbott, A. (1995). "Things of Boundaries." *Social Research*, 62(4), 857–882.
(2001). *Chaos of Disciplines*. Chicago: University of Chicago Press.
Abel, R. (1980). "Redirecting Social Studies of Law." *Law and Society Review*,
14, 803–829.
(1985). "Comparative Sociology of Legal Professions: An Exploratory
Essay." *American Bar Foundation Research Journal*, 10(1), 1–79.
(1989). *American Lawyers*. New York: Oxford University Press.
(1995a). *Politics by Other Means: Law in the Struggle against Apartheid,
1980–1994*. New York: Routledge.
(1995b). *The Law and Society Reader*. New York: New York University
Press.
(1998). "Speaking Law to Power: Occasions for Cause Lawyering." In *Cause
Lawyering: Political Commitment and Professional Responsibilities*, edited by
Austin Sarat & Stuart Scheingold (pp. 69–117). Oxford: Oxford University Press.
(2010). "Law and Society: Project and Practice." *Annual Review of Law and
Social Science*, 6(1), 1–23.
Abramovich, V., & Courtis, C. (2002). *Los derechos sociales como derechos
exigibles*. Madrid: Trotta.
Abrams, K. (1991). "Hearing the Call of Stories." *California Law Review*,
79, 971.
Acemoglu, D., & Robinson, J. (2012). *Why Nations Fail: The Origins of Power,
Prosperity and Poverty*. New York: Crown Business.
Ackerman, B. A. (1984). *Reconstructing American Law*. Cambridge, MA:
Harvard University Press.
Ackerman, B. A., & Rosenkrantz, C. (1991). "Tres conceptos de la democra-
cia constitucional." In Fundamentos y alcances del control judicial de
constitucionalidad, Cuadernos y debates – Centro de Estudios Constitucionales, (29), 15–31.
Agrikoliansky, E. (2003). "Usages choisis du droit: le service juridique de la
ligue des droits de l' homme (1970–1990): entre politique et raison
humanitaire." *Sociétés Contemporaines*, 52, 61–84.
Albarracín, M. (2011). *Movilización legal para el reconocimiento de parejas del
mismo sexo*. Bogota: Universidad de los Andes.

Alberdi, J. B. (1981). *Bases y puntos de partida para la organización política de la República Argentina.* Buenos Aires: Plus Ultra.

Alexander, J. (1987). *Twenty Lectures.* New York: Columbia University Press.

Alexander, M. (2012). *The New Jim Crow.* New York: The New Press.

Alexy, R. (1993). *Teoría de los derechos fundamentales.* Madrid: Centro de Estudios Constitucionales.

Alves da Fonseca, M. (2013a). *Michel Foucault et le droit.* Paris: L'Harmattan.

Amselek, P. (1997). "La part de la science dans les activités de juristes." Recueil Dalloz, Chronique, (39), 337–342.

Anderson, P. (1979). *El Estado Absolutista.* Madrid: Siglo Veintiuno Editores.

Aristotle. (1974). *La politique.* Paris. Retrieved from Ladrange.

Arnaud, A. J. (1973). *Essai d'analyse structurale du Code civil français.* Paris: Librairie Générale de Droit et de Jurisprudence.

(1975). *Les juristes face à la société.* Paris: PUF.

(1981). *Critique de la raison Juridique.* Paris: LGDJ.

(1988). *Dictionnaire encyclopédique de théorie et sociologie du droit.* Paris: LGDJ.

(1989). "Le droit, un ensemble peu convivial." *Droit et Société,* 1(11–12), 79–95.

(1991). "Du jeu fini au jeu ouvert. Réflexions additionnelles sur le Droit post-moderne." *Droit et Société,* 1(17–18), 39–55.

(1993). "Droit: le système et l'ensemble." In *Niklas Luhmann, observateur du droit,* Collection *Droit et Société* (25), edited by Andre Jean Arnaud & Pierre Guibentif (pp. 147–166). Paris: LGDJ.

(1998a). *Entre modernité et mondialisation.* Paris: LGDJ.

(1998b). *Le droit trahi par la sociologie.* Paris: LGDJ.

(2009). "Présentation : Autour d'un dialogue imaginaire entre Michel Villey et Friedrich A. Hayek." *Droit et Société,* 1(71), 9–25.

(2013a). "Du dia-logein au transgredir : en guise d'ouverture." In *Droit, arts, sciences humaines et sociales: (dé)passer les fontières disciplinaires,* edited by Sandrine Chassagnard-Pinet, Pierre Lemay, Céline Regulski, & Dorothée Simonneau (pp. 39–53). Paris: LDGJ.

(2013b). "The Transplanetary Journey of a Legal Sociologist." In *Law and Intersystemic Communication: Understanding "Structural Coupling,"* edited by Alberto Febbrajo & Gorm Harste (pp. 17–30). New York: Routledge.

(2014). *La Gouvernance, un outil de participation.* Paris: Lextenso Éditions.

Arnaud, A. J., & Andrini, S. (1995). *Jean Carbonier, Renato Treves et la sociologie du droit. Archéologie d'une discipline. Entretiens et Pièces.* Paris: LGDJ.

Arnaud, A. J., & Fariñas Dulce, M. (1998). *Introduction à l'analyse sociologique des systèmes juridiques.* Brussels: Bruylant.

(2012). *Jean Carbonnier: Un juriste dans la cité.* Paris: LDGJ.

Arnold, M. (1971). "The Function of Criticism at the Present Time." In *Critical Theory since Plato*, edited by Hazard Adams (pp. 592–603). New York: Harcourt, Brace, Jovanovich.

Assier-Andrieu, L. (1996). *Le droit dans les sociétés humaines*. Paris: Nathan. (2011). *Les avocats. Identité, culture et devenir*. Paris: L'Extenso.

Audren, F. (2016). "Le 'moment 1900' dans l'histoire de la science juridique française." In *Critique sociale et critique sociologique du droit en Europe et aux Etats-Unis*, edited by Olivier Jouanjan & Élizabeth Zoller (pp. 55–74). Paris: Editions Panthéon-Assas.

Audren, F., & Halpérin, J.-L. (2013). *La culture juridique française. Entre Mythes et réalités*. Paris: CNRS Editions.

Auerbach, J. (1976). *Unequal Justice: Lawyers and Social Change in Modern America*. New York: Oxford University Press.

Austin, J. L. (1962). *How to Do Things with Words*. Cambridge, MA: Harvard University Press.

Ayres, I., & Braithwaite, J. (1992). *Responsive Regulation: Transcending the Deregulation Debate*. New York: Oxford University Press.

Bacon, F. (2001). *Essays, Civil and Moral*. Cambridge: Collier and Son Company.

Bailleaux, A., & Ost, F. (2013). "Droit, contexte et interdisciplinarité : refondation d'une démarche." *Revue Interdisciplinaire D'études Juridiques*, 70, 25–44.

Balbus, I. D. (1977). "Commodity Form and Legal Form: An Essay on the Relative Autonomy of the Law." *Law and Society Review*, 11, 143–156. (1996). "Commodity Form and Legal Form: An Essay on the Relative Autonomy of the Law." In *The Sociology of Law*, edited by Javier Treviño (pp. 140–148). New York: St. Martin's Press.

Balkin, J. M. (1987). "Deconstructive Practice and Legal Theory." *The Yale Journal*, 96, 743–786.

Banakar, R. (2003). *Merging Law and Sociology: Beyond the Dichotomies in Socio-legal Research*. Berlin: Galda & Wilch.

Banakar, R., & Travers, M. (2002). "Law and Sociology." In *An Introduction to Law and Social Theory*, edited by Reza Banakar & Max Travers (pp. 345–352). Portland: Hart Publishing.

Bancaud, A. (1993). *La haute magistrature entre politique et sacerdoce*. Paris: LGDJ.

Bancaud, A., & Dezalay, Y. (1984). "La sociologie juridique comme enjeu social et professionel." *Revue Interdisciplinaire D' Études Juridiques*, 12, 1–29.

Bankowski, Z., & Mungham, G. (1976). *Images of Law*. London: Routledge.

Baratta, A. (1986). *Criminología crítica y crítica del derecho penal. Introducción a la sociología jurídico-penal*. Mexico City: Siglo XXI.

Barclay, S., Jones, L., & Marshall, A.-M. (2011). "Two Spinning Wheels: Studying Law and Social Movements." *Studies in Law, Politics and Society*, 54, 1–16.

Barrow, C. W. (1993). *Critical Theories of the State: Marxist, Neo-Marxist Post-Marxist*. Madison: University of Wisconsin Press.

Bart, K., Van Beers, B., & Poort, L. (2016). *Symbolic Legislation Theory and Development in Biolaw*. Geneva: Springer.

Barthes, R. (1980). *Mitologías*. Mexico City: Siglo XXI.

Bartlett, K. (2012). "Feminist Legal Scholarship: A History through the Lens of the California Law Review." *California Law Review, 100*, 381–429.

Bastard, B., & Ackerman, W. (1993). "Une coopération conflictuelle : les relations entre les barreaux et les tribunaux de grande instance." *Droit et Société, 1*(23–24), 59–77.

Bastard, B., & Mouhanna, C. (2007). *Une justice dans l'urgence. Le traitement en temps réel des affaires pénales*. Paris: PUF.

Baudot, P.-Y., & Revillard, A. (Eds.). (2014). *L'Etat des droits. La pratique des droits dans l'action publique*. Paris: Presses de Sciences Po.

Baum, D. (1997). *Smoke and Mirrors: The War on Drugs and the Politics of Failure*. Boston: Little Brown.

Bauman, R. W. (1996). *Critical Legal Studies: A Guide to the Literature*. New York: Westview Press.

Beaud, O. (2006). "La distinction entre droit public et droit privé : un dualisme que résiste aux critiques." In *The Public Law/Private Law divide. Une entente assez cordiale?*, edited by Mark Freedland & Jean-Bernard Auby (pp. 21–39). Oxford: Hart.

Becker, C. H. (1925). *Vom Wesen der deutschen Universitat*. Leipzig: Verlag Quelle und Meyer.

Becker, G. (1993a). *Human Capital: A Theoretical and Empirical Analysis with Special Reference to Education*. Cambridge: Cambridge University Press.

(1993b). "Nobel Lecture: The Economic Way of Looking at Behavior." *Journal of Political Economy, 101*, 385.

Becker, H. (1963). *Outsiders: Studies in the Sociology of Deviance*. New York: Free Press.

Beckett, K., & Hoffman, B. (2014). "Challenging Medicine: Law, Resistance and the Cultural Politics of Childbirth." In *The Law and Society Reader II*, edited by Erik Larson & Patrick Schmidt (pp. 276–284). New York: New York University Press.

Beirne, P., & Quinney, R. (Eds.). (1982). *Marxism and Law*. New York: John Wiley & Sons.

Belleau, M. C. (1999). "Les juristes inquiets: classisisme juridique et critique du droit au début du XXe siècle en France." *Les Cahiers de Droit, 40*(3), 507–544.

Belley, J. G. (1986). "L'Etat et la régulation juridique des sociétés globales. Pour une problématique du pluralisme juridique." *Sociologie et Sociétés*, 18(1), 11–32.

Bereni, L. (2009). "Faire de la diversité une richesse pour l'entreprise. La transformation d'une contrainte juridique en catégorie managériale." *Raisons politiques*, 3(35), 87–105.

Berger, P., & Luckmann, T. (1966). *The Social Construction of Reality: A Treatise in the Sociology of Knowledge*. New York: Anchor Books.

Berger, R., Searles, P., & Neuman, L. W. (1988). "The Dimensions of Rape Reform Legislation." *Law and Society Review*, 22, 329–358.

Berman, H. (1983). *Law and Revolution: The Formation of Western Legal Tradition*. Cambridge, MA: Harvard University Press.

(2003). *Law and Revolution: The Impact of the Protestant Reformation on the Western Legal Tradition*. Cambridge, MA: Harvard University Press.

Bessy, Ch. (2015). *L'Organisation des activités des avocats*. Paris: LGDJ.

Biland, E., & Israël, L. (2011). "À l'école du droit : les apports de la méthode ethnographique à l'analyse de la formation juridique." *Les Cahiers Du Droit*, 52(3–4), 619–658.

Biland, E. & Vanneuville, R. (2012). "Government Lawyers and the Training of Senior Civil Servants. Maintaining Law at the Heart of the French State." *International Journal of Legal Profession*, 19(1), 29–54.

Bisharat, G. (1990). "Courting Justice? Legitimation in Lawyering under Israeli Occupation." *Law and Social Inquiry*, 20(2), 349–405.

Bixio, Andre. (1994). *Sociología del diritto. Guida alla laurea in Scienze Politiche*. Bologna: Il Mulino.

Black, D. (1972). "The Boundaries of Legal Sociology." *Yale Law Journal*, 81, 1086–1100.

(1976). *The Behavior of Law*. New York: Academic Press.

(1995). "The Epistemology of Pure Sociology." *Law and Social Inquiry*, 20, 829–870.

Blanco Valdés, R. L. (1998). *El valor de la Constitución*. Madrid: Alianza Universidad.

Blanquer, J.-M., & Millet, M. (2015). *L'invention de l'Etat. Léon Duguit et Maurice Hauriou et lnaissance du droit public modern*. Paris: Odile Jacob.

Blum, L. (1965). *L'Oeuvre de Leon Blum*. Paris: Albin Michel.

Blumer, H. (1945). "Collective Behavior." In *New Outline of the Principles of Sociology*, edited by Alfred McClung Lee & Robert Ezra Park (pp. 67–121). New York: Barnes and Noble.

(1969). *Symbolic Interactionism: Perspectives and Method*. Englewood Cliffs, NJ: Prentice Hall.

Bobbio, N. (2005). *Teoría general de la política*. Madrid: Trotta.

Boigeol, A. (2007). "Le genre comme ressource dans l'accès des femmes au 'gouvernement du barreau': l'exemple du barreau de Paris." *Genèses, 67*, 66–88.

Boigeol, A., & Dezalay, Y. (1997). "De l'agent d'affaires au barreau : les conseils juridiques et la construction d'un espace professionnel." *Genèses, 27*, 49–68.

Boigeol, A., & Willemez, L. (2005). "France: Fighting for Survival: Unification, Differentiation and Representation of the French Bar." In *Reorganization and Resistance: Legal Professions Confront a Changing World*, edited by William Felstiner (pp. 41–65). Portland, OR: Hart Publishing.

Boltanski, L. (1990). *L'amour et la justice comme compétence*. Paris: Métailié.

Bonafé-Schmitt, J.-P. (1992). *La médiation: une justice douce, Syros Alternatives*. Paris: Syros.

Bonnecase, J. (1924). *l'Ecole de l'exégèse en droit civil*. Paris: E. de Boccard.

Bourdieu, P. (1964). *Les Héritiers. Les étudiants et la culture*. Paris: Minuit.

(1977). *Outline of a Theory of Practice*. New York: Cambridge University Press.

(1980). *Le sens pratique*. Paris: Minuit.

(1986). "La force du droit: éléments pour une sociologie du champ juridique." *Actes de La Recherche En Sciences Sociales, 64*, 3–19.

(1987). "The Force of Law: Toward a Sociology of the Juridical Field." *Hastings Law Journal, 38*, 814–853.

(1989). *La noblesse d'état: Grand corps et grandes écoles*. Paris: Minuit.

(1990). "Droit et passe-droit." *Actes de La Recherche En Sciences Sociales, 81–82*, 86–96.

(1991). "Les juristes, gardiens de l'hypocrisie collective." In *Normes juridiques et régulation sociale*, edited by François Chazel & Jacques Comaille (pp. 95–99). Paris: LDGJ.

(1994). *Raison Pratiques: Sur la théorie de l'action*. Paris: Seuil.

(1997). "De la maison du roi à la raison d'État. Un modèle de la genèse du champ bureaucratique." *Actes de La Recherche En Sciences Sociales, 1*(118), 55–68.

(2000). *Les Structures Sociales de l'Economie*. Paris: Seuil.

(2012). *Sur l'État: Cours au Collège de France (1989–1992)*. Paris: Seuil.

Bourdieu, P., & Wacquant, L. J. D. (1992). *An Invitation to Reflexive Sociology*. Chicago: University of Chicago Press.

Bowen, J., & Bentaboulet, M. (2002). "On the Institutionalization of the 'Human and Social Science' in France." *Anthropological Quarterly, 75*(3), 537–555.

Boyle, J. (1985). "The Politics of Reason: Critical Legal Theory and Local Social Thought." *University of Pennsylvania Law Review, 133*(4), 685–780.

Bredemeier, H. (1962). "Law as an Integrative Mechanism." In *Law and Sociology*, edited by W. M. Evan (pp. 73–90). New York: Free Press.

Brigham, J. (1987). *The Cult of the Court*. Philadelphia: Temple University Press.

——— (1996). *The Constitution of Interest: Beyond the Politics of Rights*. New York: New York University Press.

——— (1998). "The Constitution of Interests: Institutionalism, CLS and New Approaches to Sociolegal Studies." *Yale Journal of Law and the Humanities*, 10(2), 421–461.

Brisbin, R. (2010). "Resistance to Legality." *Annual Reviews of Law and Social Science*, 6, 25–44.

Brown, W., & Halley, J. E. (Eds.). (2002). *Left Legalism/Left Critique*. Durham: Duke University Press.

Brunet, P. (2014). "Le 'positivisme' français dans la lumière du Nord. Le réalisme juridique scandinave et la doctrine française." *Revus*, 24, 2–18.

——— (2015). "Argument sociologique et théories de l'interprétation: beaucoup d'interprétation très peu de sociologie." In *L'argument sociologique en droit. Pluriel et singularité*, edited by Dominique Fenouillet (pp. 101–116). Paris: Dalloz.

Brunetière, F. (1897). "Dans l'Est americain." *Revue Des Deux Mondes*, 92–123.

Buchanan, M. (1994). "Context, Continuity and Difference in Poverty Law Scholarship." *University of Miami Law Review*, 48(5), 999–1062.

Bumiller, K. (1988). *The Civil Rights Society: The Social Construction of Victims*. Baltimore: Johns Hopkins University Press.

Burawoy, M., Burton, A., Ferguson, A. A., & Fox, K. J. (1991). *Ethnography Unbound, Power Resistance in Modern Metropolis*. Berkeley: University of California Press.

Burchell, G. (1991). *The Foucault Effect: Studies in Governmentality*. Chicago: University of Chicago Press.

Butler, J. (1990). *Gender Trouble: Feminism and the Subversion of Identity*. New York: Routledge.

——— (1992). "Contingent Foundations: Feminism and the Question of Postmodernism." In *Feminists Theorize the Political*, edited by Judith Butler & Joan W. Scott (pp. 3–21). New York: Routledge.

Caillosse, J. (1996). "Droit public – droit privé. Sens et portée d'un partage académique." *Actualité juridique*, 4, 67–90.

——— (2004). "Pierre Bourdieu, Lector juris: Anti-juridisme et science du droit." *Droit et Société*, 56–57, 17–37.

——— (2011). "La sociologie politique du droit, le droit et les juristes." *Droit et Société*, 77, 189–206.

Cain, M., & Hunt, A. (1979). *Marx and Engels on Law*. New York: Academic Press.

Calabresi, G. (2016) *The Future of Law and Economics: Essays in Reform and Recollection*. New York: Yale University Press.

(1970). *The Cost of Accidents: A Legal and Economic Analysis*. New Haven: Yale University Press.

Calavita, K. (1996). "The New Politics of Immigration: 'Balanced-Budget Conservatism' and the Symbolism of Proposition 187." *Social Problems*, 43, 284–305.

(2001). "Blue Jeans, Rape, and the 'De-Constitutive' Power of Law." *Law and Society Review*, 35(1), 89–116.

(2002). "Engaged Research, 'Goose Bumps' and the Role of the Public Intellectual." *Law and Society*, 36, 5–20.

(2010). *Invitation to Law and Society: An Introduction to the Study of Real Law*. Chicago: University of Chicago Press.

Campos, P., Schlag, P., & Smith, S. (1996). *Against the Law*. Durham: Duke University Press.

Capeller, W., & De, M. (2009) *L'engrénage de la repression. Stratégies sécuritaires et politiques criminelles au Brésil*. Collection *Droit et Société*. Paris: LDGJ.

Capitant, H. (1898). *Introduction à l'étude du droit civil – Notions générales*. Paris: A. Pédone.

Carbonnier, J. (1978). *Sociologie Juridique*. Paris: PUF.

(2001). *Flexible droit. Pour une sociologie du droit sans rigueur*. Paris: LDGJ.

(2007). "La sociologie juridique et son emploi en législation. Communication de Jean Carbonnier à l'académie des sciences morales et politiques." *L'Année Sociologique*, 57(2), 393–401.

Carlin, J. (1962). *Lawyers on Their Own: The Solo Practitioner in an Urban Setting*. San Francisco: Austin and Winfield Publishers.

Carré de Malberg, R. (1922). *Contribution à la théorie générale de l'Etat*. Paris: Sirey.

Carty, A. (1992). *Law and Development*. New York: New York University Press.

Centeno, M. & Ferraro, A. (2013). *State and Nation Making in Latin America and Spain*. New York: Cambridge University Press.

Chambliss, E. (2008). "When Do Facts Persuade? Some Thoughts on the Market for 'Empirical Legal Studies.'" *Law and Contemporary Problems*, 71(2), 17–40.

Chambliss, W. (1999). *Power, Politics and Crime*. Boulder: Westview Press.

Champy, F., & Israël, L. (2009). "Professions et engagement public." *Société Contemporaines*, 1(73), 7–19.

Chappe, V. A. (2010). "La qualification juridique est-elle soluble dans le militantisme ? Tensions et paradoxes au sein de la permanence juridique d'une association antiraciste." *Droit et Société*, 76(3), 543–567.

Charboneau, S., & Padioleau, J. G. (1980). "La mise en oeuvre d'une politique publique réglementaire: le défrichement des bois et forêts." *Revue française de sociologie*, 1(21), 49–75.

Charle, C. (2003). "Les références étrangères des universitaires. Essai de comparaison entre la France et l'Allemagne. 1870–1970." *Actes de La Recherche En Sciences Sociales*, 3(148), 8–19.

Chassagnard-Pinet, S. (2013). "La science du droit dans son rapport aux sciences humaines et sociales. Approche historique et comparée." In *Droit, arts, sciences humaines et sociales: (dé)passer les fontières disciplinaires*, edited by Sandrine Chassagnard-Pinet, Pierre Lemay, Céline Regulski, & Dorothée Simonneau (pp. 39–53). Paris: LDGJ.

Chassagnard-Pinet, S., Lemay, P., Regulsky, C., & Simonneau, D. (2013). *Droit, arts, sciences humaines et sociales: (dé)passer les frontières disciplinaires*. Paris: LGDJ.

Chazel, F. (1991). "Émile Durkheim et l'élaboration d'un 'programme de recherche' en sociologie du droit." In *Normes juridiques et régulation sociale*, edited by François Chazel & Jacques Comaille (pp. 27–38). Paris: LGDJ.

Chazel, F., & Commaille, J. (Eds.). (1991). *Normes juridiques et régulation sociale*. Paris: LDGJ.

Chevallier, J. (1993). "Les interprètes du droit." In *La doctrine juridique*, edited by Yves Poirmeur & Alain Bernard (pp. 259–282). Paris: PUF.

(1997). "La fin des écoles?" *Revue Du Droit Public*, 3, 679–700.

(2003). *L'Etat post-moderne*. Paris: LGDJ.

(2006). "Pour une sociologie du droit constitutionnel." In *L'architecture du droit. Mélanges en l'honneur de Michel Troper*, edited by Denys de Béchillon, Véronique Champeil-Desplats, Pierre Brunet, & Eric Millard (pp. 281–298). Paris: Economica.

Chodorow, N. J. (1989). *Feminism and Psychoanalytic Theory*. New Haven: Yale University Press.

Chomsky, N. (1993). "World Order and Its Rules: Variations on Some Themes." *Journal of Law and Society*, 20(2), 145–165.

Clark, D. (Ed.). (2012a). *Comparative Law and Society*. Cheltenham: Edward Elgar.

(2012b). "History of Comparative Law and Society." In *Comparative Law and Society*, edited by David Clark (pp. 1–38). Cheltenham: Edward Elgar.

Coase, R. (1960). "The Problem of Social Cost." *Journal of Law and Economics*, 3, 1–44.

Cohen, F. (1937). "Fundamental Principles of the Sociology of Law." *Illinois Law Review*, 31, 1128–1134.

Cohen, A., & Vauchez, A. (2011). "The Social Construction of Law: The European Court of Justice and Its Legal Revolution Revisited." *Annual Reviews of Law and Social Science*, 7, 417–431.

Cohen-Tanugi, L. (2007). *Le droit sans l'Etat*. Paris: PUF.
(2015). *What's Wrong with France*. Paris: Grasset.
Coleman, J., & Lange, J. (1993). *Law and Economics*. New York: New York University Press.
Collins, H. (1986). *The Law of Contract*. London: Weidenfeld & Nicolson.
Collins, R. (1994). *Four Sociological Traditions*. Oxford: Oxford University Press.
Colliot-Thélène, C. (2009). "Pour une politique des droits subjectifs: la lutte pour les droit comme lutte politique." *L'Année Sociologique*, 59(1), 232–258.
Comack, E. (2006). "Theoretical Approaches in the Sociology of Law: Theoretical Excursions." In *Locating Law: Race/Class/Gender/Sexuality Connections*, edited by Elizabeth Comack (pp. 18–67). Black Point, NS: Fernwood Publishing.
Commaille, J. (1983). "The Law and Science: Dialectics between the Prince and the Maidservant." *Law and Policy*, 10, 253–265.
(1989). "La sociologie du droit en France. Les ambiguïtés d'une specialisation." *Sociologia Del Diritto*, 16, 19.
(2000). *Territoires de justice; une sociologie politique de la carte judiciaire*. Paris: PUF.
(2003a). "Droit et politique." In *Dictionnaire de la culture juridique*, edited by D. Alland and S. Rials (pp. 477–481). Paris: PUF.
(2003b). "Sociologie juridique." In *Dictionnaire de la culture juridique*, edited by D. Alland and S. Rials (pp. 1423–1427). Paris: PUF.
(2007a). "La construction d'une sociologie spécialisée. Le savoir sociologique et la sociologie juridique de Jean Carbonnier." *L'Année Sociologique*, 57(2), 275–299.
(2007b). "La justice entre détraditionnalisation, néoliberalisation et démocratisation. Vers une théorie de sociologie politique de la justice." In *La fonction politique de la justice*, edited by Jacques Commaille & Martin Kaluszynski (pp. 295–321). Paris: La Découverte.
(2010). "De la 'sociologie juridique' à une sociologie politique du droit." In *La juridisation du politique*, edited by Jacques Commaille, Laurence Dumolin, & Cécile Robert (pp. 29–51). Paris: LDGJ.
(2012). "Preface." In *Jean Carbonnier. Un juriste dans la cité*, edited by Andre Jean Arnaud (pp. 5–12). Paris: LDGJ.
(2013). *Sociologie politique du droit. Quels acquis? Quels perspectives? Propos conclusifs – Journées en l'honneur de Jacques Commaille*. Paris: ENS – Cachan.
(2015). *A quoi nous sert le droit?* Paris: Gallimard.
(2016). "Les enjeux politiques d'un régime de connaissance sur le droit. La sociologie du droit de Georges Gurvitch." *Droit et Société*, 94, 547–564.

Commaille, J., Commaille, J. F. P., Dumoulin, L., & Robert, C. (2000). *La juridicisation du politique: Leçons scientifiques*. Paris: LGDJ.

Commaille, J., & Duran, P. (2009). "Pour une sociologie politique du droit: presentation." *L'Année Sociologique*, 59(1), 11–28.

Commaille, J., & Kaluszynski, M. (Eds.). (2007). *La fonction politique de la justice*. Paris: La Découverte.

Commaille, J., & Perrin, J.-F. (1985). "Le modèle de Janus de la sociologie du droit." *Droit et Société*, 1(1), 119–134.

Commaille, J., Demoulin, L., & Robert, C. (2010). *La juridicisation du politique*. Paris: LGDJ.

Conti, J. (2014). "The Good Case: Decisions to Litigate at the World Trade Organization." In *The Law and Society Reader II*, edited by Erik Larson & Patrick Schmidt (pp. 24–31). New York: New York University Press.

Coombe, R. J. (1998). "Contingent Articulations: A Critical Cultural Studies of Law." In *Law in the Domains of Culture*, edited by A. Sarat & T. R. Kearns (pp. 21–64). Ann Arbor: University of Michigan Press.

Correas, O. (1993). "La sociología jurídica. Un ensayo de definición." *Revista Latinoamericana de Política, Filosofía y Derecho*, 12, 23–53.

Corten, O. (2003). "La persistance de l'argument légaliste : éléments pour une typologie contemporaine des registres de légitimité dans une société libérale." *Droit et Société*, 50, 185–203.

Coskun, D. (2007). *Law as Symbolic Form: Ernst Cassirer and the Anthropocentric View of Law*. Dordrecht: Springer.

Costa, P. (2012). "Histoire, théorie et histoire de théories." In *Comment écrit-on l'histoire Constitutionnelle?*, edited by Carlos-Miguel Herrera and Arnaud Le Pillouer (pp. 19–56). Paris: Kimé.

Cotterrell, R. (1983). "The Sociological Concept of Law." *Journal of Law and Sociology*, 10, 241.

(1989). *The Politics of Jurisprudence: A Critical Introduction to Legal Philosophy*. London: Butterworths.

(1990). "Sociology of Law in Britain: Its Development and Present Prospects." In *Developing Sociology of Law: A World-Wide Documentary Enquiry*, edited by V. Ferrari (pp. 779–803). Milano: Giuffre.

(1991). "The Durkheimian Tradition in the Sociology of Law." *Law and Society Review*, 25(4), 923–946.

(1992). *The Sociology of Law: An Introduction*. London: Butterworths.

(1998). "Why Must Legal Ideas Be Interpreted Sociologically?" *Journal of Law and Society*, 25, 171–192.

(2004). "Law in Social Theory and Social Theory in the Study of Law." In *The Blackwell Companion to Law and Society*, edited by Austin Sarat (pp. 15–29). Malden: Blackwell Publishing.

(2006). *Law, Culture and Society: Legal Ideas in the Mirror of Social Theory*. Aldershot: Ashgate.

(2007). "Images of Europe in Sociolegal Traditions." In *European Ways of Law: Towards a European Sociology of Law*, edited by David Nelken & Volkmar Gessner (pp. 21–39). Oxford: Hart Publishing.

(2012). "Comparative Sociology of Law." In *Comparative Law and Society*, edited by David Clark (pp. 39–60). New York: Edward Elgar.

Coutin, S. (2001). "Cause Lawyering in the Shadow of the State." In *Cause Lawyering and the State in a Global Era*, edited by Austin Sarat & Stuart Scheingold (pp. 117–140). New York: Oxford University Press.

Cramer, R. (1986). "Eléments biographiques et bibliographiques pour une étude de l'apport de Georges Gurvitch à la théorie et à la sociologie du droit." *Droit et Société*, 4, 457–467.

Crenshaw, K. (2002). "The First Decade: Critical Reflections, or 'A Foot on the Closing Door'." *UCLA Law Review*, 49, 1343.

Crenshaw, K. W. (1988). "Race, Reform and Retrenchment: Transformation and Legitimation in Anti-Discrimination Law." *Harvard Law Review*, 101(7), 1331–1387.

Crenshaw, K. et al. (1995). "Introduction." In *Critical Race Theory: The Key Writings that Formed the Movement*, edited by Kimberly Crenshaw (pp. 13–32). New York: New Press.

Crozier, B. (1935). "Constitutionality of Discrimination Based Sex." *Boston University Law Review*, 15, 723.

Cuin, C. H., & Gresle, F. (2002). *Histoire de la sociologie*. Paris: La Découverte.

Curry, T. (2012). "Shut Your Mouth When You're Talking to Me: Silencing the Idealist School of Critical Race Theory through a Culturalogic Turn in Jurisprudence." *Georgetown Law Journal of Modern Critical Race Studies*, 3(1), 1–38.

Dahrendorf, R. (1969). "Law Faculties and the German Upper Class." In *Sociology of Law*, edited by Vilhelm Aubert (pp. 294–309). London: Penguin Books.

Darian-Smith, E. (2013). *Laws and Societies in Global Contexts*. Cambridge, MA: Cambridge University Press.

(2015). "The Constitution of Identity: New Modalities of Nationality." In *The Handbook of Law and Society*, edited by Austin Sarat & Patricia Ewick (pp. 351–366). Chichester: Wiley Blackwell.

De Aquino, T. (1988). *Summa Theologica I IIae*. Madrid: BAC.

De Galembert, C. (2008). "Le voile en procès." *Droit et Société*, 66, 11–31.

De la torre, J. A. (2006). *El derecho como arma de liberación en América Latina. Sociología del derecho y uso alternativo del derecho*. San Luis de Potosí: Universidad Autónoma de San Luis de Potosí.

De Saussure, F. (1945). *Curso de Lingüística General*. Buenos Aires: Losada.

De Sutter, L., & Gutwirth, S. (2004). "Droit et cosmopolitique. Notes sur la contribution de Bruno Latour à la pensée du droit." *Droit et Société*, 56–57, 259–289.

Dean, M. (2009). *Governmentality: Power and Rule in Modern Society*. London: Sage Publications.

Deflem, M. (2008). *Sociology of Law: Visions of a Scholarly Tradition*. Cambridge, MA: Cambridge University Press.

——— (2010). *Sociology of Law*. Cambridge, MA: Cambridge University Press.

Del Vecchio, G. (1964). *Historia de la filosofía del derecho*. Barcelona: Bosch.

Delgado, R. (1987). "The Ethereal Scholar: Does Critical Legal Studies Have What Minorities Want?" *Harvard Civil Liberties Law Review*, 22, 302–322.

Delgado, R., & Stefancic, J. (2013). *Critical Race Theory: An Introduction*. New York: New York University Press.

Dellay, J. D., & Mader, L. (1981). "Que faire des objectifs dans une étude de mise en oeuvre de la législation?" *Revue Suisse de Sociologie*, 7, 385–397.

Delpeuch, T., & Vassileva, M. (2009). "Contribution à une sociologie politique des entrepreneurs internationaux de transferts de réformes judiciaires." *L'Année Sociologique*, 59(2), 371–402.

Delpeuch, T., Dumoulin, L., & De Galembert, C. (2014). *Sociologie du droit et de la justice*. Paris: Armand Colin.

Demogue, R. (1911). *Les notions fondamentales en droit privé (La Mémoire du Droit)*. Paris: Arthur Rousseau.

Demoulin, L., & Licoppe, C. (2011). "La visioconférence dans la justice pénale: retour sur la fabrique d'une politique publique." *Les Cahiers de La Justice*, 2, 29–52.

Derrida, J. (1976). *On Grammatology*. Baltimore: John Hopkins University Press.

——— (2002). "Force of Law: The 'Mystical Foundations of Authority'." In *Acts of Religion*, edited by Jacques Derrida & Gil Anidjar (pp. 228–98). New York: Routledge.

Devon, C. & Roithmayr, D. (2014). "Critical Race Theory Meets Social Science." *Annual Revue of Law and Social Sciences*, 10, 149–167.

Dezalay, Y. (1990). "Juristes purs et marchands de droit. Division du travail de domination symbolique et aggiornamento dans le champ du droit." *Politix*, 3(10), 70–91.

——— (1992). *Marchands de droit*. Paris: Fayard.

——— (1993). "La production doctrinale comme objet et terrain de luttes politiques et professionnelles." In *La doctrine juridique*, edited by Yves Poirmeur & Alain Bernard (pp. 230–239). Paris: PUF.

Dezalay, Y., & Garth, B. (2002). "Legitimating the New Legal Orthodoxy." In *Global Prescriptions: The Production, Exportation, and Importation of a New Legal Orthodoxy*, edited by Yves Dezalay & Bryan Garth (pp. 306–334). Ann Arbor: University of Michigan Press.

Dezalay, Y., Sarat, A., & Silbey, S. (1989). "D'une démarche contestataire a un savoir méritocratique. Eléments pour une histoire sociale de la sociologie juridique Américaine." *Actes de La Recherche En Sciences Sociales*, 78, 79–90.

Dicey, A. V. (1905). *Lectures on the Relation between the Law and Public Opinion in England during the Nineteenth Century*. London: MacMillan.

Di-Maggio, P., & Powell, W. (1991). *The New Institutionalism in Organizational Analysis*. Chicago: University of Chicago Press.

Dingwall, R. (2003). "The LSA and the 'Pax Americana'." *Law and Society Review*, 37(2), 315–322.

(2007). "Sociology of Law." In *Blackwell Encyclopedia of Sociology*, edited by George Ritzer & Michael Ryan (pp. 2560–2564). Oxford: Blackwell Publishing.

Dos Santos, W. G. (1987). *Ciudadanía e justiça, a politica social na ordem Brasileira*. Rio de Janeiro: Campus.

Droit et Société. (2015). "Lettre – manifeste : 'Le sens d'une revue académique'." *Droit et Société*, 3(91), 459–462.

Dudas, J., Goldberg-Hiller, J., & McCann, M. (2015). "The Past, Present, and Future of Rights Scholarship." In *The Handbook of Law and Society*, edited by Austin Sarat & Patricia Ewick (pp. 367–381). Malden: Wiley Blackwell.

Dufour, A. (1974). "Droit et langage dans l'Ecole historique du droit." *Archives de Philosophie Du Droit*, 19, 115–180.

Duguit, L. (1889). "Le droit constitutionnel et la sociologie." *Revue Internationale de L'enseignement*, 28, 484–505.

(1922). *Le droit social, le droit individuel et les transformations de l'Etat: conférences faîtes à l'Ecole des Hautes Etudes Sociales*. Paris: F. Alcan.

Duguit, L., Fouillée, A., Demogue, R., & Charmont, J. (1916). *Modern French Legal Philosophy*. Boston: Boston Book Company.

Dulong, D. (1997). *Moderniser la politique. Aux origines de la Ve République*. Paris: L'Harmattan.

Dupré de Boulois, X., & Kaluszynski, M. (2011). *Le droit en révolution. Regard sur la critique du droit des années 1970 à nos jours*. Paris: LDGJ.

Dupret, B. (2006). *Droit et sciences sociales*. Paris: Armand Collin.

(2010). "Droit et sciences sociales. Pour un respécification praxéologique." *Droit et Société*, 75(2), 315–335.

Duran, P. (1993). "Piloter l'action publique avec ou sans le droit." *Politiques et Management Public*, 11(4), 24.

(1999). *Penser l'action publique*. Paris: LGDJ.

Durkheim, E. (1899). "Deux lois de l'évolution pénale." *L'Année Sociologique*, 4, 65–95.

(1963). *Les règles de la méthode sociologique*. Paris: Flammarion.

(1993). *La division du travail social*. Paris: PUF.

Duxbury, N. (1995). *Patterns of American Jurisprudence*. Oxford: Clarendon Press.

Dworkin, R. (1977). *Taking Rights Seriously*. Cambridge, MA: Harvard University Press.

(1985). *A Matter of Principle*. Cambridge, MA: Harvard University Press.

Edelman, L. (1992). "Legal Ambiguity and Symbolic Structures: Organization Mediation of Civil Rights Law." *American Journal of Sociology*, 97(6), 1531–1576.

(2004). "Rivers of Law and Contested Terrains: A Law and Society Approach to Economic Rationality." *Law and Society Review*, 38, 181–197.

(2016). *Working Law: Courts, Corporations, and Symbolic Civil Rights*. Chicago: University of Chicago Press.

Edelman, L., & Stryker, R. (2005). "A Sociological Approach to Law and the Economy." In *The Handbook of Economic Sociology*, edited by Neil Smelser & Richard Swedberg (pp. 526–551). Princeton: Princeton University Press.

Edelman, L., & Suchman, M. (1997). "The Legal Environment of Organizations." *Annual Review of Sociology*, 23, 479–515.

Edelman, M. (1971). *Politics as Symbolic Action: Mass Arousal and Quiescence*. Chicago: Markham.

Ehrlich, E. (1922). "The Sociology of Law." *Harvard Law Review*, 36, 94–109.

(1936). *Principles of Sociology of Law*. Cambridge, MA: Harvard University Press.

Elias, N. (1986). *El proceso de la civilización. Investigaciones psicogenéticas y sociogenéticas*. Mexico City: FCE.

Ellickson, R. (2000). "Trends in Legal Scholarship: A Statistical Study." *The Journal of Legal Studies*, 29, 517–543.

Ellmann, S. (1995). "Struggle and Legitimation." *Law and Social Inquiry*, 20(2), 340.

Emirbayer, M. (1997). "Manifesto for a Relational Sociology." *American Journal of Sociology*, 103(2), 281–237.

Encinas de Muñagorri, R., Hannette-Vauchez, S., Herrera, C. M., & Leclerc, O. (2016). *L'Analyse juridique de (x). Le droit parmi les sciences sociales*. Paris: Kimé.

Engel, D. (1999). "Making Connections: Law and Society Researchers and Their Subjects." *Law and Society Review*, 33(1), 3–16.

Engels, F. (1955). "The Housing Question." In *Karl Marx and Friedrich Engels Selected Works* (Vol. 1, pp. 546–634). Moscow: Foreign Languages Publishing House.

Epp, C. R. (1998). *The Rights Revolution*. Chicago: University of Chicago Press.

Epstein, L., & King, G. (2002). "Building an Infrastructure for Empirical Research." *Journal of Legal Education*, 53, 311–320.

Erlanger, H. (2005). "Organizations, Institutions, and the Story of Shmuel: Reflections on the 40th Anniversary of the Law and Society Association." *Law and Society Review*, 39(1), 1–10.

Erlanger, H., Garth, B., Larson, J., Mertz, E., Nourse, V., & Wilkins, D. (2005). "Foreword: Is It Time for a New Legal Realism?" *Wisconsin Law Review*, 2, 335–364.

Escalante, F. (2017) *Historia mínima del neoliberalismo*. México: Colegio de México.

Esquirol, J. (2008). "The Failed Law of Latin America." *The American Journal of Comparative Law*, 56, 75–124.

(2011). "Renewing Latin American Legal Studies." Institute for Global Law and Policy. Retrieved from www.harvardiglp.org/new-thinking-new-writing/interview-with-iglp-contributor-prof-jorge-esquirol.

Etienne, M. (1973). "The Ethics of Cause Lawyering: An Empirical Examination of Criminal Defense Lawyers as Cause Lawyers." *The Journal of Criminal Law and Criminology*, 95, 1195–1260.

Evan, W. (1980). "Law as an Instrument of Social Change." In *The Sociology of Law: A Social-Structural Perspective*, edited by William Evan (pp. 554–562). New York: W. Evan.

Ewald, F. (1986). *L'etat providence*. Paris. Grasset.

Ewick, P. (2006). "Consciousness as Ideology." In *The Blackwell Companion for the Sociology of Law*, edited by A. Sarat (pp. 80–94) Oxford: Blackwell Publishers.

(2008). "Embracing Eclecticism." *Studies in Law, Politics and Society*, 41, 1–18.

Ewick, P., & Sarat, A. (2015). "On the Emerging Maturity of Law and Society: An Introduction." In *The Handbook of Law and Society*, edited by Austin Sarat & Patricia Ewick (pp. xiii–xx). Malden: Wiley Blackwell.

Ewick, P., & Silbey, S. (1992). "Conformity, Contestation and Resistance: An Account of Legal Consciousness." *New England Law Review*, 26, 731–749.

(1998). *The Common Place of Law: Stories from Everyday Life*. Chicago: University of Chicago Press.

Ewick, P., Kagan, R. A., & Sarat, A. (Eds.). (1999). *Social Science, Social Policy, and the Law*. New York: Russel Sage Foundation.

Faria, J. E. (1988). *Eficácia jurídica e violência simbólica. O direito como instrumento de transformação social*. São Paulo: Universidade de São Paulo.

Felstiner, W. (2005). *Reorganisation and Resistance: Legal Professions Confront a Changing World*. Oxford: Hart Publishing.

Felstiner, W., & Sarat, A. (1992). "Enactments of Power: Negotiating Reality and Responsibility in Lawyer-Client Interaction." *Cornell Law Review*, 77, 1447–1498.

Felstiner, W., Abel, R., & Sarat, A. (1981). "The Emergence and Transformation of Disputes: Naming, Blaming, Claiming." *Law and Society Review*, 15, 631–654.

Fineman, M. (2015). "Feminist Legal Theory." *Journal of Gender, Social Policy and Law*, 13(1), 13–32.

Fioravanti, M. (1999). *Constituzione*. Bologne: Il Mulino.

(2001). *Constitución: de la antigüedad a nuestros días*. Madrid: Trotta.

Firestone, S. (1970). *The Dialectic of Sex: The Case for Feminist Revolution*. New York: William Morrow and Company, Inc.

Fisher, W., Horwitz, M., & Reed, T. (1993). *American Legal Realism*. New York: Oxford University Press.

Fiss, O. (1986). "The Death of the Law." *Cornell Law Review*, 72, 1–16.

Fitzpatrick, P. (1992). *The Mythology of Modern Law: Sociology of Law and Crime*. London: Routledge.

Fletcher, G. P. (1998). "Comparative Law as a Subversive Discipline." *American Journal of Comparative Law*, 46, 683–700.

Flood, J. (1983). *Barrister's Clerks: The Law's Middlemen*. Manchester: Manchester University Press.

Foucault, M. (1975). *Surveiller et Punir*. Paris: Gallimard.

(1980a). *Power/Knowledge: Selected Interviews and Other Writings*. New York: Pantheon.

(1980b). *La verdad y las formas jurídicas*. Barcelona: Gedisa.

Fourcade, M. (2009). *Economists and Societies: Discipline and Profession in the United States, Britain, and France, 1870 to 1990*. Princeton: Princeton University Press.

France, A. (1894). *Le Lys rouge*. Paris: Calmann-Lévy.

France, P., & Vachez, A. (2017). *Sphère publique, Intérêts privés*. Paris: Science Po.

François, B. (1996). *Naissance d'une constitution*. Paris: Presses de Sciences Po.

Fraser, N. (1998). "Social Justice in the Age of Identity Politics: Redistribution, Recognition, and Participation." In *The Tanner Lectures on Human Values*, edited by Grethe B. Peterson (Vol. 19, pp. 1–67). Salt Lake City: University of Utah Press.

(2000). *De la redistribución al reconocimiento. Dilemas de la justicia en la era postsocialista*. Madrid: The New Left.

Freeman, A. (1978). "Legitimizing Racial Discrimination through Antidiscrimination Law: A Critical Review of Supreme Court Doctrine." *Minnesota Law Review*, 62, 1049.

Freeman, M. (2001). *Introduction to Jurisprudence*. London: Sweet and Maxwell Ltd.

(2006). *Law and Sociology*. Oxford: Oxford University Press.

Freidson, E. (1984). "The Changing Nature of Professional Control." *Annual Review of Sociology*, 10, 1–20.

Friedman, L. (1985). *A History of American Law.* New York: Touchstone Book.

(1989). "Sociology of Law and Legal History." *Sociologia Del Diritto,* 16(2), 7–17.

(2005). "Coming to Age: Law and Society Enters an Exclusive Club." *Annual Reviews of Law and Social Science,* 1, 1–16.

Friedman, L., Pérez-Perdomo, R., & Gómez, M. (2012). *Law in Many Societies.* Stanford: Stanford University Press.

Friedrichs, D. (2006). *Law in Our Lives.* Los Angeles: Roxbury Publishing Company.

Frug, M. J. (1992). "A Postmodern Feminist Legal Manifesto." *Harvard Law Review,* 105, 1045.

Fuller, L. (1964). "The Morality of Law." *Harvard Law Review,* 78, 1281.

Gabel, J. (1975). *False Consciousness: An Essay on Reification.* New York: Harper & Row.

Gabel, P. (1980). "Reification in Legal Reasoning." *Research in Law and Sociology,* 3, 25–51.

(1984). "Roll Over Beethoven." *Stanford Law Review,* 36, 1–55.

Gabel, P., & Harris, P. (1983). "Building Power and Breaking Images: Critical Legal Theories and the Practice of Law." *New York University Review of Law and Social Change,* 11, 369–412.

Gaillet, A. (2016). "Contre le formalism de la 'jurisprudence de concepts': Philipp Heck et la 'jurisprudence des intérêts' en Allemagne." In *Critique social et critique sociologique du droit en Europe et aux Etats-Unis,* edited by Olivier Jouanjan & Élizabeth Zoller (pp. 195–222). Paris: Editions Panthéon-Assas.

Galanter, M. (1974). "Why the 'Haves' Come Out Ahead: Speculations on the Limits of Legal Change." *Law and Society Review,* 9, 1.

(1985). "The Legal Malaise, Or Justice Observed." *Law and Society Review,* 19, 537.

(2005). *Lowering the Bar: Lawyer Jokes and Legal Culture,* Madison: Univeristy of Wisconsin Press.

Galligan, D. (2007). *Law in Modern Society.* Oxford: Oxford University Press.

Ganne, Y. (2016). "La sociologie dans les doctrines contemporaines du droit aux Etats-Unis: entre héritage et renouveau." In *Critique social et critique sociologique du droit en Europe et aux Etats-Unis,* edited by Olivier Jouanjan & Élizabeth Zoller (pp. 273–308). Paris: Editions Panthéon-Assas.

Garapon, A. (1995). "The French Legal Culture and the Shock of Globalization." *Social and Legal Studies,* 4, 493–505.

(1996). *Les gardien de promesses. Justice et démocratie.* Paris: Odile Jacob.

(2007). "La place paradoxale de la culture juridique américaine dans la mondialisation." In *European Ways of Law: Towards a European Sociology of Law*, edited by David Nelken & Volkmar Gessner (pp. 71–92). Oxford: Hart Publishing.

(2010). *La raison du moindre Etat*. Paris: Odile Jacob.

Garapon, A., & Papadopoulos, I. (2003). *Juger en Amérique et en France*. Paris: Odile Jacob.

García-Villegas, M. (1993). *La eficacia simbólica del derecho*. Bogota: Uniandes.

——— (1997). "Las fronteras del derecho." *Pensamiento Jurídico*, 8, 25–50.

——— (2001). *Sociología Jurídica. Teoría y sociología del derecho en Estados Unidos*. Bogota: Universidad Nacional de Colombia.

——— (2002). "Law as Hope: Constitution and Social Change in Latin America." *Wisconsin International Law Journal*, 20, 353–370.

——— (2003a). "Symbolic Power without Symbolic Violence? Critical Legal Comments on Legal Consciousness Studies." *International Journal for the Semiotics of Law*, 16, 363–393.

——— (2003b). "Symbolic Power without Symbolic Violence." *Florida Law Review*, 55(1), 157–189.

——— (2004). "On Bourdieu's Legal Thought." *Droit et Société*, 1, 57–70.

——— (2006). "Comparative Sociology of Law: Legal Fields, Legal Scholarships, and Social Sciences in Europe ante The United States." *Law and Social Inquiry*, 31(2), 343–382.

——— (2009a). "Champs juridiques et sciences sociales en France et aux Etats-Unis." *L'Année Sociologique*, 59(1), 29–62.

——— (2010). *Sociología y crítica del derecho*. México City: Fontamara.

——— (2012a). "Constitucionalismo aspiracional: Derecho, democracia y cambio social en América Latina." *Análisis Político*, 25(75), 89–110.

——— (2012b). "La sociologie du droit de Jean Carbonier." In *Les Actes Jean Carbonier* (pp. 1112–1118). Paris: Le Senat.

——— (2014). *La eficacia simbólica del derecho. Sociología política del campo jurídico en América Latina*. Bogota: Random House.

——— (2015). *Les pouvoirs du droit*. Paris: LGDJ.

——— (2016). "A Comparison of Sociopolitical Legal Studies." *Annual Review of Law and Social Science*, 12, 25–44.

García-Villegas, M., & Ceballos, M.-A. (2016). *Democracia, justicia y sociedad. Diez años de investigación en Dejusticia*. Bogotá: Dejusticia.

García-Villegas, M., & Lejeune, A. (2011). "La sociologie du droit en France: de deux sociologies à la création d'un projet pluridisciplinaires." *Revue Interdisciplinaire D'études Juridiques*, 66, 1–139.

García-Villegas, M., & Saffón, M. P. (2011). *Crítica jurídica comparada*. Bogota: Universidad Nacional de Colombia.

García-Villegas, M., & Uprimny, R. (2006). *El control judicial de los estados de excepción en Colombia*. Bogota: Norma.

García-Villegas, M., Jaramillo, I. C., & Restrepo, E. (2007). "Estudio preliminar." In *Crítica jurídica. Teoría y sociología jurídica en los Estados Unidos*, edited by Mauricio García-Villegas, Isabel Cristina Jaramillo, & Esteban Restrepo (pp. 7–65). Bogota: Universidad Nacional and Universidad de los Andes.

Gardner, J. (1980). *Legal Imperialism*. Madison: University of Wisconsin Press.

Gargarella, R. (2005). *El derecho a la protesta*. Buenos Aires: Ad-Hoc.

(2011a). *200 años de constitucionalismo en América Latina. 1810–2010*. Buenos Aires: Ad-Hoc.

(2011b). "Pensando sobre la reforma constitucional en América Latina." In *El derecho en América Latina; un mapa para el pensamiento jurídico del siglo XXI*, edited by César Rodíguez Garavito (pp. 87–108). Buenos Aires: Siglo XXI.

(2014). "Latin American Constitutionalism: Social Rights and the 'Engine Room' of the Constitution." In *Law and Society in Latin America*, edited by César Rodríguez Garavito (pp. 83–92). New York: Routledge.

Garland, D. (1990). *Punishment and Modern Society*. Chicago: University of Chicago Press.

Garland, D., & Sparks, R. (2000). *Criminology and Social Theory*. Oxford: Oxford University Press.

Garth, B., & Dezalay, Y. (1996). *Dealing in Virtue: International Commercial Arbitration and the Construction of a Transnational Legal Order*. Chicago: University of Chicago Press.

Garth, B., & Sterling, J. (1998). "From Legal Realism to Law and Society: Reshaping Law for the Last Stages of the Social Activist State." *Law and Society Review, 22*(2), 409–471.

Garzón, I., & Botero, A. (2012). "El debate público sobre cuestiones éticas y religiosas en Colombia: algunas lecciones habermasianas." In *Tolerancia y derecho; un análisis de los derechos LGBTI*, edited by Andrés Botero (pp. 171–199). Medellín: Universidad de Medellín.

Gazzaniga, J. L. (1994). "Quand les avocats forment les juristes et la doctrine." *Droits, 20*, 31–41.

Geertz, C. (1983). *Local Knowledge: Further Essays in Interpretive Anthropology*. New York: Basic Books.

Geiger, T. (1969). *On Social Order and Mass Society*. Chicago: University of Chicago Press.

Gény, F. (1899). *Méthode d'interprétation et sources en droit privé positif*. Paris: A. Chevalier-Marescq.

Gessner, V., & Budak, A. C. (1998). *Emerging Legal Certainty: Empirical Studies on the Globalization of Law*. Dartmouth: Ashgate.

Gessner, V., & Nelken, D. (2007a). *European Ways of Law: Towards a European Sociology of Law*. Oxford: Hart Publishing.

(2007b). "Introduction: Studying European Ways of Law." In *European Ways of Law: Towards a European Sociology of Law*, edited by David Nelken & Volkmar Gessner (pp. 1–17). Oxford: Hart Publishing.

Giddens, A. (1984). *The Construction of Society: Outline of the Theory of Structuration*. Berkeley: University of California Press.

Gilligan, C. (1993). *In a Different Voice: Psychological Theory and Women's Development*. Cambridge, MA: Harvard University Press.

Gjerdingen, D. (1983). "The Coase Theorem and the Psychology of Common-Law Thought." *Southern California Law Review*, 56, 711.

Golder, B., & Fitzpatrick, P. (2009). *Foucault's Law*. New York: Routledge.

Gómez de la Serna, R. (2014). "Peor que el infierno." In *Antología de la literatura fantástica*, edited by Jorge Luis Borges, Adolfo Bioy Casares, & Silvina Ocampo (pp. 189–190). Buenos Aires: Sudamericana.

Gómez, L. (2004). "A Tale of Two Genres: On the Real and Ideal Links between Law and Society and Critical Race Theory." In *The Blackwell Companion to Law and Society*, edited by Austin Sarat (pp. 435–452). Malden: Blackwell Publishers.

(2012). "Looking for Race in All the Wrong Places." *Law and Society Review*, 46(2), 221–245.

Gordon, R. (1984). "Critical Legal Histories." *Stanford Law Review*, 57, 36.

(1988). "The Independence of Lawyers." *Boston University Law Review*, 68, 83.

(1998). "Some Critical Theories on Law and Their Critics." In *The Politics of Law: A Progressive Critique*, edited by David Kairys (3rd ed., pp. 641–662). New York: Basic Books.

Gordon, R. W. (1987). "Unfreezing Legal Reality: Critical Approaches to Law." *Florida State University Law Review*, 15, 195.

Gordon, R. W., & Horwitz, M. (Eds.). (2014). *Law, Society and History: Themes in the Legal Sociology and Legal History of Lawrence Friedman*. Cambridge: Cambridge University Press.

Grattet, R., & Jenness, V. (2008). "Transforming Symbolic Law into Organizational Action: Hate Crime Policy and Law Enforcement Practice." *Social Forces*, 87, 501.

Greenhouse, C. (2015). "Durkheim in the United States: 1900." In *Critique social et critique sociologique du droit en Europe et aux Etats-Unis*, edited by Olivier Jouanjan & Élizabeth Zoller (pp. 35–54). Paris: Editions Panthéon-Assas.

Griffiths, J. (2006). "The Idea of Sociology of Law and Its Relation to Law and Sociology." In *Law and Sociology: Current Legal Issues*, edited by Michael Freeman (Vol. 8, pp. 49–68). Oxford: Oxford University Press.

Grossman, J., Kritzer, H., & Macaulay, S. (2014). "Do the 'Haves' Still Come Out Ahead?" In *The Law and Society Reader II*, edited by Erik Larson & Patrick Schmidt (pp. 13–15). New York: New York University Press.

Guibentif, P. (2002). "The Sociology of Law as a Sub-Discipline of Sociology." *Portuguese Journal of Social Sciences*, 1(3), 175–184.

(2010). *Foucault, Luhmann, Habermas, Bourdieu; une génération repense le droit*. Paris: LGDJ.

Gupta, A. (1995). "Blurred Boundaries: The Discourse of Corruption, the Culture of Politics, and the Imagined State." *American Ethnologist, 22*(2), 375–402.

Gurr, T. (1970). *Why Men Rebel*. Princeton: Princeton University Press.

Gurvitch, G. (1931). *L'idée du droit social; Notion et système du droit social: Histoire doctrinale depuis le XVIIIe siècle jusqu'à la fin du XIXe siècle*. Paris: Sirey.

(1935). *L'Expérience juridique et la philosophie pluraliste du droit*. Paris: A. Pedone.

(1940). *Éléments de sociologie juridique*. Paris: Aubier.

(1942). *Sociology of Law*. New York: Philosophical Library.

Gusfield, J. (1963). *Symbolic Crusade: Status Politics and the American Temperance Movement*. Urbana: University of Illinois Press.

Habermas, J. (1998). *Facticidad y validez. Sobre el derecho y el Estado democrático de derecho en términos de teoría del discurso*. Madrid: Trotta.

Hall, S. (1996). "The Problem of Ideology: Marxism without Guarantees." In *Stuart Hall: Critical Dialogues in Cultural Studies*, edited by David Morley & Kuan-Hsing Chen (pp. 24–45). New York: Routledge.

Halley, J. E. (1993). "Reasoning about Sodomy: Act and Identity in and after Bowers v. Hardwick." *Virginia Law Review, 79*, 1721.

Halpérin, J. L. (Ed.). (2011a). *Paris, capital juridique (1804–1950). Etude de socio-histoire sur la faculté de droit de Paris*. Paris: Editions Rue d'Ulm.

(2011b). *Un gouvernement de professeurs: réalité ou illusion?* Paris: Edition Rue d'Ulm.

(2015). *L'indépendance de l'avocat en France au XIXe et XXe siècle*. In *L'indépendence des avocats: le long chemin d'une liberté*, edited by Louis Assier-Andrieu. Paris: Dalloz.

Handler, J. (1992). "Postmodernism, Protest and the New Social Movements." *Law and Society Review, 26*, 697–732.

Handler, J., & Hasenfeld, Y. (2007). *Blame Welfare, Ignore Poverty and Inequality*. Cambridge: Cambridge University Press.

Haney López, I. F. (1994). "The Social Construction of Race: Some Observations on Illusion, Fabrication, and Choice." *Harvard Civil Rights-Civil Liberties Law Review, 29*, 1.

Harari, Y. N. (2015). *Sapiens: A Brief History of Humankind*. New York: HarperCollins.

Harris, A. (1990). "Race and Essentialism in Feminist Legal Theory." *Stanford Law Review, 42*(3), 481–616.

Harris, C. I. (1993). "Whiteness as Property." *Harvard Law Review, 106*, 1709–1791.

Harrison, J. (2003). *Law and Economics*. St. Paul: Thomson West.

Hart, H. L. A. (1961). *The Concept of Law*. Oxford: Clarendon Press.

(1970). "Jhering's Heaven of Concepts and Modern Analytical Jurisprudence." In *Essays in Jurisprudence and Philosophy*. Oxford: Oxford University Press.

(1983). "American Jurisprudence through English Eyes: The Nightmare and the Noble Dream." In *Essays in Jurisprudence and Philosophy*, edited by H. L. A. Hart (pp. 123–144). Oxford: Oxford University Press.

Hauriou, M. (1910). *Principes du droit publique*. Paris: Larose et Ténin.

Hawkins, K. (2003). *Law as Last Resort*. Oxford: Oxford University Press.

Heinz, J. P., & Laumann, E. O. (1982). *Chicago Lawyers: The Social Structure of the Bar*. New York: Russel Sage Foundation.

Heinz, J., Laumann, E., Nelson, R., & Michelson, E. (2014). "The Changing Character of Lawyers' Work: Chicago in 1975 and 1995." In *The Law and Society Reader II*, edited by Erik Larson & Patrick Schmidt (pp. 141–146). New York: New York University Press.

Heise, M. (2002). "The Past, Present, and Future of Empirical and Experimental Legal Scholarship: Judicial Decisionmaking as a Case Study." *University of Illinois Law Review*, 4, 819–850.

Held, D., & Roger, C. (2013). *Global Governance at Risk*. Cambridge: Polity Press.

Herget, J., & Wallace, S. (1987). "The German Free Law Movement at the Source of American Legal Realism." *Virginia Law Review*, 73(2), 399–455.

Herrera, C. M. (2002). *Les juristes de gauche sous la république de Weimar*. Paris: Kimé.

(2003a). *Par le droit, au-delà du droit. Textes sur le socialisme juridique*. Paris: Kemé.

(2003b). *Droit et Gauche; pour une identification*. Quebec: Les Press de l'Université de Laval.

(2003c). *Les juristes face au politique. Le droit, la gauche, la doctrine sous la III République*. Paris: Editions Kimé.

(2016). "Droits sociaux et politiques chez Gurvitch." *Droit et Société*, 94, 513–524.

Herrera, C. M., & Le Pillouer, A. (Eds.). (2012). *Comment écrit-on l'histoire constitutionnelle?* Paris: Kimé.

Hespanha, A. M. (2005). *Cultura Jurídica Europeia. Síntese de um Milênio*. Florianópolis: Boiteux.

(2011). "Taking the History Seriously: The Exégetas as Themselves Tell It." Presented at the V Congreso Brasilero de Historia del derecho, Curitiba, Brasil.

Hesselink, M. (2001). *The New European Legal Culture*. Deventer: Kluwer.

Heurtin, J., & Molfessis, N. (2006). *La sociologie du Droit de Max Weber*. Paris: Dalloz.

Hirschl, R. (2004). *Towards Juristocracy: The Origins and Consequences of the New Constitutionalism*. Cambridge, MA: Harvard University Press.

Holger, S. (2015). "Empirical Comparative Law." *Annual Review of Law and Social Sciences*, 11, 131–153.

Holmes, O. W. (1881). *The Common Law*. Boston: Little Brown and Company.

(1897). "The Path of the Law." *Harvard Law Review*, 10, 457.

(1920). "The Path of the Law." In *Collected Legal Papers*, edited by O. W. Holmes (pp. 167–202). New York: Harcourt, Brace and Company.

Holston, J. (2008). *Insurgent Citizenship: Disjunctions of Democracy and Modernity in Brazil*. Princeton: Princeton University Press.

Honneth, A., & Joas, H. (1988) *Social Action and Human Nature*. Cambridge: Cambridge University Press.

Horowitz, I. (1993). *The Decomposition of Sociology*. New York: Oxford University Press.

Horwitz, M. J. (1992). *The Transformation of American Law: 1870–1960*. New York: Oxford University Press.

Hoyos, I. M. (2005). "Entre el delito del aborto y el derecho a abortar." In *La Constitucionalización de Las Falacias. Antecedentes a una sentencia*, edited by Ilva Myriam Hoyos (pp. 4–114). Bogota: Temis.

Hunt, A. (1978). *The Sociological Movement in Law*. Philadelphia: Temple University Press.

(1982). "Emile Durkheim: Towards a Sociology of Law." In *Marxism and Law*, edited by Piers Beirne and Richard Quinney (pp. 27–43). New York: John Wiley & Sons.

(1985). "The Ideology of Law: Advances and Problems in Recent Applications of the Concept of Ideology to the Analysis of Law." *Law and Society Review*, 11, 19.

(1990). "The Big Fear: Law Confronts Postmodernism." *McGill Law Journal*, 35(3), 507–540.

(1993). *Explorations in Law and Society: Toward a Constitutive Theory of Law*. London: Routledge.

(1994). *Foucault and Law: Toward a Sociology of Law and Governance*. London: Pluto Press.

Hunt, E., & Colander, D. (2013). *Social Science: An Introduction to the Study of Society*. New York: Pearson Higher.

Hurst, J. W. (1956). *Law and the Conditions of Freedom in the Nineteenth-Century United States*. Madison: University of Wisconsin Press.

Hutchinson, A. (1992). "Doing the Right Thing? Toward a Postmodern Politics." *Law and Society Review*, 26, 773–787.

(1989). *Critical Legal Studies*. Totowa: Rowman & Littlefield.

Hutchinson, D. (2003). "Centennial Tribute Essay: Elements of the Law." *University of Chicago Law Review*, 70, 141.

Hutter, B. (1988). *The Reasonable Arm of the Law?* Oxford: Clarendon Press.

Iglesias, E., & Valdés, F. (2001). "LatCrit at Five: Institutionalizing a Post-subordination Future." *Denver University Law Review*, 78, 1249.

Israël, L. (2001). "Usages militants du droit dans l'arène judiciaire : le cause lawyering." *Droit et Société*, 3(49), 793–824.

(2005). *Robes noires, années sombres. Avocats et magistrats en résistance pendant la Seconde Guerre mondiale.* Paris: Fayard.

(2008a). "Question(s) de méthodes. Se saisir du droit en sociologie." *Droit et Société*, 69–70, 381–395.

Israel, L. (2008b). "Présentation; dossier: Quelles méthodes pour la sociologie du droit et de la justice." *Droit et Société*, 2(69–70), 325–329.

Israël, L. (2009a). *L'Arme du droit.* Paris: Presses de SciencesPo.

(2009b). "Résister par le droit? Avocats et magistrats dans la Résistance (1941–1944)." *L'Année Sociologique*, 59(1), 149–176.

(2012a). "Conseil de sociologues. Bruno Latour et Dominique Sshnapper face au droit." *Genèses*, 87(2), 136–152.

(2012b). "Le rôle du droit dans la formation des élites." *Clio@themis. Revue Electronique D'histoire Du Droit*, 5, 1–9.

(2013). "Legalise It! The Rising Place of Law in French Sociology." *International Journal of Law in Context*, 9(2), 262–278.

Israël, L., & Mouralis, G. (2005). "Les magistrats, le droit positif et la morale. Usages sociaux du positivisme et du naturalisme juridique en France sous Vichy en Allemagne depuis 1945." In *Sur la portée sociale du droit*, edited by Liora Israël, Guillaume Sacriste, Antoine Vauchez, & Laurent Willemez (pp. 61–78). Paris: PUF–CURAPP.

Israël, L., & Pelisse, J. (2004). "Quelques éléments sur les conditions d'une importation (Note liminaire à la traduction du texte de S. Silbey et P. Ewick)." *Terrains & Travaux*, 1(6), 101–111.

Israël, L., & Vanneuville, R. (2014). "Enquêter sur la formation au droit en France : l'exemple des formations extra-universitaires." *Revue Interdisciplinaire D'Etudes Juridiques*, 72, 141–162.

(2017). "Legal Training and the Reshaping of French Elite: Lessons from an Ethnography of Law Classes in Two French Elite Higher Education Institutions." *Journal of Education and Work*, 30(2), 156–167.

Israël, L., Sacriste, G., Vauchez, A., & Willemez, L. (2005a). "Introduction." In *Les usages sociaux du droit*, edited by Danièle Lochak (pp. 10–18). Paris: PUF.

(Eds.). (2005b). *Sur la portée sociale du droit.* Paris: PUF.

Jaggar, A. (1983). *Feminist Politics and Human Nature.* Lanham: Rowman & Littlefield.

Jamin, C. (2012). *La cuisine du droit.* Paris: Lextenso Éditions.

Jaramillo, I. C. (2010). "The Social Approach to Family Law: Some Conclusions from the Canonical Family Law Treatises of Latin America." *American Journal of Comparative Law*, 58(4), 843.

Jaramillo, I. C., & Alfonso, T. (2008). *Mujeres, cortes y medios: la reforma judicial del aborto*. Bogota: Siglo del Hombre – Uniandes.

Jaurès, J. (1964). "Discours à la jeunesse." In *L'esprit du socialisme: Six discours et études*, edited by Jean Jaurès (pp. 55–67). Paris: Gonthier.

Jeammaud, A. (1987). *La crítica jurídica en Francia*. Puebla: Universidad Autónoma de Puebla.

Jellinek, G. (1981). *Teoría General del Estado*. Buenos Aires: Albatros.

Jenness, V., & Smyth, M. (2011). "The Passage and Implementation of the Prison Rape Elimination Act: Legal Endogeneity and the Uncertain Road from Symbolic Law to Instrumental Effects." *Stanford Law and Policy Review*, 22, 489–527.

Jestaz, P., & Jamin, C. (2004). *La doctrine*. Paris: Dalloz.

Johnson, S. (1751). "The Rambler N° 110." The Rambler, (110), 164–168. London.

Johnston, L. (1992). *The Rebirth of Private Policing*. New York: Routledge.

Josserand, L. (1927). *De l'esprit des droits et de leur relativité*. Paris: Dalloz.

Jouanjan, O. (2016a). "Le souci du social: Le 'moment 1900' de la doctrine et de la pratique juridiques." In *Critique social et critique sociologique du droit en Europe et aux Etats-Unis*, edited by Olivier Jouanjan & Élizabeth Zoller (pp. 134–222). Paris: Editions Panthéon-Assas.

(2016b). "Pourquoi des jurists en temps de détresse?" In *Critique social et critique sociologique du droit en Europe et aux Etats-Unis*, edited by Olivier Jouanjan & Élizabeth Zoller (pp. 223–251). Paris: Editions Panthéon-Assas.

Jouanjan, O., & Zoller, E. (2016). *Critique social et critique sociologique du droit en Europe et aux Etats-Unis*. Paris: Editions Pantéon-Assas.

Junqueira, E. (2001). *Através do Espelho. Ensaios de sociologia do direito*. Rio de Janeiro: Letracapital.

Kagan, R. A. (2001). *Adversarial Legalism: The American Way of Law*. Cambridge, MA: Harvard University Press.

(2007). "American and European Ways of Law: Six Entrenched Differences." In *European Ways of Law: Towards a European Sociology of Law*, edited by David Nelken & Volkmar Gessner (pp. 41–70). Oxford: Hart Publishing.

Kagan, R. A., Krygier, M., & Winston, K. (Eds.). (2002). *Legality and Community: On the Intellectual Legacy of Philip Selznick*. New York: Rowman & Littlefield.

Kahn, P. (1999). *The Cultural Study of Law: Reconstructing Legal Scholarship*. Chicago: Chicago University Press.

Kairys, D. (1998). *The Politics of Law: A Progressive Critique*. New York: Basic Books.

Kalman, L. (1996). *Strange Career of Legal Liberalism*. New Haven: Yale University Press.

Kanowitz, L. (1963). *Women and the Law: The Unfinished Revolution*. Albuquerque: University of New Mexico Press.

Kant de Lima, R. (1995). *The Brazilian Puzzle: Culture on the Boundaries of the Western World*. New York: Columbia University Press.

Kant, E. (1797). *Métaphysique des Mœurs*. Paris: Vrin.

Karpik, L. (1989). "Le désintéressement." *Annales. Economie, Société, Civilisations*, 3, 733–751.

(1995). *Les avocats. Entre l'Etat, le public et le marché. XIIIe-XXe siècle*. Paris: Gallimard.

Karpik, L., Halliday, T., & Feeley, M. (2007). *Fighting for Political Freedom: Comparative Studies of the Legal Complex for Political Change*. Oxford: Hart Publishing.

Kay, H. (1972). "Making Marriage and Divorce Safe for Women." *California Law Review*, 60, 1683.

Keck, M., & Sikkink, K. (1998). *Activists beyond Borders: Advocacy Networks in International Politics*. Ithaca: Cornell University Press.

Keck, T. (2014). "Beyond Backlash: Assessing the Impact of Judicial Decisions on LGBT Rights." In *The Law and Society Reader II*, edited by Erick Larson & Patrick Schmidt (pp. 62–70). New York: New York University Press.

Kelman, M. (1987). *A Guide to Critical Legal Studies*. Cambridge, MA: Harvard University Press.

Kelsall, M. S. (2009). "Symbolic, Shambolic or Simply Sui Generis? Reflections from the Field on Cambodia's Extraordinary Chambers." *Law in Context*, 27(1), 154.

Kelsen, H. (1997). *Théorie générale du droit et de l'Etat*. Brussels: Bruylant.

Kennedy, D. (1976). "Form and Substance in Private Law Adjudication." *Harvard Law Review*, 89, 1685.

(1979). "The Structure of Blackstone's Commentaries." *Buffalo Law Review*, 28, 205.

(1981). "Critical Labor Law Theory: A Comment." *Industrial Relations Law Journal*, 4, 503.

(1995). "An Autumn Weekend." In *After Identity: A Reader on Law and Culture*, edited by Dan Danielsen & Karen Engle (pp. 191–209). New York: Routledge.

(1997). *A Critique of Adjudication*. Cambridge, MA: Harvard University Press.

(1998). "Law and Economics from the Perspective of Critical Legal Studies." In *The New Palgrave Dictionary of Economics and the Law*, edited by Peter Newman (pp. 465–474). London: Palgrave Macmillan.

(2002). "The International Human Rights Movement: Part of the Problem?" *Harvard Human Rights Journal*, 15, 101–125.

(2006). "The Globalization of Law and Legal Thought: 1859–2000." In *The New Law and Economic Development*, edited by David Trubek & Alvaro Santos (pp. 19–73). Cambridge: Cambridge University Press.

Kessler, L. (2011). "Feminism for Everyone." *Seattle University Law Review*, 34, 679.

King, D., & Le Galès, P. (2017). *Reconfiguring European States in Crisis*. Oxford: Oxford University Press.

Kornhauser, L. (2008). *The Economic Analysis of Law*. Redwood City: Stanford University Press.

Kourilsky, C. (1998). *Socialisation juridique et conscience du droit*. Paris: LGDJ.

Kramer, L. (2004). *The People Themselves: Popular Constitutionalism and Judicial Review*. Oxford: Oxford University Press.

Krieger, L. (1998). "Civil Rights Perestroika: Intergroup Relations after Affirmative Action." *California Law Review*, 86, 1251.

Krishnan, J. (2006). "Lawyering for a Cause and Experiences from Abroad." *California Law Review*, 94(2), 575–616.

Krygier, M. (2016). "The Rule of Law: Past, Present and Two Possible Futures." *Annual Review of Law and Social Science*, 12, 199–229.

Kuty, O., & Schoenaers, F. (2010). "La modernisation de la justice." *La Revue Nouvelle*, 1, 28–30.

Laclau, E., & Mouffle, C. (1985). *Hegemony and Socialist Strategy: Towards a Radical Democratic Politics*. London: Verso.

Lambert, E. (1928). *Etudes de droit commun législatif*. Paris: V. Giard & E. Brière.

Lamont, M. (2012). "How Has Bourdieu Been Good to Think With?" *Sociological Forum*, 22, 228–237.

Lampert, R. (2010). "A Personal Odyssey toward a Theme: Race and Equality in the United States: 1948–2009." *Law and Society Review*, 44(3/4), 432–462.

Lane, P. (1998). "Ecofeminism Meets Criminology." *Theoretical Criminology*, 2, 235–248.

Larson, E., & Schmidt, P. (Eds.). (2014). *The Law and Society Reader II*. New York: New York University Press.

Larson, M. S. (1977). *The Rise of Professionalism: A Sociological Analysis*. Berkeley: University of California Press.

Lascoumes, P. (1990). "Normes juridiques et mise en œuvre des politiques publiques." *L'Année Sociologique*, 40, 43–71.

(1991). "Le droit comme science sociale. La place de E. Durkheim, dans les débats entre juristes et sociologues à la charnière des deux derniers siècles (1870–1914)." In *Normes juridiques et régulation sociale*, edited by François Chazel & Jacques Comaille (pp. 39–49). Paris: LDGJ.

(1995). *Actualité de Max Weber pour la sociologie du droit.* Paris: LDGJ.

Lascoumes, P., & Galès, P. (2005). *Gouverner par les instruments.* Paris: Press de Science Po.

Lascoumes, P., & Le Bourhis, J. P. (1996). "Des 'passe-droits' aux passes du droit. La mise en œuvre sociojuridique de l'action publique." *Droit et Société, 32,* 51–73.

Lascoumes, P., & Nagels, C. (2014). *Sociologie des élites délinquantes. De la criminalité en col blanc à la corruption politique.* Paris: Armand Colin.

Lascoumes, P., & Serverin, E. (1986). "Théories et pratiques de l'effectivité du droit." *Droit et Société, 2*(1), 127–250.

Lassalle, F. (1964). *¿Qué es una constitución?* Buenos Aires: Siglo XXI.

Lasswell, H., & McDougal, M. (1943). "Legal Education and Public Policy: Professional Training in the Public Interest." *Yale Law Journal, 53,* 203.

Latour, B. (2004). *La fabrique du droit. Une ethnographie du Conseil d'Etat.* Paris: La Découverte.

(2010). *The Making of Law.* Cambridge: Polity Press.

Latour, B., & Woolgar, S. (1986). *Laboratory Life: The Construction of Scientific Facts.* Princeton: Princeton University Press.

Le Beguec, G. (2003). *La République des avocats.* Paris: Armand Collin.

Le Goff, J. (2016). "Poursuivre le débat avec George Gurvitch." *Droit et Société, 94,* 495–502.

Le Roy, E. (1978). "Pour une anthropologie du Droit." *Revue Interdisciplinaire D'Etudes Juridiques, 1,* 71–100.

Ledford, K. F. (1996). *From General Estate to Special Interest: German Lawyers 1878–1933.* Cambridge: Cambridge University Press.

Legendre, P. (1974). *L'amour du censeur. Essai sur l'ordre dogmatique.* Paris: Seuil.

(1995). "Qui dit légiste, dit loi et pouvoir. Entretien avec Pierre Legendre." *Politix, 32*(8), 23–44.

Legrand, P. (1999). *Le droit comparé.* Paris: PUF.

Legrand, P., & Munday, R. (Eds.). (2003). *Comparative Legal Studies: Traditions and Transitions.* Cambridge: Cambridge University Press.

Leiter, B. (2003). "In Praise of Realism (and against 'Nonsense Jurisprudence')." *University of Texas Law Review, 1,* 820.

Lejeune, A. (2011a). *Le droit au Droit. Les juristes et la question sociale en France.* Paris: Editions des Archives Contemporaines.

(2011b). "Les professionnels du droit comme acteurs du politique. Revue critique de la littérature nord-américaine et enjeux pour une importation en Europe continentale." *Sociologie Du Travail, 53*(2), 216–233.

Lemaitre, J. (2008). "Legal Fetishism: Law, Violence, and Social Movements in Colombia." *Revista jurídica de la Universidad de Puerto Rico, 77*(2), 493–511.

(2009). *El derecho como conjuro. Fetichismo legal, violencia y movimientos sociales.* Bogotá: Universidad de los Andes.

(2015). "Law and Globalism: Law without the State as Law without Violence." In *The Handbook of Law and Society,* edited by A. Sarat & P. Ewick (pp. 433–445). Malden: Wiley Blackwell.

Lempert, R. (2010). "A Personal Odyssey toward a Theme: Race and Equality in the United States: 1948–2009." *Law and Society Review,* 44(3/4), 432–462.

Lenoble, J., & Ost, F. (1980). *Droit, Mythe et raison.* Brussels: Facultés Universitaires de Saint-Louis.

Lenoir, R. (2003). *Généalogie de la morale familiale.* Paris: Seuil.

Lerner, M. (1973). "Constitution and Court as Symbols." *The Yale Law Journal,* 46, 1290–1319.

Levine, F. (1990). "Goose Bumps and 'the Search for Signs of Intelligence Life' in Sociolegal Studies." *Law and Society Review,* 24(1), 7–34.

Levitsky, S. (2015). "Law and Social Movements: Old Debates and New Directions." In *The Handbook of Law and Society,* edited by Austin Sarat & Patricia Ewick (pp. 382–398). Malden: Wiley Blackwell.

Lévy, E. (1909). *Capital et travail.* Paris: Parti Socialiste.

Lévy-Bruhl, H. (1955). *Aspects sociologiques du droit.* Paris: Rivière.

Littleton, C. (1987). "Reconstructing Sexual Equality." *California Law Review,* 75, 1279.

Llewellyn, K. (1930). "A Realistic Jurisprudence: The Next Step." *Columbia Law Review,* 30(4), 431–465.

(1994). "Una teoría del derecho realista: el siguiente paso." In *El ámbito de lo jurídico,* edited by P. Casanovas & José Juan Moreso (pp. 244–293). Barcelona: Crítica.

Lochak, D. (1989a). "La doctrine sous Vichy ou les mésaventures du positivisme." In *Les usages sociaux du droit,* edited by Danièle Lochak (pp. 252–285). Paris: PUF–CURAPP.

(1989b). *Les usages sociaux du droit.* Paris: PUF.

Locke, J. (1946). *The Second Treatise of Civil Government and a Letter Concerning Toleration.* Oxford: B. Blackwell.

Loiselle, M. (2000). "L'analyse du discours de la doctrine juridique; l'articulation de perspectives interne et externe." In *Les méthodes au concret. Démarches, formes de l'expérience et terrains d'investigation en science politique,* edited by Myriam Bachir (p. 188). Paris: PUF.

Lopés, J. R. de L., & Freitas, R. (2015). "Law and Society in Brazil at the Crossroads: A Review." *Annual Reviews of Law and Social Science,* 11, 91–103.

López, D. (2004). *Teoría impura del derecho. La transformación de la cultura jurídica latinoamericana.* Bogota: Legis.

Lovell, G., McCann, M., & Taylor, K. (2016). "Covering Legal Mobilization: A Bottom-Up Analysis of *Wards Cove v. Atonio.*" *Law and Social Inquiry*, *41*, 61–99.

Luhmann, N. (1983). *Sistema jurídico y dogmática jurídica.* Madrid: Centro de Estudios Constitucionales.

(1985). *A Sociological Theory of Law.* London: Routledge and Kegan Paul.

Macaulay, S. (1979). "Lawyers and Consumer Protection Law." *Law and Society Review*, *14*, 115.

(1984). "Law and Behavioral Science: Is There any There?" *Law and Policy*, *6*, 149–187.

(1987). "Images of Law in Everyday Life: The Lessons of School, Entertainment, and Spectator Sports." *Law and Society Review*, *21*(2), 185–218.

Macaulay, S., Friedman, L., & Mertz, E. (2007). *Law in Action.* New York: Foundation Press.

MacCoun, R. (1993). "Drugs and the Law: A Psychological Analysis of Drug Prohibition." *Psychological Bulletin*, *113*(3), 497–512.

MacDonald, G. (2002a). *Social Context and Social Location in the Sociology of Law.* Peterborough: Broadview Press.

(2002b). "Theory and the Canon: How the Sociology of Law Is Organized." In *Social Context and Social Location in the Sociology of Law*, edited by Gayle MacDonald (pp. 13–22). Peterborough: Broadview Press.

MacKenzie, D. (2002). "Reducing the Criminal Activities of Known Offenders and Delinquents: Crime Prevention in the Courts and Corrections." In *S Evidence-Based Crime Prevention*, edited by Lawrence Sherman, David Farrington, B. Welsh, & Doris MacKenzie (pp. 330–404). London: Routledge.

MacKinnon, C. A. (1982). "Feminism, Marxism, Method, and State: An Agenda for Theory." *Signs*, *7*, 515–544.

(1987). *Feminism Unmodified: Discourses on Life and Law.* Cambridge, MA: Harvard University Press.

(1989). *Toward a Feminist Theory of the State.* Cambridge, MA: Harvard University Press.

(1991). "From Practice to Theory, or What Is a White Woman Anyway?" *Yale Law Journal and Feminism*, *4*(1), 13–22.

Madsen, M., & Dezalay, Y. (2002). "The Power of the Legal Field: Pierre Bourdieu and the Law." In *An Introduction to Law and Social Theory*, edited by Reza Banakar & Max Travers (pp. 189–207). Oxford: Hart Publishing.

Maine, H. J. S. (1861). *Ancient Law: Its Connection with the Early History of Society and Its Relations to Modern Ideas.* London: John Murray.

Mannheim, K. (1936). *Ideology and Utopia.* New York: Harcourt, Brace.

March, J. G., & Olsen, J. P. (1989). *Rediscovering Institutions: The Organizational Basis of Politics.* New York: Free Press.

Marchis, L. (1914). "Une visite aux universités du centre des Etats Unies." *Revue Internationale de L'enseignement*, 68, 7.

Marshall, A., & Crocker Hale, D. (2014). "Cause Lawyering." *Annual Review of Law and Social Science*, 10, 301–320.

Marx, K. (1842). "Debates on Law on Thefts of Wood." *Rheinische Zeitung*, issues 298, 300, 303, 305, and 307.

Marx, K., & Engels, F. (2000). *Manifiesto Comunista*. Buenos Aires: Ediciones Elaleph.

Matteucci, N. (1988). *Organización del poder y libertad*. Madrid: Trotta.

McAdam, D. (1982). *Political Process and the Development of Black Insurgency, 1930–1970*. Chicago: University of Chicago Press.

McAdam, D., McCarthy, J., & Zald, M. (1996). *Comparative Perspectives on Social Movements: Political Opportunities, Mobilizing Structures and Cultural Framing*. Cambridge: Cambridge University Press.

McCann, M. (1992). "Resistance, Reconstruction, and Romance in Legal Scholarship." *Law and Society Review*, 26, 733–749.

(1994). *Rights at Work: Pay Equity Reform and the Politics of Legal Mobilization*. Chicago: University of Chicago Press.

(2004). "Law and Social Movements." In *The Blackwell Companion to Law and Society*, edited by Austin Sarat (pp. 506–522). Malden: Blackwell Publishing.

(2006). "Law and Social Movements: Contemporary Perspectives." *Annual Review of Law and Social Science*, 2, 17–38.

McCann, M., & March, T. (1995). "Law and Everyday Forms of Resistance: A Socio-Political Assessment." In *Studies in Law, Politics, and Society* (15), edited by Austin Sarat (pp. 207–236). London: JAI Press.

McCann, M., & Silverstein, H. (1998). "Rethinking Law's 'Allurements': A Relational Analysis of Social Movements Lawyers in the United States." In *Cause Lawyering: Political Commitment and Professional Responsibilities*, edited by Austin Sarat & Stuart Scheingold (pp. 261–292). New York: Oxford University Press.

McCloskey, D. (1988). "The Rhetoric of Law and Economics." *Michigan Law Review*, 86(4), 752–767.

Mead, G. (1934). *Mind, Self and Society from the Standpoint of a Social Behaviorist*. Chicago: University of Chicago Press.

Mekki, M. (2013). "L'ouverture disciplinaire et la théorie sociologique du droit : un approche renouvelée de l'objet droit?" In *Droit, arts, sciences humaines et sociales: (dé)passer les fontières disciplinaires*, edited by Sandrine Chassagnard-Pinet, Pierre Lemay, Céline Regulski, & Dorothée Simonneau (pp. 111–142). Paris: LDGJ.

Menger, A. (1899). *The Right to the Whole Produce of Labour: The Origin and Development of the Theory of Labour's Claim to the Whole Product of Industry*. London: Macmillan.

Merry, S. (1985). "Concepts of Law and Justice among Americans: Ideology and Culture." *Legal Studies Forum*, 9, 59–70.

(1988). "Legal Pluralism." *Law and Society Review*, 22(5), 869–896.

(2001). "Spatial Governmentality and the New Urban Social Order: Controlling Gender Violence through Law." *American Anthropologist*, 103(1), 16–29.

Merry, S. E. (1990). *Getting Justice and Getting Even: Legal Consciousness among Working-Class Americans*. Chicago: University of Chicago Press.

(1995). "Resistance and the Cultural Power of Law." *Law and Society*, 29, 11–26.

(2014). "Rights, Religion and Community: Approaches to Violence against Women in the Context of Globalization." In *The Law and Society Reader II*, edited by Erik Larson & Patrick Schmidt (pp. 313–320). New York: New York University Press.

Merryman, J. H. (1975). "Legal Education There and Here: A Comparison." *Stanford Law Review*, 27(3), 859–878.

(1994). *The Civil Law Tradition: Europe, Latin America, and East Asia*. Charlottesville: Michie Co.

Mertz, E. (1994). "Conclusion: A New Social Constructionism for Sociolegal Studies." *Law and Society Review*, 28(5), 1243–1266.

(2007). *The Language of the Law School: Learning to "Think Like a Lawyer."* London: Oxford University Press.

(Ed.). (2008). *The Role of Social Science in Law*. Aldershot: Ashgate.

(2014). "A New Social Constructionism for Social Studies." In *The Law and Society Reader II*, edited by Eric Larson & Patrick Schmidt (pp. 176–181). New York: New York University Press.

Mezey, N. (2015). "Mapping a Cultural Studies of Law." In *The Handbook of Law and Society*, edited by Austin Sarat & Patricia Ewick (pp. 39–55). Malden: Wiley Blackwell.

Miaille, M. (1976). *Une Introduction Critique au Droit*. Paris: Maspero.

(1985). *El Estado del Derecho*. Puebla: Universidad Autónoma de Puebla.

Migdal, J. S. (2001). *State in Society: Studying How States and Societies Transform and Constitute One Another*. Cambridge: Cambridge University Press.

(2011). "El Estado en la sociedad. Una nueva definición del Estado. (Para superar el estrecho mundo del rigor)." In *Estados Fuertes, Estados débiles*, edited by Joel Samuel Migdal (pp. 15–66). Mexico City: FCE.

Milet, M. (2000). *Les professeurs de droits citoyens*. Paris: Paris II.

(2001). "L'autonomisation d'une discipline. La création de l'agrégation de science politique." *Revue D'histoire de Sciences Humaines*, 4, 95–116.

(2012). "Les publicistes français et la CED, controverses doctrinal et engagement civique." *Relations Internationales*, 149(1), 101–113.

Miller, R., & Sarat, A. (1980). "Grievances, Claims, and Disputes: Assessing the Adversary Culture." *Law and Society Review*, 15, 525–566.

Minda, G. (1995). *Postmodern Legal Movements: Law and Jurisprudence at Century's End*. New York: New York University Press.

Minow, M. (1987). "Interpreting Rights: An Essay for Robert Cover." *Yale Law Journal*, 96(8), 1860–1915.

Moore, W. J., & Newman, R. (1985). "The Effects of Right-to-Work Laws: A Review of the Literature." *Industrial and Labor Relations Review*, 38, 571–585.

Moran, R. (2010). "What Counts as Knowledge? A Reflection on Race, Social Science, and the Law." *Law and Society Review*, 44(3–4), 515–551.

Morand, C.-A. (1993). *Evaluation législative et lois expérimentales*. Aix-en-Provence: Presses Universitaires d'Aix-Marseille.

Morin, E. (1994). "Sur l'interdisciplinarité." *Bulletin Interactif du Centre Inter-nationale de Recherches et Etudes transdisciplinaires*, 2. Available at http://ciret-transdisciplinarity.org/bulletin/b2c2.php.

Morril, C., & Mayo, K. (2015). "Charting the 'Classics' in Law and Society: The Development of the Field over the Past Half-Century." In *The Handbook of Law and Society*, edited by Austin Sarat & Patricia Ewick (pp. 18–36). Chichester, West Sussex: Wiley Blackwell.

Mottini, E., Brunet, P., & Zevounou, L. (Eds.). (2014). *Usages de l'interdisci-plinarité du droit*, Paris: Press Universitaire de Paris Ouest.

Mouly, C., & Atias, C. (1993). "Faculty Recruitment in France." *The American Journal of Comparative Law*, 41(3), 401–411.

Muir-Watt, H. (2000). "La fonction subversive du droit compare." *Revue Internationale de Droit Comparé*, 52(3), 503–527.

Munger, F. (1998). "Mapping Law and Society." In *Crossing Boundaries: Traditions and Transformations in Law and Society Research*, edited by Austin Sarat (pp. 21–80). Chicago: Northwestern University Press.

(2004). "Rights in the Shadow of Class: Poverty, Welfare, and the Law." In *The Blackwell Companion to Law and Society*, edited by Austin Sarat (pp. 330–353). Malden: Blackwell Publishing.

Nelken, D. (1984). "Law in Action or Living Law? Back to the Beginning in Sociology of Law." *Legal Studies*, 4, 157–174.

(1986). "Beyond the Study of 'Law and Society'? Henry's Private Justice and O'Hagan's The End of Law?" *Law & Social Inquiry*, 11, 323–338.

(1995). "Understanding/Invoking Legal Culture." *Social Legal Studies*, 4, 435–452.

(1996). "Can There Be a Sociology of Legal Meaning?" In *Law as Commu-nication*, edited by David Nelken (pp. 107–128). Aldershot: Dartmouth.

(2001). *Adapting Legal Cultures*. Oxford: Hart Publishing.

(2002). "Comparative Sociology of Law." In *An Introduction to Law and Social Theory*, edited by Reza Banakar & Max Travers (pp. 329–344). Portland: Hart Publishing.

(Ed.). (2012). *Using Legal Culture*. London: Wildy, Simmonds & Hill Publishing.

(2016). "Comparative Legal Research and Legal Culture: Facts, Approaches, and Values." *Annual Review of Law and Social Sciences, 12,* 45–62.

Nelson, R. L., Trubek, D., & Solomon, R. (1991). *Lawyer's Ideals, Lawyer's Practice: Transformation in the American Legal Profession*. Ithaca: Cornell University Press.

Newburn, T. (2007). *Criminology*. Cullompton: Willan Publishing.

Nicolescu, B. (2002). *Manifesto of Transdisciplinarity*. New York: State University of New York Press.

Noguera, A. (2006). "Durkheim y Weber: surgimiento de la sociología jurídica y teorización del derecho como instrumento de control social." *Revista Investigaciones Sociales, 10*(17), 395–411.

Nonet, P., & Selznick, P. (1978). *Law and Society in Transition: Toward Responsive Law*. New York: Octagon.

Noreau, P. (2009). "De la force symbolique du droit." In *La force normative, naissance d'un concept*, edited by Catherine Thiberge (pp. 137–150). Paris: LGDJ.

Noreau, P., & Arnaud, A.-J. (1998). "The Sociology of Law in France: Trends and Paradigms." *Journal of Law and Society, 25*(2), 257–273.

Nourse, V., & Shaffer, G. (2009). "Varieties of New Legal Realism: Can a New World Order Prompt a New Legal Theory?" *Cornell Law Review, 95,* 61–137.

Novoa Monreal, E. (1980). *El derecho como obstáculo al cambio social*. Mexico City: Siglo XXI.

Nussbaum, M. (2014). *For Love of Country?* Boston: Vintage Books.

O'Donnell, G. (1994). "Delegative Democracy." *Journal of Democracy, 5*(1), 55–69.

(1998). *Polyarchies and the (Un)Rule of Law in Latin America*. Notre Dame: University of Notre Dame.

Obasogie, O. (2010). "Do Blind People See Race? Social and Theoretical Considerations." *Law and Society Review, 44*(3–4), 585–616.

Ocqueteau, F. (2006). *Mais qui donc dirige la police? Sociologie des commissaires*. Paris: Armand Colin.

Ocqueteau, F., & Warfman, D. (2011). *La sécurité privé en France*. Paris: PUF.

Odorisio, R., Celoria, M.-C., Petrella, G., & Pulitano, D. (1970). *Valori socio-culturalli della giurisprudeza*. Bari: Laterza.

Olivera, L. (2015). *Manual de sociología jurídica*. Petrópolis: Editora Vozes.

Olsen, F. (1983). "The Family and the Market: A Study of Ideology and Legal Reform." *Harvard Law Review, 96,* 1497.

(1984). "Statutory Rape: A Feminist Critique of Rights Analysis." *Texas Law Review*, 63, 387.

Ost, F. (2013). *La Nature hors la loi. L'Ecologie à l'Epreuve du droit*. Paris: La Découverte.

(2016). *A quoi sert le droit?* Brussels: Bruylant.

Ost, F., & Van de Kerchove, M. (1978). "Possibilité et limites d'une science du droit." *Revue Interdisciplinaire D'études Juridiques*, 1, 11–39.

(1987). *Jalons pour une Théorie Critique du Droit*. Brussels: Facultés Universitaires de Saint Louis.

(1991). "De la scène au balcon. D'où vient la science du droit?" In *Normes juridiques et régulation sociale*, edited by François Chazel & Jacques Commaille (pp. 67–80). Paris: LGDJ.

(2001). *Elementos para una teoría crítica del derecho*. Bogota: Universidad Nacional–Facultad de Derecho, Ciencias Políticas y Sociales.

(2002). *De la pyramide au réseau. Pour une théorie dialectique du droit*, Brussels: Publications des Facultés Universitaires Saint-Louis.

Ostrom, E. (1990). *Governing the Commons: The Evolution of Institutions for Collective Action*. New York: Cambridge University Press.

Papachristos, A. (1988). "Sociologie législative." In *Dictionnaire encyclopédique de théorie et sociologie du droit*, edited by Andre Jean Arnaud (pp. 387–389). Brussels: LGDJ.

Parsons, T. (1954). "A Sociologist Looks at the Legal Profession." In *Essays in Sociological Theory*, edited by Talcott Parsons (pp. 370–385). New York: Free Press.

(1962). "The Law and Social Control." In *Law and Sociology: Exploratory Essays*, edited by William M. Evan (pp. 56–72). New York: The Free Press of Glencoe.

(1968). "Law and Sociology: A Promising Courtship." In *The Path of the Law from 1967*, edited by Arthur Sutherland (pp. 47–54). Cambridge, MA: Harvard University Press.

(1977). "Law as an Intellectual Stepchild." *Sociological Inquiry*, 47, 11–58.

Pasquino, P. (1998). *Sieyés. L'invention de la Constitution en France*. Paris: Odile Jacob.

Pasukanis, E. (1979). *La théorie générale du droit et le marxisme*. Paris: EDI.

Paterson, A. (1982). *The Law Lords*. London: MacMillan.

Patiño Santa, J. (1992). *Apertura económica y justicia*. Cali: Hojas de Papel Editores.

Pavlich, G. (2000). *Critique and Radical Discourses on Crime*. Aldershot: Ashgate.

(2011). *Law and Society Redefined*. Oxford: Oxford University Press.

Pécaut, D. (1996). "La Sociologie à la VIe section." In *Une école pour les sciences sociales. De la VIe section à l'Ecole des hautes études en sciences sociales*, edited by Nathan Watchel & Jacques Revel (pp. 145–166). Paris: Editions du CERF.

Pelisse, J. (2003). "Consciences du temps et consciences du droit chez les salariés à 35 heures." *Droit et Société*, *53*, 164.

(2005). "A-t-on conscience du droit ; autour de legal consciousness studies." *Genèses*, *2*(59), 114–130.

Peller, G. (1985). "The Metaphysics of American Law." *California Law Review*, *73*, 1152–1290.

Perea, J. F. (1997). "The Black/White Binary Paradigm of Race." *California Law Review*, *85*, 1213.

Perelman, C. (1984). *Le raisonnable et le déraisonnable en droit*. Paris: LGDJ.

Perelman, C., & Olbrechts-Tyteca, L. (1976). *Trattato dell'argomentazione. La nuova retorica*. Turin: Einaudi.

Petrazycki, L. (1955). *Law and Morality*. Cambridge, MA: Harvard University Press.

Piketty, T. (2013). *Le Capital au XXIe siècle*. Paris: Seuil.

Pinto, L. (1989). "Du 'pépin' au Litige de consommation." *Actes de la recherche en sciences sociales*, *76–77*, 65–81.

Piven, F., & Cloward, R. (1979). *Poor People's Movements*. New York: Vintage Books.

Planiol, M. (1899). *Traité élémentaire de Droit civil*. Paris: LGDJ.

Planiol, M., & Ripert, G. (1925). *Traité pratique de droit civil français*. Paris: Librairie générale de droit et de jurisprudence.

Pogge, T. (2008). *World Poverty and Human Rights*. Cambridge: Cambridge University Press.

Pollak, M. (1988). "La place de Max Weber dans le champ intellectuel français." *Droit et Société*, *9*, 189–203.

Posner, R. (1975). "An Economic Approach to Law." *Texas Law Review*, *53*, 757.

(1977). *The Economic Analysis of Law*. Boston: Little, Brown and Co.

(1990). *The Problems of Jurisprudence*. Cambridge, MA: Harvard University Press.

(1995). *Overcoming Law*. Cambridge, MA: Harvard University Press.

(2014). *Economic Analysis of Law*. New York: Aspen.

Poulantzas, N. (1972). *Political Power and Social Classes*. London: New Left Books.

(1973). "The Problem of the Capitalist State." In *Ideology in Social Science*, edited by Robin Blackburn (pp. 238–253). New York: Vintage Books.

Pound, R. (1912). "The Scope and Purpose of Sociological Jurisprudence." *Harvard Law Review*, *24*, 591–619.

(1927). "Sociology and Law." In *The Social Sciences and Their Interrelations*, edited by William Fielding Ogburn (pp. 319–328). New York: Houghton Mifflin.

(1943). "Sociology of Law and Sociological Jurisprudence." *The University of Toronto Law Journal*, 5(1), 1–20.

(1967). *Interpretation of Legal History*. Gloucester: Peter Smith Publisher Inc.

Pressman, J., & Wildavsky, A. (1973). *Implementation: How Great Expectations in Washington Are Dashed in Oakland; or, Why It's Amazing that Federal Programs Work at All, This Being a Saga of the Economic Development Administration as Told by Two Sympathetic Observers Who Seek to Build Morals on a Foundation of Ruined Hopes*. Berkeley: University of California Press.

Priban, J. (2007). *Legal Symbolism: On Law, Time and European Identity*. Aldershot: Ashgate Publishing.

Quinney, R. (1970). *The Social Reality of Crime*. New Brunswick: Little Brown & Company.

(1974). *Critique of Legal Order: Crime Control in Capitalist Society*. Brunswick: Transaction Publishers.

Raiser, T. (1999). *Das lebende Recht. Rechstssoziologie in Deutschland*. Baden-Banen: Nomos.

Rajagopal, B. (2005). "The Role of Law in Counter-Hegemonic Globalization and Global Legal Pluralism: Lessons from the Narmanda Valley Struggle in India." *Leiden Journal of International Law*, 18, 345–387.

Reimann, M. (1993). *The Reception of Continental Ideas in the Common Law World. 1820–1920*. Berlin: Duncker & Humblot.

Revillard, A., Bereni, K., Debauche, A., & Latour, E. (2009). "A la recherche d'une analyse sur le droit dans les écrits francophones." *Nouvelles Questions Féministes*, 28(2), 4–10.

Rheinstein, M. (1954). *Max Weber on Law in Economy and Society*. Cambridge, MA: Harvard University Press.

Riesenfeld, S. (1937). "A Comparison of Continental and American Legal Education." *Michigan Law Review*, 36(1), 31–55.

Roach Anleu, S. L. (2000). *Law and Social Change*. London: Sage Publications.

Robespierre, M. (1970). *Oeuvres*. New York: Burt Franklin.

Robinson, E. (1934). "Law: An Unscientific Science." *Yale Law Journal*, 44, 235–367.

Rocher, G. (1996). "Droit, pouvoir et domination." In *Etudes de sociologie du droit et de l'éthique*, edited by Guy Rocher (pp. 235–258). Montréal: Thémis.

Rodotà, S. (2013). *Il diritto di avere diritti*. Roma-Bari: Laterza.

Rodríguez Garavito, C. A. (2001). "Globalization, Judicial Reform and the Rule of Law in Latin America: The Return of Law and Development." *Beyond Law*, 7, 13–42.

Rodríguez Garavito, C. (2006). "Globalización, reforma judicial y estado de derecho." *¿Justicia para todos? Sistema judicial, derechos sociales y* *democracia en Colombia*, edited by Rodrigo Uprimny, César Rodríguez Garavito, & Mauricio García-Villegas (pp. 405–469). Bogota: Grupo Editorial Norma.

(2011). "Beyond the Courtroom: The Impact of Judicial Activism on Socioeconomic Rights in Latin America." *Texas Law Review*, 89, 1669.

(Ed.). (2014). *Law and Society in Latin America*. New York: Routledge.

Roelofs, J. (1982). "Judicial Activism as Social Engineering: A Marxist Interpretation of the Warren Court." In *Supreme Court Activism and Restraint*, edited by Stephen Halpern & Charles Lamb (pp. 249–270). Lexington, MA: Lexington Books.

Rojas, F., & Moncayo, V. M. (1978). *Luchas obreras y política sindical en Colombia*. Bogotá: La Carreta.

Romano, S. (1946). *L'ordinamento giuridico*. Firenze: Sansoni.

Rose-Ackerman, S. (1988). "Progressive Law and Economics – And the New Administrative Law." *The Yale Law Journal*, 98, 341.

Rosenberg, G. N. (1991). *The Hollow Hope: Can Courts Bring about Social Change?* Chicago: University of Chicago.

Rousseau, J. J. (1915). *The Political Writings of Jean-Jacques Rousseau* (Vol. 1), edited by Charles Edwyn Vaughan. Cambridge: Cambridge University Press.

(1964). "Du contrat social." In *Oeuvres complètes* (Vol. t. 3, pp. 280–470). Paris: Gallimard.

Roussel, V. (2002). *Affaires de juges; les magistrats dans les scandales politiques en France (1990–2000)*. Paris: La découverte.

(2003) "La judiciarisation du politique, réalités et faux semblants." *Mouvements*, 29(4), 13–18.

(2004). "Les droits et ses formes. Eléments de discussion de la sociologie du droit de Pierre Bourdieu." *Droit et Société*, 56–57, 41–55.

Rubio, M. (1999). *Crimen e impunidad. Precisiones sobre la violencia*. Bogota: Tercer Mundo.

Sabine, G. H. (1961). *A History of Political Thought*. New York: Holt, Rinehart & Wiston.

Sachs, J. (1998). *Globalization and the Rule of Law*. New Haven: Yale University Law School.

Saffón, M. P., & García-Villegas, M. (2011). "Critique du droit au Brésil, en Argentine et en Colombie." In *Le droit en révolution. Regards sur la critique du droit des années 1979 à nos jours*, edited by Xavier Dupré de Boulois & Martine Kaluszinski (pp. 149–172). Paris: LDGJ.

Saleilles, R. (1904). *La théorie possessoire du Code civil allemand*. Paris: F. Pichon.

Sallaz, Z. (2007). "Bourdieu in American Sociology." *Annual Review of Sociology*, 33, 21–41.

Santos, B. de S. (1977). "The Law of the Oppressed: The Construction and Reproduction of Legality in Pasargada Law." *Law and Society Review*, 12(1), 5–126.

———. (1987). "Law: A Map of Misreading. Toward a Postmodern Conception of Law." *Journal of Law and Society*, 14(3), 279–302.

———. (1989). "Room for Manoeuver: Paradox, Program, or Pandora's Box?" *Law and Social Inquiry*, 4, 149–164.

———. (1995a). "Three Metaphors for a New Conception of Law: The Frontier, the Baroque, and the South." *Law and Society Review*, 29, 569–585.

———. (1995b). *Toward a New Common Sense: Law, Science and Politics in the Paradigmatic Transition*. New York: Routledge.

———. (1998a). "Oppositional Postmodernism and Globalization." *Law and Social Inquiry*, 23, 121–139.

———. (1998b). *Reinventar a Democracia*. Lisboa: Gradiva.

———. (2000a). *A crítica da razão indolente. Contra o desperdício da experiência*. Porto: Edições Afrontamento.

———. (2000b). "Law and Democracy: (Mis)trusting the Global Reform of Courts." In *Global Institutions, Case Studies in Regulation and Innovation*, edited by J. Jenson and Boaventura de Sousa Santos (pp. 252–284). Aldershot: Ashgate.

———. (2002). *Toward a New Legal Common Sense*. London: Butterworths.

———. (2003a). *La caída del Angelus Novus. Ensayos para una nueva teoría social y una nueva práctica política*. Bogota: ILSA – Universidad Nacional de Colombia.

———. (2003b). "Nuestra América: la formulación de un nuevo paradigma subalterno de reconocimiento y redistribución." In *La caída del Angelus Novus: ensayos para una nueva teoría social y una nueva práctica política*, edited by Boaventura de Sousa Santos (pp. 81–124). Bogota: ILSA – Universidad Nacional de Colombia.

———. (2009a). *La reinvención del Estado y el Estado plurinacional*. Buenos Aires: CLACSO & Waldhuter Editores.

———. (2009b). *Sociología jurídica crítica. Para un nuevo sentido común en el derecho*. Bogota: ILSA.

———. (2010). *Refundación del Estado en América Latina. Perspectivas desde una epistemología del Sur*. La Paz: Plural Editores.

———. (2014). *Derechos humanos, democracia y desarrollo*. Bogota: Dejusticia.

———. (2016). *Epistemologies of the South: Justice against Epistemicide*. New York: Routledge.

Santos, B. de S., & García-Villegas, M. (2001). *El Caleidoscopio de las justicias en Colombia*. Bogota: Uniandes – Siglo del Hombre.

Santos, B. de S., & Grijalva, A. (2012). *Justicia indígena, plurinacionalidad e interculturalidad en Ecuador*. Quito: Abya Yala.

Santos, B. de S., & Rodríguez-Garavito, C. A. (2005). *Law and Globalization from Below: Towards a Cosmopolitan Legality*. Cambridge: Cambridge University Press.

(2006). "Introduction: Expanding the Economic Canon and Searching for Alternatives to Neoliberal Globalization." In *Another Production Is Possible: Beyond the Capitalist Canon*, edited by Boaventura de Sousa Santos (pp. xvii–lx). London: Verso.

Sarat, A. (1985). "Legal Effectiveness and Social Studies of Law: On the Unfortunate Persistence of a Research Tradition." *Legal Studies Forum*, 9, 21–31.

(1990a). "Off to Meet the Wizard: Beyond Validity and Reliability in the Search for a Post-Empiricist Sociology of Law." *Law and Social Inquiry*, 15, 155–170.

(1990b). "The Law Is All Over: Power, Resistance and Legal Consciousness of the Welfare Poor." *Yale Journal of Law and the Humanities*, 2, 343–379.

(2000). "Redirecting Legal Scholarship in Law Schools." *Yale Journal of Law and the Humanities*, 12(1), 129–140.

(2004a). *The Blackwell Companion for the Sociology of Law*. Oxford: Blackwell Publishers.

(2004b). "Vitality Amidst Fragmentation: On the Emergence of Post-Realist Law and Society Scholarship." In *The Blackwell Companion to Law and Society*, edited by Austin Sarat (pp. 1–11). Oxford: Blackwell Publishers.

(2009). *Revisiting Rights*. Bingley: Emerald.

(Ed.). (2010). *Sovereignty, Emergency, Legality*. Cambridge: Cambridge University Press.

Sarat, A., & Ewick, P. (Eds.). (2015). *The Handbook of Law and Society*. Malden: Wiley Blackwell.

Sarat, A., & Kearns, T. R. (1998). *Law in the Domains of Culture*. Ann Arbor: University of Michigan Press.

Sarat, A., & Scheingold, S. (1998). *Cause Lawyering: Political Commitments and Professional Responsibilities*. New York: Oxford University Press.

(2005). *The Worlds Cause Lawyers Make: Structure and Agency in Legal Practice*. Redwood City: Stanford University Press.

(2008). *The Cultural Lives of Cause Lawyers*. Cambridge: Cambridge University Press.

Sarat, A., & Silbey, S. (1988). "The Pull of the Policy Audience." *Law and Policy*, 10, 97–166.

Sarat, A., & Simon, J. (2003). *Cultural Analysis, Cultural Studies, and the Law: Moving Beyond Legal Realism*. Durham: Duke University Press.

Sarat, A., Constable, M., Engel, D., Hans, V., & Lawrence, S. (1998). *Crossing Boundaries: Traditions and Transformations in Law and Society Research*. Evanston: Northwestern University Press.

Savigny, F. K. V. (2001). "Essence et valeur des universités allemandes." *Revue d'histoire des facultés de droit et de science juridique*, 23, 173–195.

Scauzillo, S. (2015). "Air Pollution from China Undermining Gains in California, Western States." *San Gabriel Valley Tribune*. www.sgvtribune.com/2015/08/11/air-pollution-from-china-undermining-gains-in-california-western-states/

Scheingold, S. (1974). *The Politics of Rights, Lawyers, Public Policy, and Political Change*. New Haven: Yale University Press.

Scheingold, S., & Sarat, A. (2004). *Something to Believe In: Politics, Professionalism, and Cause Lawyering*. Stanford: Stanford University Press.

Schlegel, J. H. (1984). "Toward an Intimate, Opinionated and Affectionate History of the Conference on Critical Legal Studies." *Stanford Law Review*, 36, 391.

(1995). *American Legal Realism and Empirical Social Science*. Chapel Hill: University of North Carolina Press.

Schnapper, D. (2010). *Une sociologie du Conseil Constitutionnel*. Paris: Gallimard.

Schoenaers, F. (2003). *Disponibilité des ressources et innovation managériale. Quelles mutations pour les juridictions du travail belges et françaises face aux évolutions de leurs environnements?* Paris: IEP.

Selznick, P. (1949). *TVA and the Grass Roots: A Study in the Sociology of Formal Organization*. Berkeley: University of California Press.

(1996). "Institutionalism 'Old' and 'New'." *Administrative Science Quarterly*, 41(2), 270.

Seron, C. (2006). *The Law and Society Cannon*. Aldershot: Ashgate.

Seron, C., & Silbey, S. (2004). "Profession, Science and Culture: An Emergent Canon of Law and Society Research." In *The Blackwell Companion to Law and Society*, edited by Austin Sarat (pp. 30–60). Malden: Blackwell Publishing.

Seron, C., Coutin, S., & Meeusen, W. (2013). "Is There a Canon of Law and Society?" *Annual Review of Law and Social Science*, 9, 287–306.

Serverin, E. (1985). *De la jurisprudence en droit privé: théorie d'une pratique*. Paris: Press Universitaire de Lyon.

(2000). *Sociologie du droit*. Paris: La Découverte.

Shaffer, G. (2008). "A New Legal Realism: Method in International Economic Law Scholarship." In *International Economic Law: The State and Future of the Discipline*, edited by Colin Picker, Isabella D. Bunn, & Douglas W. Arner (pp. 29–42). Oxford: Hart.

(2016). "Theorizing Transnational Legal Orders." *Annual Review of Law and Social Sciences*, 16, 231–253.

Shavell, S. (2004). *Foundations of Economic Analysis of Law*. Cambridge, MA: Harvard University Press.

Shelden, R. (2010). "On Richard Quinney, Critique of Legal Order." In *Classic Writings in Law and Society*, edited by Javier A. Treviño (pp. 329–341). Brunswick: Transaction Publishers.

Shihata, I. F. I. (1995). "Judicial Reform in Developing Countries and the Role of the World Bank." In *Judicial Reform in Latin American and the Caribbean*, edited by Malcolm Rowat & Waleed Haider Malik (pp. 2–13). Washington, DC: World Bank.

Sieder, R., & Ansolabehere, K. (2017). *Routledge Handbook of Law and Society in Latin America*. London: Routledge.

Siegel, R. B. (1997). "Why Equal Protection No Longer Protects: The Evolving Forms of Status-Enforcing State Action." *Stanford Law Review*, 49, 1111.

Sieyès, E. (2002). *Qu'est-ce que le Tiers état?* Paris: Editions du Boucher.

Silbey, S. (1987). "Critical Traditions in Law and Society Research." *Law and Society Review*, 21, 165.

(1997). "Let Them Eat Cake: Globalization, Postmodern Colonialism,and the Possibilities of Justice." *Law and Society Review*, 31(2), 207–235.

(1998). "Ideology, Power and Justice." In *Power and Justice in Law and Society Research*, edited by B. Garth & A. Sarat (pp. 272–308). Evanston: Northwestern University Press.

(2000). "From the Editor." *Law and Society Review*, 34, 859.

(2005). "After Legal Consciousness." *Annual Reviews of Law and Social Science*, 1, 323–368.

(Ed.). (2008). *Law and Science*. Aldershot: Ashgate.

(2012/2013). "Images in/of Law." *New York Law School Review*, 57, 171–183.

Silbey, S., & Bittner, E. (1982). "The Availability of Law." *Law and Policy*, 4(4), 339–434.

Singer, P. (2004). *One World: The Ethics of Globalization*. New Haven: Yale University Press.

Skocpol, T., & Somers, M. (1980). "The Uses of Comparative History in Macrosocial Inquiry." *Comparative Studies in Society and History*, 22(2), 174–197.

Smart, C. (1989). *Feminism and the Power of Law*. London: Routledge.

Smith, P. (2000). "Feminist Jurisprudence." In *A Companion to Philosophy of Law and Legal Theory*, edited by Dennis Patterson (pp. 302–311). Oxford: Blackwell Publishers.

Somers, M., & Roberts, C. (2008). "Toward a New Sociology of Rights: A Genealogy of 'Buried Bodies' of Citizenship and Human Rights." *Annual Reviews of Law and Social Science*, 4, 385–425.

Soubiran-Paillet, F. (1994). "Quelles voix(es) pour la sociologie du droit en France aujourd'hui?" *Genèse*, 15, 142–153.

(2000). "Juristes et sociologues français d'après guerre: une rencontre sans lendemain." *Gènese, 41,* 125–140.

Spanou, C. (1989). "Le droit instrument de la contestation sociale? Les nouveaux mouvements sociaux face au droit." In *Les usages sociaux du droit,* edited by Danièle Lochak (pp. 33–43). Paris: PUF.

Spelman, E. (1988). *Inessential Woman: Problems of Exclusion in Feminist Thought.* Boston: Beacon Press.

Spencer, H. (1898). *The Principles of Sociology.* New York: D. Appleton and Company.

Spire, A. (2008). *Accueillir ou reconduire. Enquête sur les guichets de l'immigration.* Paris: Raisons d'Agir.

(2012). *Faibles et puissants face à l'impôt.* Paris: Raisons d'Agir.

Stark, B. (2015). *International Law and Its Discontents: Confronting Crisis.* Cambridge: Cambridge University Press.

Stiglitz, J. (2013). *The Price of Inequality.* New York: W. W. Norton and Company.

Stone, A. (1985). "The Place of Law in the Marxian Structure-Superstructure." *Law and Society Review, 19,* 39–67.

Stone, M., Wall, I., & Douzinas, C. (2014). *New Critical Legal Thinking: Law and the Political.* New York: Routledge.

Strebeig, F. (2009). *Equal: Women Reshape American Law.* London: Norton and Company.

Stryker, R. (2007). "Half Empty, Half Full, or Neither: Law, Inequality, and Social Change in Capitalist Democracies." *Annual Review of Law and Social Science, 3,* 69–97.

Suchman, M., & Mertz, E. (2010). "Toward a New Legal Empiricism: Empirical Legal Studies and Legal Realism." *Annual Review of Law and Social Science, 2010*(6), 555–579.

Sumner, W. G. (1940). *Folkways: A Study of the Sociological Importance of Usages, Manners, Customs, Mores and Morals.* Boston: Ginn and Company.

Sunstein, C. (Ed.). (2000). *Behavioral Law and Economics.* Cambridge: Cambridge University Press.

Supiot, A. (2005). *Homo juridicus: essai sur la fonction anthropologique du droit.* Paris: Seuil.

(2010). *L'Esprit de Philadelphie. La justice sociale face au marché total.* Paris: Seuil.

Sutter, L. (2017) *Zizek and the Law.* New York: Routledge.

Sutton, J. (2001). *Law/Society, Origins, Interactions and Change.* London: Pine Forge Press.

(2013). "Symbols and Substance: Effects of California's Three Strikes Law on Felony Sentencing." *Law and Social Inquiry, 47*(1), 37–71.

Tamanaha, B. (2001). *A General Jurisprudence of Law and Society*. New York: Oxford University Press.

(2006). *Law as a Means to an End: Threat to the Rule of Law*. Cambridge: Cambridge University Press.

(2012). *Failing Law Schools*. Chicago: University of Chicago Press.

Tarde, G. de. (1993). *Les lois de l'imitation*. Paris: Editions Kimé.

Taylor, M. (1988). *Rationality and Revolution*. Cambridge: Cambridge University Press.

Teitel, R. (1997). "Transitional Jurisprudence: The Role of Law in Political Transformation." *The Yale Law Journal*, 106, 209–280.

The Yale Law Journal. (1981). "Papers from the Yale Law Journal Symposium on Legal Scholarship: Its Nature and Purposes." *The Yale Law Journal*, 90, 5.

Théry, I. (2010). *Des humains comme les autres. Bioéthic, anonymat et genre de don*. Paris: Editions de L'EHESS.

Thévenot, L. (1992). "Jugements ordinaires et jugements de droit." *Annales ESC*, 47(6), 1279–1299.

(2006). "L'action à bon droit : jugements ordinaires et jugements de droit." In *L'action au pluriel. Sociologie des régimes d'engagement* (La Découverte), edited by Laurent Thévenot (pp. 157–181). Paris: Thévenot Laurent.

Thompson, E. P. (1975). *Whigs and Hunters: The Origin of the Black Act*. New York: Pantheon Books.

Thornhill, C. (2017). *The Sociology of Constitutions*. Cambridge: Cambridge University Press.

Tilly, C. (1978). *From Mobilization to Revolution*. New York: McGraw-Hill Publishing Company.

(1990). *Coercion, Capital, and European States*. Oxford: Blackwell.

(2005). "Regimes and Contention." In *The Handbook of Political Sociology: States, Civil Societies, and Globalization*, edited by Thomas Janosky, Robert Alford, Alexander Hicks, & Mildred Schwartz (pp. 423–440). Cambridge: Cambridge University Press.

Timasheff, N. (2007). *An Introduction to the Sociology of Law*. New Brunswick: Transaction Publishers.

Tocqueville, A. (1856). *L'ancien régime et la Révolution*. Paris: Gallimard.

Todorov, T. (2002). "Right to Intervene or Duty to Assist?" In *Human Rights, Human Wrongs*, edited by Nicholas Owen (pp. 26–48). Oxford Amnesty Lectures. Oxford: Oxford University Press.

Tomasic, R. (1985). *The Sociology of Law*. London: Sage Publications.

Tomlins, C. (2000). "Framing the Field of Law's Disciplinary Encounters: A Historical Narrative." *Law and Society Review*, 34(4), 911–972.

(2007). "How Autonomous Is Law?" *Annual Review of Law and Social Science*, 3, 45–68.

(2012). "What Is Left of the Law and Society Paradigm after Critique? Revisiting Gordon's "Critical Legal History." *Law and Social Inquiry*, 37(1), 155–166.

Travers, M. (1993). "Putting Sociology Back onto the Sociology of Law." *Journal of Law and Society*, 20(4), 438–451.

(2001). "Sociology of Law in Britain." *The American Sociologist*, Summer, 32(2), 26–40.

(2010). *Understanding Law and Society*. New York: Routledge.

Trebilcock, M., & Mota-Prado, M. (2014). *Advanced Introduction to Law and Development*. Cheltenham: EdwarElgar.

Treves, R. (1966). *La sociologia del diritto*. Milano: Edizioni di Comunità, Diritto et cultura moderna.

(1995). "La sociologie du droit: un débat." In *Jean Carbonnier, Renato Treves et la sociologie du droit*, edited by Simona Andrini & André-Jacques Arnaud (pp. 187–206). Paris: LGDJ.

Treviño, A. J. (1996). *The Sociology of Law: Classical and Contemporary Perspective*. New York: Martin's Press.

(2001). *Talcott Parsons Today: His Theory and Legacy in Contemporary Sociology*. New York: Rowman & Littlefield.

(2007). *Classic Writings in Law and Society*. New Brunswick: Transaction Publishers.

(2010). *Classical Writings in Law and Society: Contemporary Comments and Criticism*. New Brunswick: Transaction Publishers.

Tronto, J. (1992). *Moral Boundaries: A Political Argument for an Ethic of Care*. New York: Routledge.

Troper, M. (2000). "Kelsen, la science du droit, le pouvoir." *Critique*, 642, 926–939.

Troper, M., & Michaut, F. (1997). *L'enseignement de la philosophie du droit*. Brussels: Bruylant.

Trubek, D. (1972). "Max Weber on Law and the Rise of Capitalism." *Wisconsin Law Review*, 3, 720–753.

(1977). "Complexity and Contradiction in Legal Order: Balbus on the Challenge of Critical Social Thought about Law." *Law and Society Review*, 11, 529–560.

(1984). "Where the Action Is: Critical Legal Studies and Empiricism." *Stanford Law Review*, 36, 576–622.

(1990). "Back to the Future: The Short, Happy Life of the Law and Society Movement." *Florida State University Law Review*, 18, 4–68.

(1996). "Law and Development: Then and Now." *Proceedings of the Annual Meeting (American Society of International Law)*, 90, 223–226.

Trubek, D., & Esser, J. (1989). "'Critical Empiricism' in American Legal Studies: Paradox, Program or Pandora's Box?" *Law and Social Inquiry*, 14, 3–52.

Trubek, D., & Galanter, M. (1974). "Scholars in Self-Estrangement: Some Reflections on the Crisis in Law and Development." *Wisconsin Law Review, 4*, 1062–1101.

Trubek, D., & Mosher, J. (2003). "New Governance, Employment Policy, and the European Social Model." In *Governing Work and Welfare in a New Economy*, edited by David Trubek & Jonathan Zeitlin (pp. 33–58). New York: Oxford University Press.

Trubek, D., & Santos, A. (2006). *The New Law and Economic Development: A Critical Appraisal.* Cambridge: Cambridge University Press.

Tunc, A. (1994). "L'importance de la doctrine dans le droit des Etats-Unis." *Droits, 20*, 75–84.

Turner, J., & Maryanski, A. (1995). *Functionalism.* California: Menlo Park.

Tushnet, M. (1984). "An Essay on Rights." *Texas Law Review, 62*, 1363–1403.

(1991). "Critical Legal Studies: A Political History." *Yale Law Journal, 100*, 1515.

(1999). *Taking the Constitution Away from the Courts.* Princeton: Princeton University Press.

(2015). *Red, White and Blue: A Critical Analysis of Constitutional Law.* Kansas City: University Press of Kansas.

Twining, W. (1985). "Talk about Realism." *New York University Law Review, 60*, 329.

(2005). "Social Science and Diffusion of Law." *Journal of Law and Society, 32*(2), 203–240.

(2009). *General Jurisprudence: Understanding Law from a Global Perspective.* Cambridge: Cambridge University Press.

Tyler, T. R. (1990). *Why People Obey the Law.* New Haven: Yale University Press.

(2006). *Why People Obey the Law.* Princeton: Princeton University Press.

(2009). "Legitimacy and Criminal Justice: The Benefits of Self-Regulation." *Ohio State Journal of Criminal Justice, 7*, 307–359.

Tyler, T. R., & Boeckmann, R. (2014). "Three Strikes and You Are Out, but Why? The Psychology of Public Support for Punishing Rule Breakers." In *The Law and Society Reader II*, edited by Erik Larson & Patrick Schmidt (pp. 223–231). New York: New York University Press.

Unger, R. (1986). *The Critical Legal Studies Movement.* Cambridge, MA: Harvard University Press.

(2015). *The Critical Legal Studies Movement: Another Time, a Greater Task.* New York: Verso.

Uprimny, R. (2011). "The Recent Transformation of Constitutional Law in Latin America: Trends and Challenges." *Texas Law Review, 89*, 1587.

(2014). "The Recent Transformation of Constitutional Law in Latin America: Trends and Challenges." In *Law and Society in Latin America*, edited by César Rodríguez-Garavito (pp. 93–111). New York: Routledge.

Uprimny, R., & García-Villegas, M. (2003). "Tribunal Constitucional e emancipação social na Colombia." In *Democratizar a Democracia. Os caminhos da democracia participativa*, edited by Boaventura de Sousa Santos (pp. 251–277). Porto: Afrontamanto.

———. (2004). "The Constitutional Court and Control of Presidential Extraordinary Powers in Colombia." In *Democratization and the Judiciary*, edited by Roberto Gargarella, Siri Gloppen, & Elin Skaar (pp. 46–69). London: Frank Cass Publishers.

Uprimny, R., Guzmán, D., & Parra, J. (2012). *La adicción punitiva. La desproporción de leyes de drogas en América Latina*. Bogota: Dejusticia. Retrieved from http://bit.ly/QMDiJl.

Vago, S. (2012). *Law and Society*. Boston: Prentice Hall.

Valdes, F. (1995). "Queers, Sissies, Dykes, and Tomboys: Deconstruction of 'Sex', 'Gender' and 'Sexual Orientation' in Euro-American Law and Society." *California Law Review, 83*, 1–377.

Valverde, M. (2010). "Spectres of Foucault in Law and Society Scholarship." *Annual Review of Law and Social Science, 6*, 45–59.

Van Caenegem, R. C. (1987). *Judges, Legislators and Professors: Chapters in European Legal History*. Cambridge: Cambridge University Press.

Van de Kerchove, M. (2013). "Science du droit, sciences humaines et sociales, fiction littéraire et artistique. Pour un épassement interdisciplinaire des frontières." In *Droit, arts, sciences humaines et sociales: (dé)passer les frontières disciplinaires*, edited by Sandrine Chassagnard-Pinet, Pierre Lemay, Céline Regulski, & Dorothée Simonneau (pp. 55–74). Paris: LDGJ.

Van Houtte, J. (1986). "La sociologie du droit ou le limites d'une science." *Droit et Société, 3*, 171–186.

Vanneuville, R. (2013). "La formation contemporaine des avocats: aiguillon d'une recomposition de l'enseignement du droit en France?" *Droit et Société, 83*, 67–82.

Vauchez, A. (2001). "Entre droit et sciences sociales; retour sur l'histoire du mouvement Law and Society." *Genèses, 45*, 134–149.

———. (2006). "La justice comme "institution politique": retour sur un objet (longtemps) perdu de la science politique." *Droit et Société, 2*(63), 491–506.

———. (2009). "Quand les juristes faisaient la loi ... Le moment Carbonnier (1963–1977), son histoire et son mythe." *Parlement[s], 1*(11), 105–116.

———. (2012). "Élite politico-administrative et barreau d'affaires." *Pouvoirs, 140*, 71–81.

———. (2013). *L'Union par le droit. L'invention d'un programme institutionnel pour l'Europe*. Paris: Presses de Sciences Po.

———. (2014). *Démocratiser l'Europe, "La République des idées."* Paris: Seuil.

Vauchez, A., & White, B. (Eds.). (2013). *The European Law as a Transnational Social Field*. Oxford: Hart Publishing.

Vauchez, A., & Willemez, L. (2007). *La justice face à ses réformateurs (1980–2006)*. Paris: PUF.

Vauchez, A., & Witte, B. (2013). *Lawyering Europe: European Law as a Transnational Social Field*. Oxford: Hart Publishing.

Vélez, V., Pérez, L., Benavidez, C., De la Cruz, A., & Solórzano, D. (2008). "Battling for Human Rights and Social Justice: A Latina/o Critical Race Analysis of Latina/o Student Youth Activism in the Wake of 2006 Anti-Immigrant Sentiment." *Social Justice*, 35, 7–27.

Vigour, C. (2007). "Les recompositions de l'institution judiciaire." In *La fonction politique de la justice*, edited by Jacques Commaille & Martin Kaluszynski (pp. 47–68). Paris: La Découverte.

(2008). "Politiques et magistrat face aux réformes de la justice en Belgique et Italie." *Revue Française D'administration Publique*, 125, 21–31.

Villey, M. (1975). *La formation de la pensée juridique moderne*. Paris: Les éditions Montchretien.

Villmoare, A. (1985). "The Left's Problems with Rights." *Legal Studies Forum*, 9, 39.

Von Humboldt, W. (1979). "Sur l'organisation interne et externe des établissements d'enseignement supériuer à Berlin." In *Philosophies de l'Université. L'idéalisme allemand et la question de l'Université*, edited by Luc Ferry, Jean Pierre Pesron, & Alain Renaut (p. 326). Paris: Payot.

Von Ihering, R. (1865a). *Geist des römischen Rechts auf den verschiedenen Stufen seiner Entwicklung. Teil 3*. Leipzig: Breitkop und Härtel.

(1865b). *Der Kampf um's Recht*. Wien: G. J. Manz'schen Buchhandlung.

(1877). *Der Zweck im Recht*. Leipzig: Breitkop und Härtel.

(1901). *L' Evolution Du Droit*. Paris: Chevalier-Marescq.

Waldron, J. (1998). "Dirty Little Secret." *Columbia Law Review*, 98(2), 510–530.

(1999). *Law and Disagreement*. Oxford: Oxford University Press.

(2006). "The Core of the Case against Judicial Review." *The Yale Law Journal*, 115, 1346–1406.

(2012). *Dignity, Rank and Rights*. Oxford: Oxford University Press.

Wallerstein, I. (1999). "L'héritage de la sociologie, la promesse de la science sociale." *Société Contemporaine*, 33–34, 159–194.

Ward, I. (1998). *An Introduction to Critical Legal Theory*. London: Cavendish Publishing Limited.

Watson, A. (2000). "Legal Transplants and European Law." Presented at the Ius Commune Lecture, Maastricht.

Weber, M. (1922). *Sociologie du droit*. Paris: PUF.

(1978). *Economy and Society*. Berkeley: University of California Press.

(1992). *Economía y sociedad*. Mexico City: Fondo de Cultura Económica.

West, R. (1988). "Jurisprudence and Gender." *University of Chicago Law Review*, 55(1), 1–72.

(1997). *Caring for Justice*. New York: New York University Press.

West, R. L. (1987). "The Difference in Women's Hedonic Lives: A Phenomenological Critique of Feminist Legal Theory." *Wisconsin Women's Law Journal*, 3, 149–215.

White, E. (1986). "From Realism to Critical Legal Studies: A Truncated Intellectual History." *Southwestern Law Journal*, 40, 819.

White, L. (1990). "Subordination, Rhetorical Survival Skills, and Sunday Shoes: Notes on the Hearing of Mrs. G." *Buffalo Law Review*, 38(1), 1–58.

Wickham, G., & Pavlich, G. (2001). *Rethinking Law, Society and Governance: Foucault's Bequest*. Oñati: Hart Publishing.

Willemez, L. (2003). "Engagement professionnel et fidélités militantes. Les avocats travaillistes dans la défense judiciaire des salariés." *Politix*, 12(62), 145–164.

Witteveen, W. (1999). "Significant, Symbolic and Symphonic Laws: Communication through Legislation." In *Semiotics and Legislation: Jurisprudential, Institutional and Sociological Perspectives*, edited by Hanneke van Schooten (pp. 27–70). Liverpool: D. Charles Publications.

Wittgenstein, L. (1988). *Investigaciones filosóficas*. Barcelona: Grijalbo.

Wolkmer, A. C. (1995). *Introdução ao Pensamento Jurídico Crítico*. São Pablo: Académica.

Wright Mills, C. (1959). *The Sociological Imagination*. Oxford: Oxford University Press.

Wyvekens, A. (2000). *L'Insertion locale de la justice pénale: Aux origines de la justice de proximité*. Paris: L'Harmattan.

Yngvesson, B. (1993). *Virtuous Citizens, Disruptive Subjects: Order and Complaint in a New England Court*. New York: Routledge.

Yoshino, K. (2002). "Covering." *Yale Law Journal*, 111, 769.

Zackin, E. (2014). "Popular Constitutionalism's Hard When You're Not Very Popular." In *The Law and Society Reader II*, edited by Erik Larson & Patrick Schmidt (pp. 55–61). New York: New York University Press.

Zagrebelzki, G. (1992). *Il diritto Mite*. Turin: Einaudi.

Zinn, H. (1990). *The Politics of History*. Urbana: University of Illinois Press.

(2002). *Disobedience and Democracy*. Cambridge: South End Press.

INDEX

CAMBRIDGE STUDIES IN LAW AND SOCIETY

Militarization and Violence against Women in Conflict Zones in the Middle East: A Palestinian Case-Study
Nadera Shalhoub-Kevorkian

Child Pornography and Sexual Grooming: Legal and Societal Responses
Suzanne Ost

Darfur and the Crime of Genocide
John Hagan and Wenona Rymond-Richmond

Fictions of Justice: The International Criminal Court and the Challenge of Legal Pluralism in Sub-Saharan Africa
Kamari Maxine Clarke

Conducting Law and Society Research: Reflections on Methods and Practices
Simon Halliday and Patrick Schmidt

Planted Flags: Trees, Land, and Law in Israel/Palestine
Irus Braverman

Culture under Cross-Examination: International Justice and the Special Court for Sierra Leone
Tim Kelsall

Cultures of Legality: Judicialization and Political Activism in Latin America
Javier Couso, Alexandra Huneeus, Rachel Sieder

Courting Democracy in Bosnia and Herzegovina: The Hague Tribunal's Impact in a Postwar State
Lara J. Nettelfield

The Gacaca Courts, Post-Genocide Justice and Reconciliation in Rwanda: Justice without Lawyers
Phil Clark

Law, Society, and History: Themes in the Legal Sociology and Legal History of Lawrence M. Friedman
Edited by Robert W. Gordon and Morton J. Horwitz

After Abu Ghraib: Exploring Human Rights in America and the Middle East
Shadi Mokhtari

Adjudication in Religious Family Laws: Cultural Accommodation: Legal Pluralism, and Gender Equality in India
Gopika Solanki

Water On Tap: Rights and Regulation in the Transnational Governance of Urban Water Services
Bronwen Morgan

Elements of Moral Cognition: Rawls' Linguistic Analogy and the Cognitive Science of Moral and Legal Judgment
John Mikhail

A Sociology of Transnational Constitutions: Social Foundations of the Post-National Legal Structure
Chris Thornhill

Mitigation and Aggravation at Sentencing
Edited by Julian V. Roberts

Institutional Inequality and the Mobilization of the Family and Medical Leave Act: Rights on Leave
Catherine R. Albiston

Authoritarian Rule of Law: Legislation, Discourse and Legitimacy in Singapore
Jothie Rajah

Law and Development and the Global Discourses of Legal Transfers
Edited by John Gillespie and Pip Nicholson

Law against the State: Ethnographic Forays into Law's Transformations
Edited by Julia Eckert, Brian Donahoe, Christian Strümpell and Zerrin Özlem Biner

Transnational Legal Ordering and State Change
Edited by Gregory C. Shaffer

Legal Mobilization under Authoritarianism: The Case of Post-Colonial Hong Kong
Waikeung Tam

Complementarity in the Line of Fire: The Catalysing Effect of the International Criminal Court in Uganda and Sudan
Sarah M. H. Nouwen

Political and Legal Transformations of an Indonesian Polity: The Nagari from Colonisation to Decentralisation
Franz von Benda-Beckmann and Keebet von Benda-Beckmann

Pakistan's Experience with Formal Law: An Alien Justice
Osama Siddique